EXCEL 2021

FOR BEGINNERS

THE COMPLETE DUMMY TO EXPERT PRACTICAL GUIDE WITH
EXAMPLES THAT TEACHES EVERYTHING YOU NEED TO
KNOW ABOUT MICROSOFT EXCEL 2021 (FORMULAS,
FUNCTIONS, VBA & MACROS INCLUSIVE)

JAMES JORDAN

CONTENTS

PREFACE

As you will be taking your time to go through this user guide for Excel 2021, there are lots of stuffs to learn. The truth is, you don't have to be a computer expert in other to make use of this user guide for Excel 2021.

Here in this book, you will be learning the fundamentals of Excel which entails what Excel is all about, its uses, and how it can be manipulated.

In the course of going through this book, you will be exposed to the basic operations on Excel which include understanding the worksheet, working with cells and also how to format the cells.

Not only that, you will be exposed to variety of formulas and functions used in Excel and the new functions added in Excel 2021. You will also get to learn how to insert formulas and functions while working on the Excel sheet and other formatting features available to the use of formulas and functions.

Features like creating of charts, changing of chart layouts and types, how to add title in charts, resizing the chart sizes and other formatting features associated with charts will be explicitly explained as you take your time to go through this guide.

Finally, there are tips and tricks to learn which will enhance your effectiveness in the use of this software. Some of the tricks and trips are shortcuts and some operations that seem very hard but in the real sense, they are very easy to perform.

Having stated what you get to gain by going through this user guide, I am sure you don't want to miss out of this golden opportunity.

See you in the next section!

INTRODUCTION

Microsoft Excel is one of the most used software applications in the world today and it comes together with some other applications found in the Microsoft office suite. This app replaced Lotus 1-2-3 as the industry standard for spreadsheets majorly because of its adaptive and flexible features.

The Microsoft Excel has become an application that is sought after in big organizations in the world today because of its features to carry out some mathematical, financial and statistical operations that could have become cumbersome when done manually and with the use of Microsoft Excel, time and energy are saved for more productive works.

Currently, with the way the world is evolving, business organizations are not just looking for a person who is computer literate rather a person who has vast knowledge on how to use Microsoft Excel and more of a reason as an individual, you can't afford to lose a job opportunity because of you lack the skills to use of Microsoft Excel.

With researches made so far, it has been discovered that Microsoft excel is one of those applications' executive heads and heads of departments must train their staff to get accustomed to ensure the smooth running of such organization and not only that, to boost the work efficiency of the organization within and outside the organizations.

Truth be told, Microsoft Excel is not an easy application to learn and use and most people find it difficult to use but guess what? In this user guide, Microsoft Excel will be taught in a way that you can easily comprehend and use.

I wish you all the best as you take a ride to exploring this book.

CHAPTER ONE

INTRODUCTION TO MICROSOFT EXCEL 2021

Excel 2021 is one of the latest applications developed by Microsoft Corporation itself with some features that have made it stand out from every other version that has been developed so far. In case you are a novice, let's quickly take a tour to what Excel is all about before diving into Excel 2021 and its basic operations.

WHAT IS EXCEL?

Excel is an application software that provides worksheets with rows and columns that helps to organize data. Space where the rows and columns intersect is known to be the cell. The Excel software was created by Microsoft Corporation and comes with the Microsoft Office Suite.

This tool is used for organizing and performing calculations and data, calculate statistics, generate pivot tables and display data in form of line graphs, histograms, and charts with a very limited three-dimension graphical display. With the Excel software, you can calculate monthly budgets, prepare payroll, track associated expenses and sort out data based on their categories or criteria.

This software is widely used these days by almost everyone because of its capacity to save time and energy and this application gives room for the updating of its features as well as introducing new features through Office 365 from time to time in a year. Researchers have proven so far that big organization in the world are ardent users of this application.

Initially, Excel was code named to be Odyssey while it was being developed before it was released on September 30, 1985.

USES OF EXCEL

Excel is one of the apps in the Microsoft Office Suite has a lot of advantages which cannot be overemphasized and here we will be talking about a few of them.

Analyzing and storing data: One of the uses of MS Excel is that it allows you to analyze data and break them down in such a way that they are displayed in form of graphs and charts in a well-organized and understood manner for its end purpose. Also, the organized data are stored systematically.

Data recovery: With the way this software is configured, it helps to recover lost or damaged file data with less or no stress.

Mathematical formulas: MS Excel allows one to tackle complex mathematical problems in a simpler and well-understood manner with less or little effort. Not only that, but MS Excel also contains a lot of mathematical formulas needed to perform the basic mathematical operation.

Security: With MS Excel, you can keep your files secure and also password them using visual basic programming or by directly securing them within the Excel file.

Online storage and access: MS excel being an outshoot of Office 365, gives the users the ability to access their files online and by implication, it means that they don't have to go around with their computers rather, they can access their files anytime anywhere using any device compatible with the use of MS excel.

Financial data: You can create your financial data like checking account, information, budgets, taxes, transactions, payrolls, invoices, receipts, forecast and the likes with the use of Excel

Forms: You can as well create form templates for handling inventory, evaluations, performance, reviews, questionnaires, timesheet, etc.

School grade or result: With Excel, teachers can create a grade sheet that helps calculate the students' grades as well as monitoring their academic performance.

Bringing of data together: This software helps to bring together different kinds of Files and documents in one location. Also, texts and images can be imported from other locations into one location with the other files and documents.

WHAT' S NEW IN EXCEL 2021?

It's no doubt that some new features have been added to the Microsoft Excel 2021 and for this study, we will be discussing the features that have made it different from other previous versions of Excel.

Automate data analyses with Excel's ideas: Ideas is one of the newly added features in Excel 2021 that helps to analyze data quickly and provides the insight needed for the data analyses. To locate Ideas in Excel, go to the Home tab of the Ribbon. Keep this in mind; you need to be actively connected to the internet to use this feature.

XLOOKUP in replacement of VLOOKUP: The XLOOKUP feature is a replacement of VLOOKUP. The XLOOKUP feature is a function used when you need to find things in a table or a range by row. Unlike the VLOOKUO that gives an appropriate match of what is being searched, the XLOOKUP gives the exact match of what is being searched for. It also allows you to search for data anywhere in the data entry.

The following syntax comes with the XLOOKUP function,

=XLOOKUP (lookup value, lookup array, return array).

Dynamic arrays: This is another feature of Excel that allows you to write a single formula that affects multiples cells simultaneously without the need to copy the formula one by one to all the cells.

In this feature, the following are made available; Filter, Sort, Sequence, Sort By, Randary and Unique.

MICROSOFT EXCEL TERMINOLOGIES

Workbook

The workbook refers to an Excel spreadsheet file. The workbook stores all of the data that you have entered and allows you to sort or calculate the results. A workbook that is accessible to be viewed and modified by multiple users on a network is called a Shared Workbook.

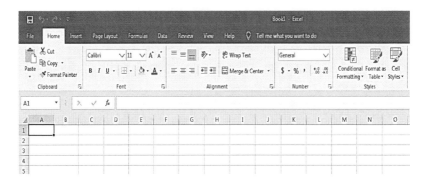

Worksheet

A worksheet is a sub-component document of a workbook. It is also called spreadsheets; you can have multiple sheets nestled in a workbook.

Tabs at the bottommost of the screen will indicate which of your worksheets you are presently working on; this is also known as an active sheet or active worksheet.

Cell

A cell is an intersection between a column and a row on a spreadsheet. Each cell in a spreadsheet can encompass any value that can be called using a virtual cell reference or called upon using a formula. Any data that you want to enter into your worksheet must be put in a cell. An Active Cell is one that is currently opened for editing.

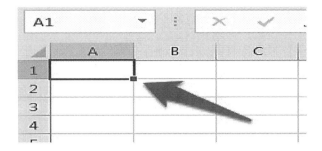

Columns and Rows

Columns and Rows refer to how your cells are aligned. Rows are aligned horizontally while columns are aligned vertically.

Column and Row Headings

These headings are the lettered and numbered gray areas located just outside of columns and rows. Clicking on a heading will select the entire row or column. You can also modify the row height or column width using the headings.

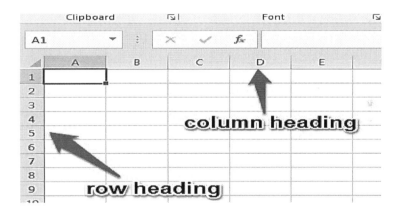

Workspace

Just like worksheets in a workbook, a workspace allows you to simultaneously open numerous files.

Ribbon

Above the workbook is a segment of command tabs known as the ribbon. A multitude of options is found behind each tab of the ribbon.

Cell Reference

A cell reference is a set of coordinates that classifies a specific cell. It's a combination of letters and numbers. For example, B3 would point to the cell situated where column B and row 3 intersect.

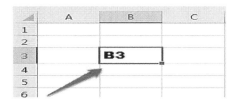

Cell Range

A Cell range is a cluster of cells that have been identified as a group based on a variety of criteria. By using a colon (:) between cell references. Excel can determine the range, also called an array. A range in a row, for example, could look like A3: D3, telling the formula to look at the cells in a row between A3 and D3, while C4: F9 would tell the formula to look at all cells in a box bounded by columns C and F and rows 4 and 9. A 3-D reference refers to a range that encompasses more than one worksheet in the same workbook.

Merged Cell

When two or more cells are united, it becomes what is known as a *merged cell*.

Template

A template is a formatted workbook or worksheet intended to help users fulfill a specific need in Excel. Examples of this include stock analysis, process map and calendar.

Operator

Operators are signs or symbols that specify which calculation must be made in an expression. Operators do not necessarily refer to simple mathematical types; comparison, concatenation, text or reference operators also exist.

Formula

A sequence inside a cell that is used to produce value is called formula. It must begin with an

equality sign (=). This could be a mathematical equation, functions, cell references, or operator. A formula is also known as an expression.

Formula Bar

Nestled between the workbook and ribbon, the Formula Bar will display the contents of an active cell. In the case of formulas, the formula bar will display all components of the formula.

Function

Functions are formulas that are pre-built into Excel. They are intended to help simplify hypothetically complex formulas in a worksheet.

Cell Formatting

This is the act of changing how a cell or its contents are displayed in the spreadsheet. When you format cells, only the visual appearance of the cells is altered; the value within the cells remains the same.

Error Code

Error Codes appear if Excel finds a problem with a formula provided.

Filter

Filters are guidelines that you can employ to choose which rows in a worksheet to display. These filters can use data such as conditions or values.

AutoFill

This enables you to copy data to more than one cell easily.

AutoSum

This feature will add up the numbers you have entered in your sheet and displays the total in a cell of your choice.

AutoFormat

This is an automatic format application to cells that match pre-determined conditions. This could be as simple as size.

Data Validation

This feature helps to avert inappropriate data from being entered into your worksheet. Data validation promotes accuracy and consistency in the data to be entered.

Pivot Table

This is a data summarization tool most commonly used to sort, average, to sum up, data automatically. The information is heaved from one table while the results are presented in another.

Pivot Chart

This type of chart provides a visual aid for pivot tables by providing graphical illustrations of the pivot table data; the user can offer a level of interactivity with the data.

Pivot Area

The pivot area is a point on the worksheet where you would drag a Pivot Table field to rearrange how a report is displayed.

Source Data

This is the information used to create your pivot table. It can either exist within the worksheet or from an external database.

Values Area

In a pivot table, Value areas are recognized as the cells that contain the instantaneous information.

Item

These are sub-categories of fields in the pivot table. If you have an area that is marked Country, the items could be the United States of America, Italy and so on.

EXCEL TOOLS

There are certain tools found in Excel, that has made the use of Excel more convenient and productive, briefly, we shall be talking about them.

Excel add-in: These are mini software that are installed into Excel to provide additional features that are not available in Excel itself. When these add-ins are added, they are located among the ribbon tools. These add-ins are developed by a third party. Examples of Excel add-ins are Filter Mate, PivotPal, Tab Hound, Paste Buddy, etc.

EXCEL FILE TYPES

The file types or extensions in Excel are very important because they provide you with information about the files before opening and allows you to save your files weather as macro-enabled files, binary files, templates, etc.

Excel workbook (.xlsx): This is the default XML-based file format for Excel 2010 and Excel 2010. This cannot save Microsoft Visual Basic for Applications (VBA) macro code or Microsoft Office Excel 4.0 macro sheet (.xlm), Xlsx files organize data in cells which are stored in worksheets and are later stored in the workbook.

- **Excel macro-enabled workbook (.xlsm):** The XML file is a macro-enabled spreadsheet for Excel 2021, Excel 365, Excel 2019, Excel 2016, Excel 2013, Excel 2010, and Excel 2007. This also contains embedded macro programmed in the Visual Basic for Application (VBA) language.

- **Excel binary worksheet (.xlsb):** This is the binary format for Excel 2010 and Excel 2007. This file format is used to create and edit a spreadsheet and it is used more than the XLSX format because it compressed to save space and it is also easier to share among users.
- **Template (.xltx):** This is a template also used for creating spreadsheets and it contains default settings and layout information used to create XLSX files. This file format cannot store Microsoft Visual Basic for Applications (VBA) macro code or Microsoft Office Excel 4.0 macro sheet. It is used to create multiple spreadsheets with common formatting and properties. With the XLTX file format, you can create documents like budgets, calendars, inventories, etc.
- **Template (.xltm):** This file format contains default settings and layout for creating micro- enabled sheets that are used in turn to create a macro-enabled workbook in Excel 2007 and Excel 2010. This Excel's file format also stores Visual Basic Application or Excel 4.0 macro sheets.
- **Excel 97- Excel 2003 workbook (.xls):** This is the default file format for Excel 2003 and it is also known as Binary Interchange File Format (BIFF).
- **Excel 97- Excel 2003 template (.xlt):** This is a template also used for creating spreadsheets and it contains default settings and layout information used to create new.XLT files and the files are saved in Excel Binary File Format.

The following are other types of Excel Files:

- Microsoft Excel 5.0/95 Workbook (.xls)
- XML Spreadsheet 2003 (.xml)
- XML Data (.xml)
- Excel Add-in (.xlam)
- Excel 4.0 (.xlw)
- Works 6.0-9.0 spreadsheet

WHERE CAN I GET MICROSOFT EXCEL?

You might have been wondering where and how you can get Microsoft Excel installed on your computer. Your days of worries are finally over. To get Microsoft Excel, there are just three ways to go about it:

- **Web Version:** You can access Microsoft Excel and any other related Office programs free on the web, and to do this, all you need is to have a Microsoft account and head to **https://www.office.com** to sign up for the free version of the app. Provided you have done this, you will be presented with the screen below to choose any app you wish to run
- **Mobile Version:** You can also get Microsoft Excel on your Android, Windows, and Apple mobile devices. To get the app on your Android devices, visit the Google Play store. For Windows devices, visit Microsoft Store and for Apple devices, visit the Apple Store.
- **Desktop Version:** You can also get Microsoft Excel and any other related Office programs on your computer. To access it, visit **https://www.office.com** on your web browser and then go to **Get Office** to see the versions of Microsoft Excel available. You will have to pay for the apps before you can use them. However, the Home version is just a trial version of 30 days and when it expires, you will have to upgrade it by paying

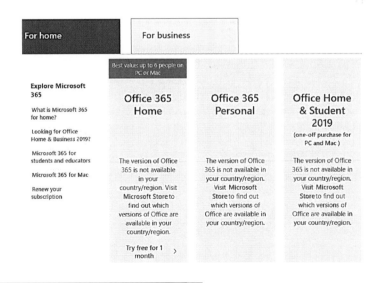

CHAPTER TWO

THE BASIC OPERATIONS ON EXCEL 2021

LAUNCHING AND QUITTING EXCEL 2021 FROM THE WINDOW

Before you launching Excel 2021 on your computer, it is expedient to understand the recommended Windows version that is permitted for it to run on is Windows 10. So, if you are using a computer with Windows 7 and 8 on it, you will need to upgrade your computer Window to Windows 10 before you can successfully install this app on it. To do this, you can visit your computer technician or go to Microsoft Office Centre to get your computer updated to the current Window.

STARTING YOUR EXCEL FROM WINDOW 10

There are different ways of starting Excel on your computer with Window 10 and we will be discussing them now.

Start button

You can launch your Excel by using the Start button using the procedure below:

- Click on the Windows icon on the screen
- Scroll downward on the alphabetical lists of apps until you locate Excel.

Search text box

Instead of opening the Window 10 Start menu, you can launch the Excel 2021 by:

- Locating the Search text box beside the Window button and type in the keyword
- Then click on enter and the app will display for launching.

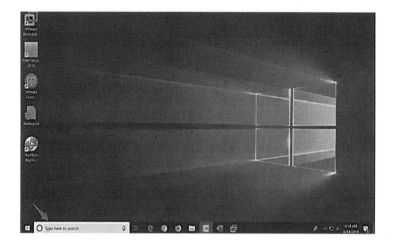

NOTE: You can also pin the app to the taskbar for easy location and to do this, right-click on the Excel program in the Start menu and then click on Pin to the Start item.

QUITTING EXCEL

In case you are done using your Excel and you wish to quit or close your Excel program, follow these simple procedures:

Press *Alt+F4* Or

Click on the Close button in the upper-right corner of the Excel Program Window.

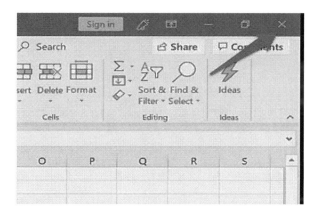

EXCEL'S START SCREEN

When you launch the Excel program, what displays on the screen is called the Start screen. This screen is divided into two; the right panel and the left panel.

The left panel has a green color with the Home icon selected which contains New Open items at the top, an Account, Feedback and options at the bottom.

The right panel shows a list of thumbnails that contains varieties of templates that can be used. Most importantly is the on the right panel is the Blank workbook which is used to open a new blank Excel workbook file.

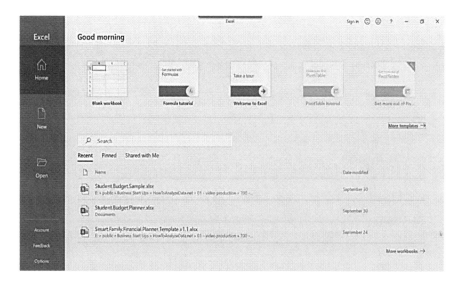

EXCEL'S RIBBON USER INTERFACE

When you open a new blank workbook, there are some features on the workbook which are necessary to work with on the blank page and these features are Excel's Ribbon interface and they are listed below into four categories:

File menu button: When you open this feature, what displays here are New, Open, Save As, Share, Export, Publish, Close and Account, and other options that allow you change the Excel's default settings

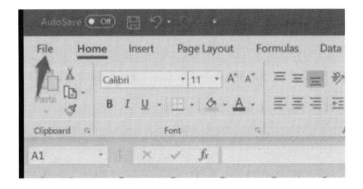

Quick Access toolbar: This is where features like AutoSave, Save, Undo and Redo are found

Ribbon: Most commands needed in Excel are found in the ribbon. They are arranged in the form of tabs from the Home through View.

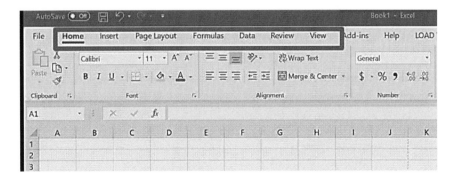

Formula bar: This shows the address of the cell being worked on alongside the content of the cell.

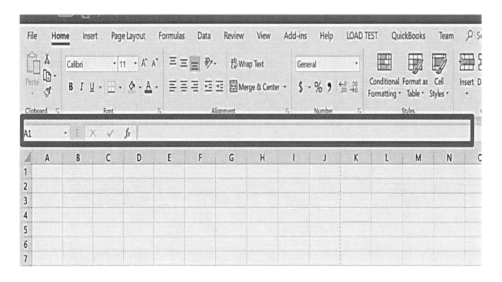

Worksheet area: This is where all the cells currently worked on are displayed for all to see with a column heading which uses letters and a row heading with numbers.

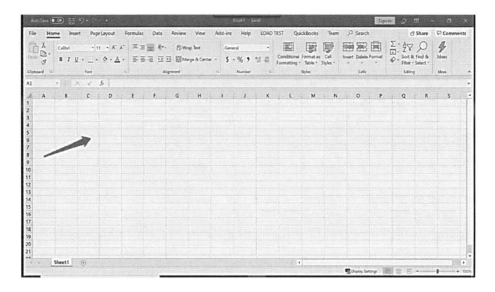

Status bar: This displays the current mode of the program and allows you to perform special operations on the worksheet. You can open a new blank worksheet with this tool as well as zooming in and zooming out.

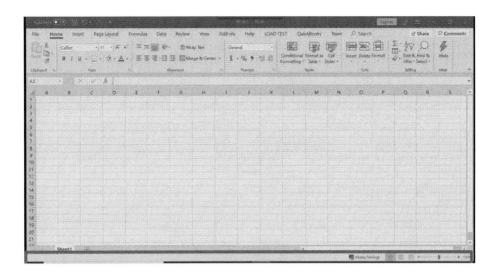

UNDERSTANDING THE WORKBOOK

We will be taking a tour on how to work on a workbook. Keep this in mind, every operation carried out on the Excel program is done right on the workbook.

The data inputted such as letters, numbers or formulas are stored on the workbook and the workbook there lies the worksheet.

A worksheet is found in a workbook and it contains 16,384 columns that are labeled by the letters of the alphabet and also contains 1,048,576 are labeled by number 1 to 1,048,576.

CREATING A NEW WORKSHEET

To create a new workbook on your Excel:

- Launch your Excel program to display the Excel start screen.

- Then click on New.

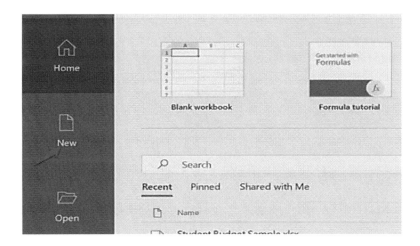

RENAMING A WORKSHEET

When you open a new Excel workbook, the default name given to it is Sheet1. You can however change the name to the one you desire and to do this,

- Right-click on the worksheet you want to rename

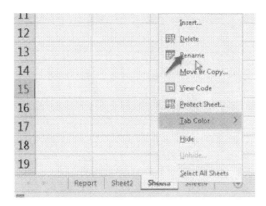

- Select the Rename option and type in the name you wish to change to and then click on enter

INSERTING A NEW WORKSHEET

To insert a new worksheet all you have to do is click on the + icon beside the worksheet.

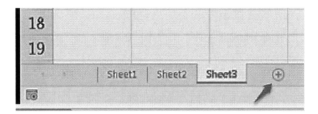

Now you can see that the new sheet has been added below in the picture

DELETING A WORKSHEET

To delete a worksheet, all you have to do is:

- Right-click on the worksheet you intend to delete

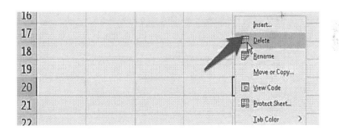

- Select the Delete option and the worksheet will be deleted from the workbook

COPYING OR MOVING A WORKSHEET

You can move or copy a worksheet with a workbook. To do this, simply follow these simple instructions:

- Right-click on the worksheet you desire to move or copy
- Click on the Copy or Move option and the location will be changed

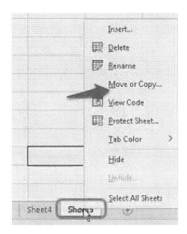

NOTE: In case you only wish to move and not copy, all you have to do is drag the worksheet to the location you.

CHANGING THE WORKSHEET COLOUR

You can change the colour of your worksheet by following this instruction:

- Right-click on the worksheet you desire to change its colour

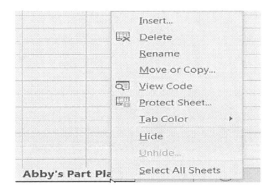

- Click on Tab colour and select the colour you want and press enter.

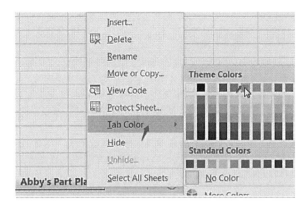

SAVING YOUR DOCUMENT

There are two different ways of saving a document in the Excel program after working on a workbook and briefly, we will explain both.

- **Save:** The save option is used when you edit a workbook that has already been on your computer. This option allows you to save the new changes made on your document. Here you don't need to create a file name and location to save.
- **Save As:** This option is used when a new document is created. Here you will need to create the file name and the location of the file. You can as well use this command to make a copy of a document but you will still need to choose a different name and location for the copied version to avoid overriding the old copied version.

To save using these commands

- Go to the Quick Access Toolbar and select the Save command.

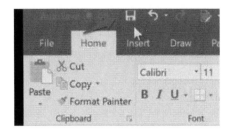

- If you are saving for the first time, click on Save As (here you will be required to create a file name and location) and if not click on Save

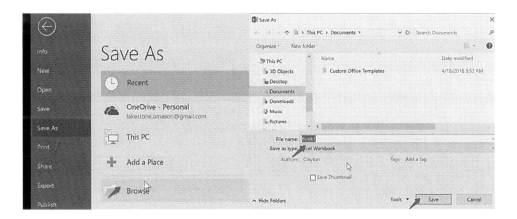

NOTE: *You can as well save your document on your OneDrive provided you sign in into Excel with your Microsoft account.*

HOW TO RECOVER YOUR DOCUMENT USING AUTOSAVE

Let's assume you lost a document and you are on how to get it, there are features made available in the Excel program that allows you to recover any lost document. All you need to do is follow the steps below:

- Relaunch your Excel program
- At the left-hand side of your workbook, click on the recovered version of the document you want.

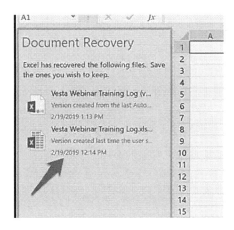

NOTE: The Excel program autosaves your documents every 10 minutes and if your computer crashes before that time, the documents may be completely lost.

EXPORTING WORKBOOKS

By default, the Excel workbooks are saved in the file format .xlsx. However, there are times there will be the need to use another file type or probably to a lesser version of the Excel program. Do not fret, all you need is to follow these simple steps:

- Open the backstage view of the Excel program and click on Export
- Then go to Create Pdf/XPS Document.

- In case you want to change the file type, go to Change File Type.

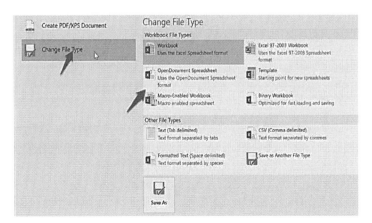

HOW TO SHARE EXCEL WORKBOOK

In case you need to share your Excel workbook to another user, all you have to do is:

- Click on the Share button on the top right corner of the Excel worksheet

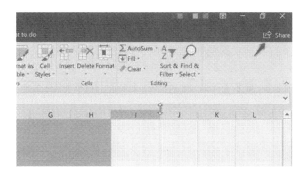

- Upload your file to OneDrive

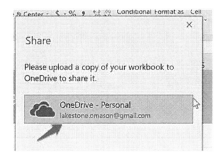

- Once it is uploaded, you can email an invitation link to your contacts to view or edit the documents.

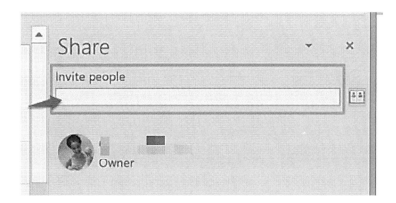

NOTE: You can as well share files by sending the files as an attachment or sending a sharing link to access the files. Just move downward on the page where you sent the invite link to get the image below

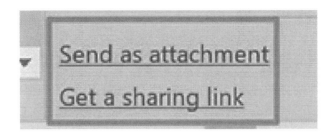

UNDERSTANDING THE CELL

The cell is where the information on the worksheet is entered. The worksheet contains thousands of rectangles that are known to be the cells. The cell, on the other hand, is an intersection of a row and a column. The Columns are tagged with letter of the alphabet (A, B, C, etc.) while the rows are tagged with numerical values (1, 2, 3, etc.)

Whenever you work with Excel, you'll enter information or content into cells. Cells are the basic building blocks of a worksheet. You'll need to learn the basics of cells and cell content to calculate, analyze and organize data in Excel.

WHAT'S A CELL?

Every worksheet is made up of thousands of rectangles which are called cells. A cell is the intersection of a row and a column. Columns are identified by letters (A, B, C), while rows are identified by numbers (1, 2, 3)

Every cell on the worksheet has its name or cell address and this is displayed at the top left corner of the worksheet

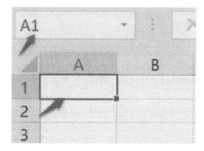

A group of cells is known as cell range; the cell range is the combination of more than two cells and for example, the cell range is written in this manner **A1: A5** or **B1: B5**

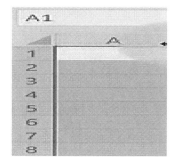

To select a cell range,

- Click, hold and drag the mouse to the cells you wish to highlight
- Release the mouse and select the cell range you desire.

INSERTING CONTENTS IN A CELL

To insert a content be it letter or numbers, all you need to do is:

- Click on the cell you wish to type into

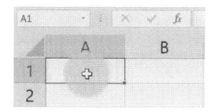

- Type the content into the cell and press Enter and the content will appear in the cell and also on the formula bar

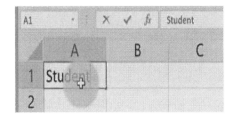

NOTE: You can delete the content of the cell by:

- *Selecting the cell content to be delete*
- *Press the Delete or Backspace to delete*

HOW TO DELETE A CELL

To delete a cell from the worksheet:

- Select the cell you wish to delete

- Select the Delete command from the Home tab from the Ribbon and follow the option that suits you

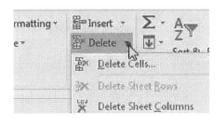

- After doing this, the cell will automatically shift up by itself.

COPYING AND PASTING CELL CONTENT

To perform this operation;

- Select the cell content you wish to copy

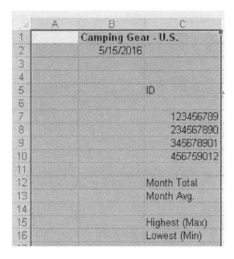

- Go to Copy command on the Home tab (you can use ctrl+C for this operation)

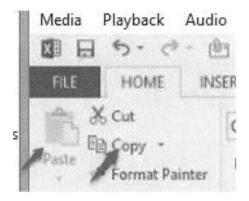

- Then select the area you wish to paste the content and then click on Paste on the Home Tab. Keep this in mind that the copied cell will have a dashed box around them for identification (you can also use ctrl+ V to paste).

DRAGGING AND DROPPING THE CELL

To save you the stress of cutting, copying and pasting of the cells, you use the dragging and dropping method to move your contents from one cell to the other. To do this, all you need to do is:

- Select the cells you desire to move
- Move the mouse on the border of the cells you have selected and drop the cells to get their contents moved
- Click, hold and drag the cells to the desired location
- Release the mouse and the cells will be moved to the desired location.

USING THE FILL HANDLE IN A CELL

The fill handle in Excel helps save the stress of copying the content from a cell to other cells in a worksheet. With the fill handle, you can quickly copy and paste the content of a cell to adjacent cells within the same row or column.

To use the fill handle:

- Select the cell you wish to duplicate its content and the fill handle appears as a small square in the bottom right corner of the selected cell

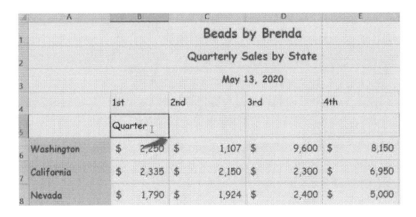

- Click, hold and drag the fill handle until all the cells you wish to fill are duplicated

	1st Quarter	2nd Quarter	3rd Quarter	4th Quarter
Beads by Brenda				
Quarterly Sales by State				
May 13, 2020				
Washington	$ 2,250	$ 1,107	$ 9,600	$ 8,150
California	$ 2,335	$ 2,150	$ 2,300	$ 6,950
Nevada	$ 1,790	$ 1,924	$ 2,400	$ 5,000

- Then release the mouse to fill the selected cell

You can as well use the fill handle to continue a series in the form of numbers (1,2,3) or days (Monday, Tuesday, Wednesday). In most cases, you will need to select more than one cell before this fill handle can work.

The pictures below will give us a clearer illustration of how to continue a series with the fill handle

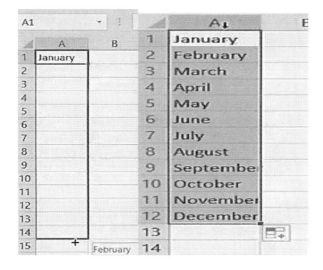

FORMATTING THE CELL

There are a lot of features available for formatting the cells and here we will be discussing on how to apply these features with simple guidelines.

CHANGING THE FONT

When the Excel program is launched, the default font that displays is the Calibri. This font is what shows when you begin to input words, numbers and the likes into the cells on the Excel worksheet. You can, however, change the font to anyone you like in the Home tab that allows for the changing of the font

To do this:

- Select the cell you wish to change its font

- Go to the Home tab, click on the Font command and change it to the desired font

CHANGING THE FONT SIZE

To change the font size, all you have to do is:

- Select the cell you wish to change its font size

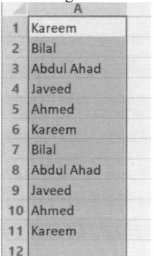

- Go to the Home tab, click on the Font command and change the font size to the one you desire.

CHANGING THE FONT COLOR

To change the font color of your cell, all you need to do is;

- Select the cell you wish to change its font colour

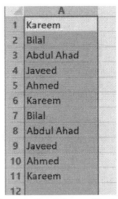

- Go to the Home tab, click on the Font Colour command and change the font size to the one you desire

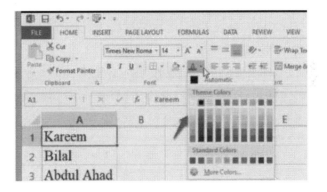

- After you must have done this, the font colour will change.

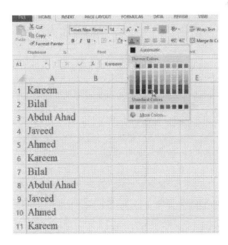

USING THE BOLD, ITALICS, AND UNDERLINED COMMANDS

- Select the cell you wish to change its font colour

- Go to the Home tab, click on bold, italics or underlined command to make the desired changes.

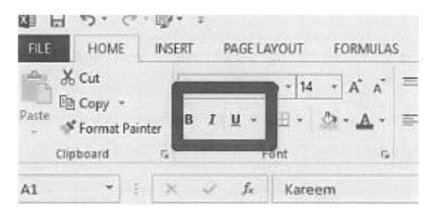

ADDING BACKGROUND COLOR USING THE FILL COLOR

The fill color allows you to add a background color to your cells making them stand out from every other part of the worksheet. You can add any color of your choice to the cell background.

To do this;

- Select the cell you wish to apply the fill colour to

- Go to the Home tab, click on the Fill colour and select the colour you want.

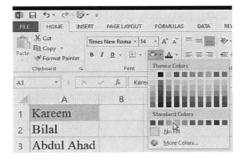

ADDING BORDERS TO CELLS

Creating a border in a worksheet helps to distinguish the cells from other cells in the worksheet. To add a border:

- Select the cell you wish to modify

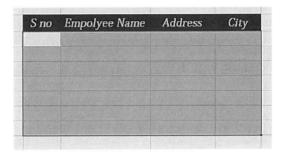

- Go to the Home tab, click on the Border command and select the border style you want

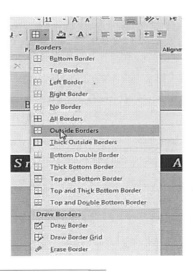

- Here on this page, the selected border will appear

S no	·Empolyee Name	Address	City
	✛		

NOTE: You can also draw the border by yourself and also add colours to the border with the Draw tools at the bottom of the Borders drop-down menu.

CHANGING THE TEXT ALIGNMENT OF YOUR BORDER

By default, the text entered into the worksheet is always at the bottom of the cell. You can change the way your cell content is displayed in such a way that makes it easy to read. To change the alignment, all you have to do is:

- Select the cell you wish to change
- From the Home tab, select the Alignment command to choose the one you prefer.

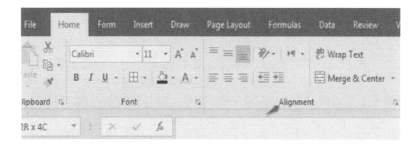

MODIFYING THE COLUMNS, ROWS, AND CELL IN A WORKSHEET

Modifying the columns, rows and cell allows you to change the height and width to different sizes you desire.

MODIFYING THE COLUMN WIDTH

To change the width of the column, all you have to do is:

- Place the mouse over the column line in the column heading and ensure that the white cross becomes a double arrow

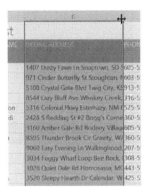

- Click, hold and drag the mouse to increase or decrease the column width.

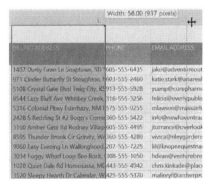

- Release the mouse. The column width will be changed.

MODIFYING THE ROW HEIGHT

To change the height of the row, all you have to do is:

- Place the mouse over the column line in the row heading and ensure that the white cross becomes a double arrow.
- Click, hold, and drag the mouse to increase or decrease the row height.
- Release the mouse and the row height will be changed.

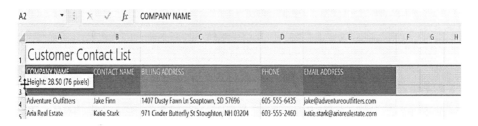

INSERTING NEW ROW

- Choose the row heading below where you desire the new row to display.
- Go to the home tab, select the insert command and click on Insert sheet rows and the new row will be seen.

INSERTING NEW COLUMN

- Choose the column heading to the right where you desire the new column to display.

- Go to the home tab, select the insert command and click on Insert sheet columns and the new sheet will be seen.

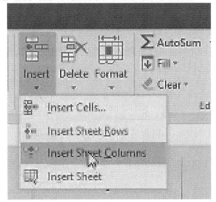

DELETING OF ROWS AND COLUMNS

In case you want to delete a row or column you don't find useful; all you need to do is:

- Select the rows and columns to be deleted.
- From the Home tab, click on the Delete command and the selected rows and columns will be deleted.

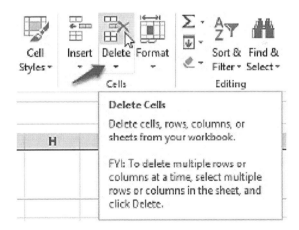

HOW TO HIDE AND UNHIDE ROWS OR COLUMNS

You can certainly hide some of your rows and columns on your worksheet while working on it and to do this:

- Select the column or row you intend to hide.
- Right-click on it and select Hide from the formatting menu.

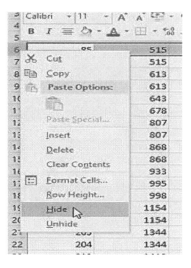

- The column or row is hidden with an indication of a green line on it.

- To unhide a column, select the columns on both sides of the hidden column.
- Right-click the mouse and select Unhide from the formatting menu and the hidden columns will appear.

WRAPPING TEXT AND MERGING CELLS

In the course of working on the worksheet, a cell may have too much content on it and you may need to wrap or merge the cell rather than increasing the size of the cell. With the use of wrapping, the texts are modified in such a way that they fit into the cell thereby adjusting the cell and displaying the content on multiple lines. Merging on its own allows you to combine or join a cell close to it by creating a large cell.

To merge cells

- Select the cell you want to merge.

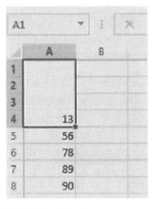

- From the Home tab, go to Merge and Centre to choose the option you desire in the listed options.

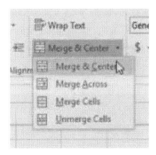

- Then the cell will be adjusted to the option chosen.

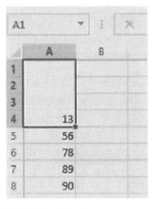

To wrap texts

- Select the cell you wish to wrap.

- From the Home tab, go to the Select Text command and the texts in the cells will be wrapped.

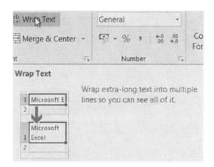

- The texts in the cells will be wrapped.

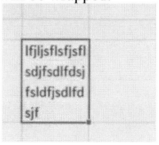

CUSTOMIZING THE DEFAULT WORKBOOK

Working on the Excel default workbook can be boring at times due to the interface of the workbook. However, you can make your Excel workbook look more captivating and exciting to work on by changing some features like the font size, font style, column width and heights, etc. which have been explained in Excel 1 under formatting the cells. To continue from there, we will be learning some other ways to customize the default workbook to suit your taste.

HOW TO CHANGE THE WORKSHEET THEME

From the Page **layout**, click on Themes to select anyone that suits your taste

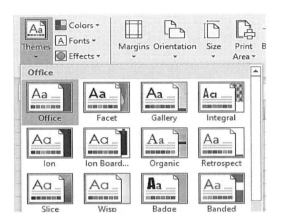

HOW TO CHANGE THE WORKSHEET THEME COLOUR

- Go to the **Page layout** and click on **Colours** to select anyone that suits your taste

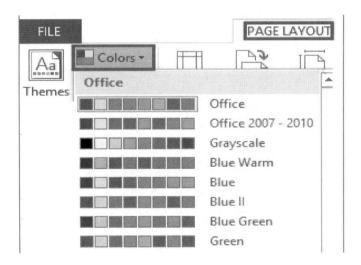

HOW TO CHANGE THE WORKSHEET THEME EFFECTS

- Go to the **Page layout** and click on **Effects** to select any that suits your taste

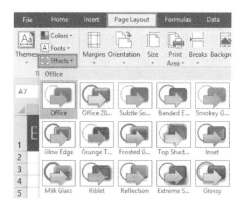

Go to the **Page layout** and click on **Fonts** to select any that suits your taste

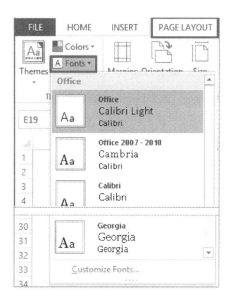

ZOOMING IN OR OUT OF THE SPREADSHEET

You can adjust the view of your default worksheet by zooming in or out. To do this, follow the steps below:

- To view 100%, go to the **View tab** and from the **Zoom group** click on **Zoom 100**
- To maximize the view of the spreadsheet, go to the **View tab** and from **the Zoom group** click **on Zoom to Selection**
- To enter a percentage or any other settings, go to the **View tab** and from **the Zoom group** click **on Zoom to Selection**

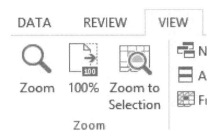

NOTE: You can use the **Zoom slider** on the status bar to zoom in or out.

ADDING MORE WORKSHEETS TO THE WORKBOOK

You can also customize your default workbook by adding more worksheets to the already existed worksheets. To do this, follow the steps below:

- Go to the **Home tab** and click on Insert
- From the **Insert drop-down arrow**, click on **Insert Sheet**

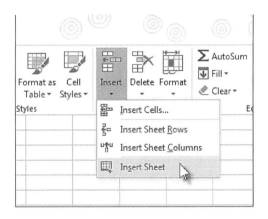

- You can also add a new worksheet by selecting the plus icon at the bottom of the worksheet

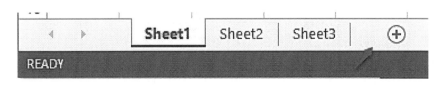

CHAPTER THREE

EXCEL TABLES AND CHARTS

WHAT IS AN EXCEL TABLE?

Excel Tables are containers for your input data. Tables tell excel that all the input data are related. Without a table, the only thing relating the data is proximity to each other.

Creating tables in Excel helps you to analyse your data. You can use table command to change a list of data into a formatted Excel table. With the Excel Table, you can use features like sorting and filtering that will give your data an organized and structured look. You can also conveniently insert formulas in the tables.

Before creating a formatted Excel Table for your data, follow the guidelines below to organize your data.

- The data must be organized and arranged in rows and columns.
- In the first row, each column must have a heading.
- Each column must contain one set of data.
- The list must have no blank rows and columns.

CREATING A TABLE

- Select all the lists of data in the worksheet to be inserted in a table

- From the **Insert tab**, go to the **Tables group** and click on **Table**

- In the **Create Table dialog box**, the range of your data automatically appears and you can make adjustments to the data range. Then check **My table has header** and click on **Ok**

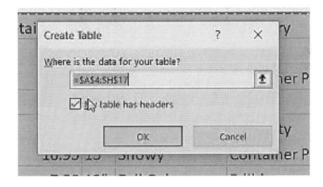

- Then the data are formatted in the Excel tables

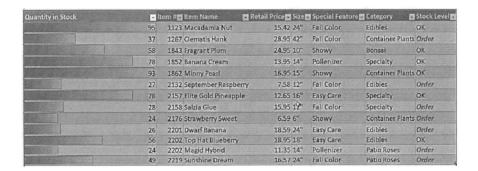

SORTING A TABLE

You can sort the data in a table by following these simple steps:

- Click on the arrow next to the **Item name** and select **Sort A to Z**

- Then click on **Ok**.

FILTERING A TABLE

You can choose to filter i.e.; select the data you wish to have displayed on your table by following these simple steps:

- Click on the arrow next to **Category** and select **Specialty**
- Then click on **Ok**.

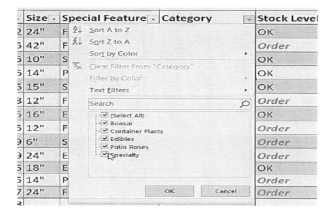

CREATING PIVOT TABLE AND CHARTS IN EXCEL

THE PIVOT TABLE

The Pivot Table is a powerful tool that is used to summarize, organize, sort, and analyze data stored in a table.

The following are the procedures on how to create a pivot table:

- Select the cell you wish to create a Pivot Table for
- From **Insert tab**, go to **Pivot Table**

- From **Choose the data that you want to analyse**, choose either **table** or **range**.
- Under **Choose where you want the Pivot Table report to be placed,** you can select **New worksheet** or **Existing worksheet**.
- Then click on **Ok**.

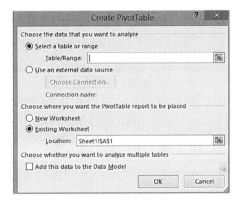

- To add a field to the Pivot table, go to the **Pivot Tables Field pane and** select the field name checkbox.

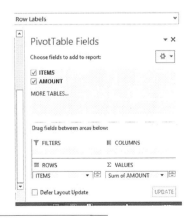

- Drag the field to the desired location with your mouse if you wish to move the field from one area to another

If you have followed the instructions above, your table will look like the image below

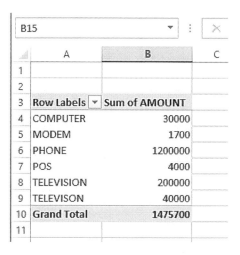

THE PIVOT CHART

The pivot chart is a visual representation of the data on the pivot table. To create a pivot chart from the pivot table, follow the instructions below:

- Select a cell in the pivot table.
- Go to Insert and click on pivot Chart.
- Then click on Ok.

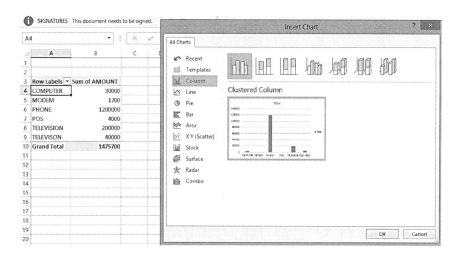

If you have followed the instructions above, your pivot table and chart will look like the image below;

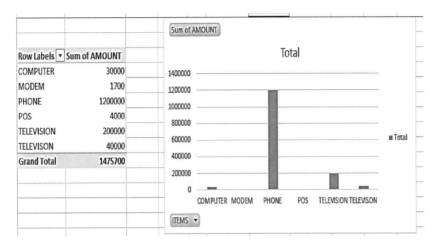

USING SLICER ON TABLES OR PIVOT TABLES

The slicer feature is used to filter data on tables or Pivot tables. It appears like a form of a button on the Excel worksheet to filter data.

To use the slicer;

- Select any cell on the table or the Pivot table
- From the **Home tab,** go to **Insert** and click on **Slicer**
- In the **Insert Slicers dialog box, select the field you want to display from the checks box**
- Then click on **Ok**

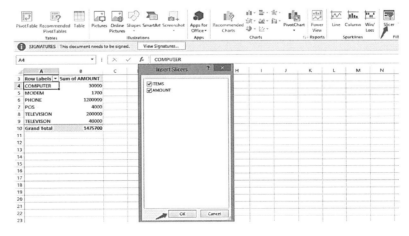

The picture below shows how the slicer looks like when used to filter data on table or Pivot table

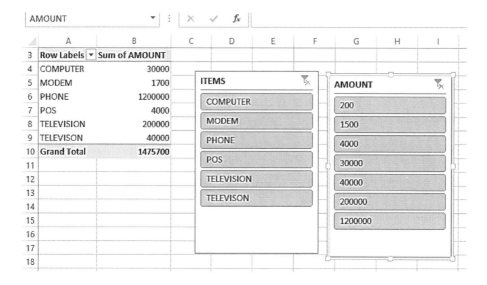

WORKING WITH CHARTS

Charts in Excel help to present data on your worksheet in a visual form thereby displaying the data which are in form of rows and columns as bars on a chart. These are varieties of charts that can be applied or used to display data. To mention a few, Excel provides charts like Pie chart, Line chart, Bar chart, Column chart, etc.

Data shown in charts are more interesting, clearer, and easier to read and understand. With the use of charts, you can evaluate your data and make comparisons between different values.

TYPES OF EXCEL CHART

There are different types of chart in Excel but briefly, we will be talking about just a few out of it.

Column Chart: This is a chart that compares values along the vertical axis and categories along the horizontal axis. There are different types of column charts such as clustered column, stacked column, 3-D stacked column, etc.

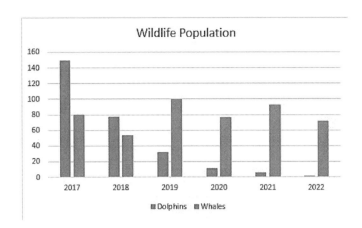

Line Chart: This is a chart that is used for showing trends in data at equal intervals e.g., months, years, days, etc. Examples of line chart are line, stacked line with markers, 100% stacked line, etc.

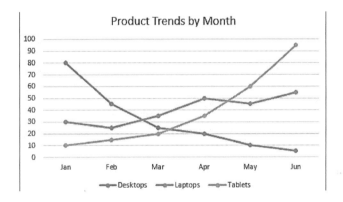

Bar Chart: Just like the column chart, the bar chart compares values along the vertical axis and categories along the horizontal axis. There are different types. The bar chart is used with large label texts. Examples of bar charts are clustered bar, stacked bar, 3-D stacked bar, etc.

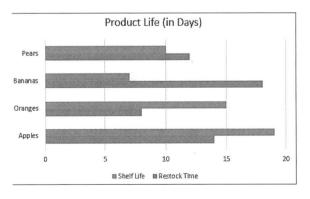

Pie Chart: This is a graph that presents or displays data in a circular graph. This chart displays information and information using a pie slice format.

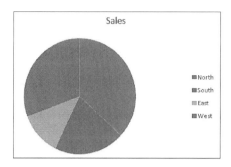

Doughnut Chart: This is a chart that shows the relationship of parts to a whole and when all pieces brought together will still amount to 100% percent just like the pie chart. The difference between the doughnut pie chart and the pie chart is that the doughnut chart can contain more than one series of data while the pie chart can only contain one data series.

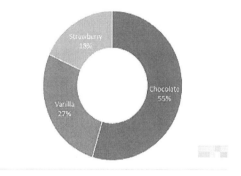

HOW TO INSERT A CHART IN EXCEL

- Select data for the chart

- Select Insert and go to Recommended Charts

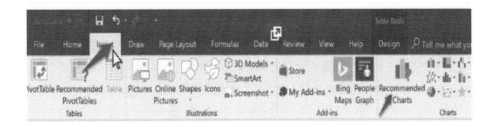

- Choose a chart on the Recommended charts tab and preview the chart

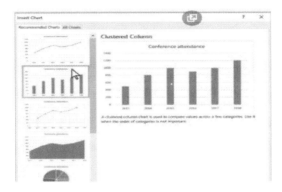

- Select the chart and click on Ok.

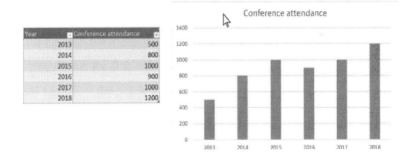

HOW TO ADD TITLE TO A CHART

When you add a title to your chart, it gives your chart a sense of purpose, and people going through your work on the Excel worksheet will be able to identify or recognize the purpose of the chart. To add a title to your chat, all you need is to do is:

- Click anywhere within the chart area

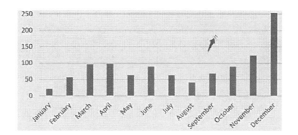

- Click on the plus sign at the upper part of the chart

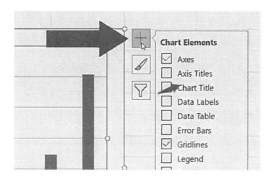

- Then click on Chart title among every other option listed

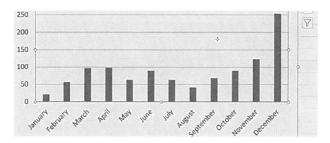

- And to change it from Chart Title, just click into the textbox to any title of your choice

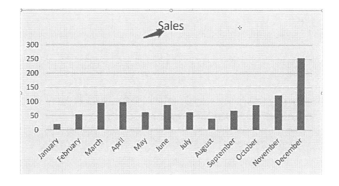

NOTE: To change the color, font size, and the font type, just right-click on the Chart title.

HOW TO CHANGE CHART TYPE IN EXCEL

There are different types of charts used in the presentation of data. In case the chart type you used in presenting your data is not suiting or appropriate, you can switch to another chart that best explained your data.

To get this done:

- Click on the chart you wish to modify

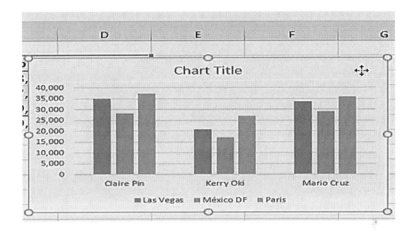

- Go to the Design tab and select Change Chart Type

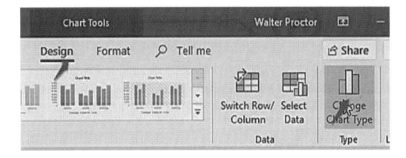

- From the Change Chart Type, a popup window will be displayed where you will have to pick your charts from Recommended charts or All charts

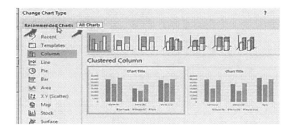

- Choose any chart you want and preview it

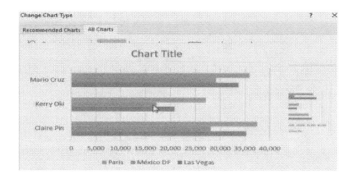

- Then click on Ok and the chart will be displayed in the worksheet.

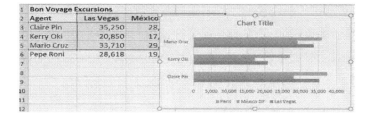

HOW TO CHANGE CHART STYLE IN EXCEL

To change the chart style in your Excel worksheet:

- Click on the chart you wish to modify

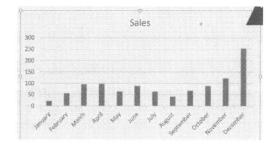

- Go to the Design tab and select Change Chart Style

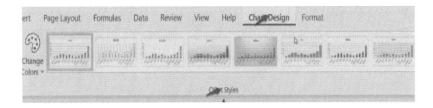

- Here on this page, the chart style will be changed.

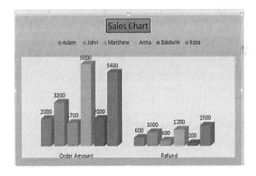

HOW TO CHANGE CHART LAYOUT IN EXCEL

- Click on the chart you wish to modify

- Go to the Design tab and select Quick Layout

- Select the Chart layout you want and the changes will be effected on the Chart

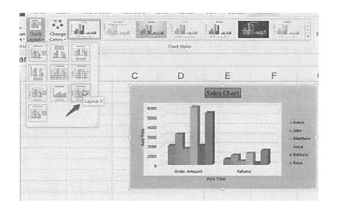

HOW TO SWITCH ROWS AND COLUMNS OF DATA IN A CHART

You can change the way charts arranges your rows and columns of your data to suit your interest. To get this done,

- Click on the chart you wish to modify

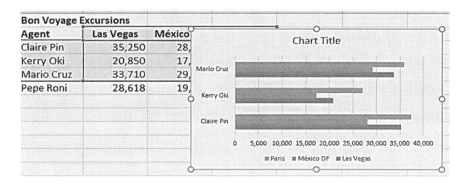

- Go to the Design tab and select Switch Row/Column

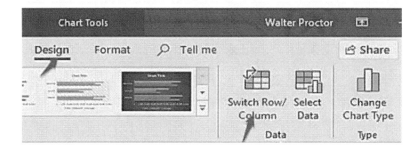

- Here on this page, the rows and columns of the data will be switched

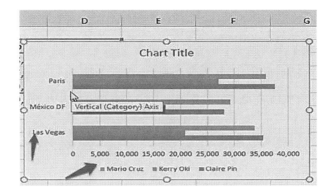

HOW TO MOVE A CHART

You can move a chart from any location on a worksheet or to a new or existing worksheet.

To move a chart within a worksheet with the mouse, drag it to the location you want but to move it to another worksheet,

- Click on the chart you wish to modify

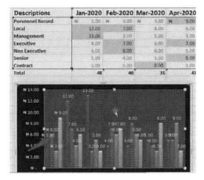

- Go to the Design tab and select Move Chart location

- After clicking on Move Chart Location, a window will pop up where you will need to choose where you want the chart to be placed

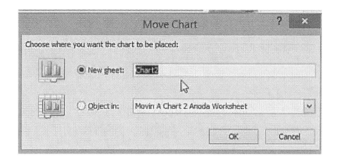

- Then click on Ok and the chart will be moved to another worksheet.

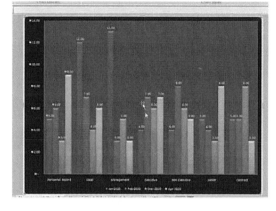

HOW TO RESIZE A CHART ON YOUR WORKSHEET

You can adjust the size of a chart to either small or big depending on what you want. To carry out this operation,

- Click on the chart to modify and at the edges of the chart, some loop handles will appear
- The loop handles allow you to change the horizontal and vertical arrangement of the chart

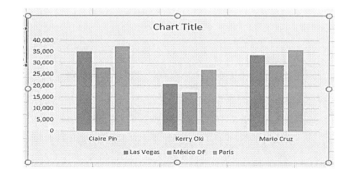

- Click on the loop handles to increase or decrease the size of the chart.

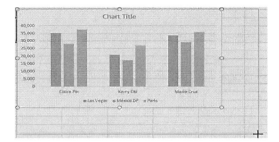

CHAPTER FOUR

CELL REFERENCING IN EXCEL

MEANING OF CELLS REFERENCING

A cell reference is an alphanumeric value or data that is used to locate or identify a cell in a worksheet. The cell reference contains one or more letters for the column and a number for the rows (A1). With the cell reference, you can locate the data you want the formula to calculate for you. Another name for cell reference is the **cell address**.

TYPES OF CELL REFERENCING

To understand the concept of cell reference better, there is a need to get familiar with the types of cell references. Therefore, we will be discussing the three types of cell references   and how they can be used:

RELATIVE REFERENCES

All cell references by default are relative references. When you copy multiple cells, they change based on their relative positions of rows and columns. For example, when you multiply B4*C4 in cell D4. When you copy into cell D5, it will become B5*C5.

To create and copy a formula using relative references, follow the steps below:

- Select the cell that will contain the formula **(D4)** and put in the formula to calculate the desired values **(B4*C4)**

- Press **Enter** and the formula will be calculated with the result displayed in the cell.

MENU ITEM	UNIT PRICE	QUANTITY	LINE TOTAL
Empanadas: Beef Picadillo	$2.99	15	$44.85
Empanadas: Chipotle Shrimp	$3.99	10	
Tamales: Chicken Tinga	$2.29	20	
Tamales: Vegetable	$2.29	30	
Arepas: Carnitas	$2.89	10	
Arepas: Queso Blanco	$2.49	20	
Empanadas: Apple Cinnamon	$3.19	40	
Beverages: Horchata	$1.89	25	
Beverages: Lemonade	$1.89	35	
Beverages: Tamarindo	$1.89	10	
		TOTAL	$44.85

- Locate the **Fill handle** in the lower part of cell D4 and then click, hold and drag down to cell D13.

MENU ITEM	UNIT PRICE	QUANTITY	LINE TOTAL
Empanadas: Beef Picadillo	$2.99	15	$44.85
Empanadas: Chipotle Shrimp	$3.99	10	
Tamales: Chicken Tinga	$2.29	20	
Tamales: Vegetable	$2.29	30	
Arepas: Carnitas	$2.89	10	
Arepas: Queso Blanco	$2.49	20	
Empanadas: Apple Cinnamon	$3.19	40	
Beverages: Horchata	$1.89	25	
Beverages: Lemonade	$1.89	35	
Beverages: Tamarindo	$1.89	10	
		TOTAL	$44.85

- Release the mouse and the formula will be to the cells selected and values in each cell will be calculated.

MENU ITEM	UNIT PRICE	QUANTITY	SALES TAX	LINE TOTAL
Empanadas: Beef Picadillo	$2.99	15		$44.85
Empanadas: Chipotle Shrimp	$3.99	10		$39.90
Tamales: Chicken Tinga	$2.29	20		$45.80
Tamales: Vegetable	$2.29	30		$68.70
Arepas: Carnitas	$2.89	10		$28.90
Arepas: Queso Blanco	$2.49	20		$49.80
Empanadas: Apple Cinnamon	$3.19	40		$127.60
Beverages: Horchata	$1.89	25		$47.25
Beverages: Lemonade	$1.89	35		$66.15
Beverages: Tamarindo	$1.89	10		$18.90
			TOTAL	$537.85

ABSOLUTE AND MULTIPLE CELL REFERENCE

An absolute cell reference is a cell reference that uses the dollar sign ($) both row and column constant when copying a formula from one cell to the other in a worksheet.

A multiple cell reference is a cell reference that uses the dollar sign to keep either the row or column constant. In most cases, the relative and absolute are commonly used.

A3	**The column and the row will not change when copied**
A$2	**The row will not change when copied**
$A2	**The column will not change when copied**

HOW TO CREATE AND COPY A FORMULA USING THE ABSOLUTE REFERENCE

In the example below, we will use 7.5% sales tax rate in cell E1 to calculate the sales tax for all data in column D. There will be a need to use absolute reference £1$E in the formula so that each reference remains constant when the formula is copied and fill to other cells in column D.

If the absolute reference is not used in a case like this, the picture below will be the outcome of what the Excel workbook will look like.

		UNIT PRICE	QUANTITY	SALES TAX	LINE TOTAL
2				TAX RATE:	7.5%
3	MENU ITEM	UNIT PRICE	QUANTITY	SALES TAX	LINE TOTAL
4	Empanadas: Beef Picadillo	$2.99	15	=(B4*C4)*E2	$48.21
5	Empanadas: Chipotle Shrimp	$3.99	10	#VALUE!	#VALUE!
6	Tamales: Chicken Tinga	$2.29	20	$2,208.19	$2,253.99
7	Tamales: Vegetable	$2.29	30	#VALUE!	#VALUE!
8	Arepas: Carnitas	$2.89	10	$65,140.30	$65,169.20
9	Arepas: Queso Blanco	$2.49	20	#VALUE!	#VALUE!
10	Empanadas: Apple Cinnamon	$3.19	40	$8,315,590.40	$8,315,718.00
11	Beverages: Horchata	$1.89	25	#VALUE!	#VALUE!
12	Beverages: Lemonade	$1.89	35	##############	##############
13	Beverages: Tamarindo	$1.89	10	#VALUE!	#VALUE!
14				TOTAL	#VALUE!

To ensure this does not occur, follow the steps below:

- Select the cell that will contain the formula **(D4)** and put in the formula to calculate the desired values **(B4*C4)*£1$E**

MENU ITEM	UNIT PRICE	QUANTITY	TAX RATE: SALES TAX	7.5% LINE TOTAL
Empanadas: Beef Picadillo	$2.99	15	=(B4*C4)*E2	⊕ $48.21
Empanadas: Chipotle Shrimp	$3.99	10	#VALUE!	#VALUE!
Tamales: Chicken Tinga	$2.29	20	$2,208.19	$2,253.99
Tamales: Vegetable	$2.29	30	#VALUE!	#VALUE!
Arepas: Carnitas	$2.89	10	$65,140.30	$65,169.20
Arepas: Queso Blanco	$2.49	20	#VALUE!	#VALUE!
Empanadas: Apple Cinnamon	$3.19	40	$8,315,590.40	$8,315,718.00
Beverages: Horchata	$1.89	25	#VALUE!	#VALUE!
Beverages: Lemonade	$1.89	35	##############	##############
Beverages: Tamarindo	$1.89	10	#VALUE!	#VALUE!
			TOTAL	#VALUE!

- Press **Enter** and the formula will be calculated with the result displayed in the cell.

	MENU ITEM	UNIT PRICE	QUANTITY	TAX RATE: SALES TAX	7.5% LINE TOTAL
4	Empanadas: Beef Picadillo	$2.99	15	$3.36	⊕ $48.21
5	Empanadas: Chipotle Shrimp	$3.99	0	#VALUE!	#VALUE!
6	Tamales: Chicken Tinga	$2.29	20	$2,208.19	$2,253.99
7	Tamales: Vegetable	$2.29	30	#VALUE!	#VALUE!
8	Arepas: Carnitas	$2.89	10	$65,140.30	$65,169.20
9	Arepas: Queso Blanco	$2.49	20	#VALUE!	#VALUE!
10	Empanadas: Apple Cinnamon	$3.19	40	$8,315,590.40	$8,315,718.00
11	Beverages: Horchata	$1.89	25	#VALUE!	#VALUE!
12	Beverages: Lemonade	$1.89	35	##############	##############
13	Beverages: Tamarindo	$1.89	10	#VALUE!	#VALUE!
14				TOTAL	#VALUE!

- Locate the **Fill handle** in the lower part of cell D4 and then click, hold and drag down to cell D13.

	MENU ITEM	UNIT PRICE	QUANTITY	TAX RATE: SALES TAX	7.5% LINE TOTAL
4	Empanadas: Beef Picadillo	$2.99	15	$3.36	$48.21
5	Empanadas: Chipotle Shrimp	$3.99	10	#VALUE!	#VALUE!
6	Tamales: Chicken Tinga	$2.29	20	$2,208.19	$2,253.99
7	Tamales: Vegetable	$2.29	30	#VALUE!	#VALUE!
8	Arepas: Carnitas	$2.89	10	$65,140.30	$65,169.20
9	Arepas: Queso Blanco	$2.49	20	#VALUE!	#VALUE!
10	Empanadas: Apple Cinnamon	$3.19	40	$8,315,590.40	$8,315,718.00
11	Beverages: Horchata	$1.89	25	#VALUE!	#VALUE!
12	Beverages: Lemonade	$1.89	35	##############	##############
13	Beverages: Tamarindo	$1.89	10	#VALUE!	#VALUE!
14				TOTAL	#VALUE!

- Release the mouse and the formula will be to the cells selected and values in each cell will be calculated.

	MENU ITEM	UNIT PRICE	QUANTITY	SALES TAX	LINE TOTAL
2				TAX RATE:	7.5%
3	MENU ITEM	UNIT PRICE	QUANTITY	SALES TAX	LINE TOTAL
4	Empanadas: Beef Picadillo	$2.99	15	$3.36	$48.21
5	Empanadas: Chipotle Shrimp	$3.99	10	$2.99	$42.89
6	Tamales: Chicken Tinga	$2.29	20	$3.44	$49.24
7	Tamales: Vegetable	$2.29	30	$5.15	$73.85
8	Arepas: Carnitas	$2.89	10	$2.17	$31.07
9	Arepas: Queso Blanco	$2.49	20	$3.74	$53.54
10	Empanadas: Apple Cinnamon	$3.19	40	$9.57	$137.17
11	Beverages: Horchata	$1.89	25	$3.54	$50.79
12	Beverages: Lemonade	$1.89	35	$4.96	$71.11
13	Beverages: Tamarindo	$1.89	10	$1.42	$20.32
14				TOTAL	$578.19

REFERENCES TO OTHER WORKSHEET

You can use the same value on one or more worksheet without the need to write or copy the formula again.

- Identify the cell you wish to reference **(D14)**, take note of the name of the worksheet **(Menu Order)**
- Open the worksheet **(Catering Invoice)** you intend to use

	MENU ITEM	UNIT PRICE	QUANTITY	SALES TAX	LINE TOTAL
3	MENU ITEM	UNIT PRICE	QUANTITY	SALES TAX	LINE TOTAL
4	Empanadas: Beef Picadillo	$2.99	15	$3.36	$48.21
5	Empanadas: Chipotle Shrimp	$3.99	10	$2.99	$42.89
6	Tamales: Chicken Tinga	$2.29	20	$3.44	$49.24
7	Tamales: Vegetable	$2.29	30	$5.15	$73.85
8	Arepas: Carnitas	$2.89	10	$2.17	$31.07
9	Arepas: Queso Blanco	$2.49	20	$3.74	$53.54
10	Empanadas: Apple Cinnamon	$3.19	40	$9.57	$137.17
11	Beverages: Horchata	$1.89	25	$3.54	$50.79
12	Beverages: Lemonade	$1.89	35	$4.96	$71.11
13	Beverages: Tamarindo	$1.89	10	$1.42	$20.32
14				TOTAL	$578.19
15					

Catering Invoice   Menu Order

- Select the cell where you wish for the value to appear**(C4)**. Type the **equal sign (=)**, the **sheet name**, an **exclamation mark (!)**, and the **cell address (='Menu Order'!E14)**

MENU ITEM	UNIT PRICE	LINE TOTAL
Menu Order	Food & beverage	T='Menu Order'!E14
Paper Goods	Plates, utensils, cups	$110.87
Rental Equipment	Tables, chairs, linens	$249.95
Service Fee	18% of food & beverage	$0.00
	TOTAL	$360.82

- Press **Enter** and the value of the reference cell will be replicated in the new worksheet and if there is any change in the **Menu Order** worksheet, it will be automatically updated on the **Catering Invoice** worksheet.

MENU ITEM	UNIT PRICE	LINE TOTAL
Menu Order	Food & beverage	$578.19
Paper Goods	Plates, utensils, cups	$110.87
Rental Equipment	Tables, chairs, linens	$249.95
Service Fee	18% of food & beverage	$104.07
	TOTAL	$1,043.08

REFERENCES TO WORKSHEETS IN OTHER WORKBOOK

You can make reference to a worksheet on another workbook. In the example below, we want to calculate the difference between two months' expenses in different workbooks. To get this done, follow the procedures below:

- Open the worksheet for the current month **(Overview)**. Select the cell that will contain the formula **(C8)** and type **=C6-** inside the selected cell.

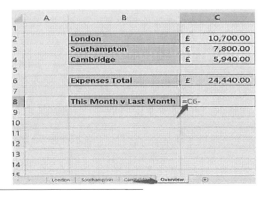

- On the View tab, click on Switch Windows and select the other workbook **(last month expenses).**

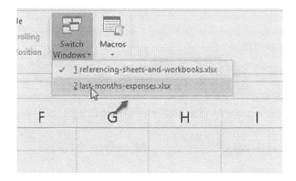

- Then click on worksheet **C6** and press **Enter**

A	B	C
	London	£ 10,950.00
	Southampton	£ 8,150.00
	Cambridge	£ 6,030.00
	Expenses Total	£ 25,130.00
	This Month v Last Month	1,400.00

fx =C6-'[last-months-expenses.xlsx]Overview'!C6

On the **Overview sheet**, the value of the reference cell will be replicated and if there is any change, it will be automatically updated on both the **Overview worksheet and Last month expenses workbook.**

A	B	C
	London	£ 10,700.00
	Southampton	£ 7,800.00
	Cambridge	£ 5,940.00
	Expenses Total	£ 24,440.00
	This Month v Last Month	-£ 690.00

CHAPTER FIVE

INTRODUCTION TO EXCEL FORMULAS & FUNCTIONS

WHAT'S A FORMULA?

Formulas in excel are statements written in the alphanumeric pattern which can perform a particular function on a cell or a range of cells based on the values from other cells or range of cells. For instance; {=Sum (A1+A2) adds up the value in cell A1 with the one in cell A2.}, {=Average (A1: A5) shows a simple average of the values from cell A1 to cell A5}.

Excel uses standard operators for formulas such as a plus sign for addition (+), a minus sign for subtraction (-), an asterisk for multiplication (*), a forward slash for division (/), and a caret (^) for exponents.

HOW TO INSERT FORMULAS IN EXCEL 2021

To create a formula, you must first understand what a cell reference is and the cell reference is what contains the cell address which is used to create a formula. With the cell reference, you can check if the formulas are accurate and you can as well change the value of the cell reference without having to change the formula. For example, the A1 and A2 in the table below is the cell reference.

=A1+A2	Adds cells A1 and A2
=C4-3	Subtracts 3 from C4
=E7/J4	Divide cell E7 by J4
=N10*1.05	Multiply cell N10 by 1.05
=R5^2	Finds the square of cell R5

To create a formula in Excel:

- Select the cell that will contain the formula.

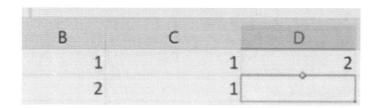

- Start typing in the formula with the equal sign preceded by the first cell address with the mathematical sign you wish to use and lastly followed by the other cell address.

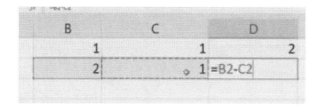

- Click the Enter key and the formula will be calculated with the value displayed in the cell.

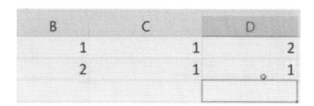

NOTE: let's assume you want to make some changes to a formula in the cell, all you have to do is just:

- Select the cell that contains the formula to be edited.

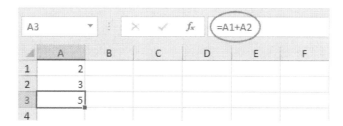

- Click on the Formula bar to make changes and a border will display on the reference cell.

- After this, press the Enter key and automatically, the formula will be updated by itself.

WHAT'S A FUNCTION?

Functions are pre-programmed formulas already available in Excel which makes it easier to perform calculations on topics like statistics, date and time arithmetic, financial calculations, engineering, and the likes. Just like the formula, you need to start the function with an equal sign before the function name.

To use a function, one must understand what an argument is. The argument is what contains what is to be calculated in form of cell addresses and they are contained or enclosed within parenthesis.

Examples of Functions are SUM, AVERAGE, COUNT, MAX, MIN, COUNTA, IF, TRIM, etc.

HOW TO INSERT A FUNCTION

Excel contains varieties of functions that can be created depending on what operation you want to carry out. To insert a function on your Excel program:

- Click on the cell that will contain the function.

- Type in first the equal sign and then the function name.

- Open the parenthesis and highlight the cells to affect the changes and then click on Enter and the final result will be displayed at the end of the cell.

B	C	D
1	1	2
2	1	1
2	2	4
4	2	2
24		
=min(B1:D4)		

You can also insert a function by using the Function command by following the steps below:

- Select a cell and click on the Insert function button above the worksheet.

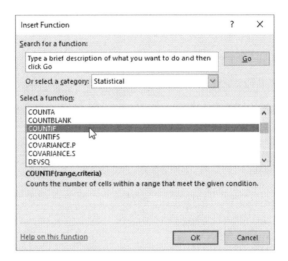

- Choose any out of the categories of functions that will be displayed then click on **Ok**.

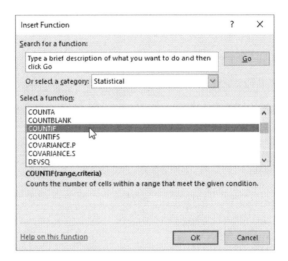

- In the next page, the Function Arguments dialogue box will appear.
- Select the range from the Range box and the criteria from the criteria box.

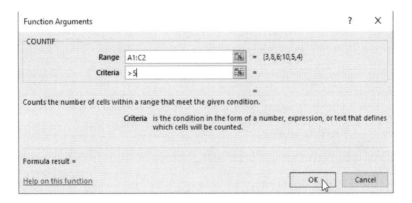

- Then click on Ok.

INTRODUCING THE FORMULAR TAB

The Excel ribbon which is located at the top of Excel contains a lot of tabs in which the formula tab is included. The Formula tab is used to insert functions, create a named range, review the formula, etc. The formula tab is divided into four groups, namely:

- *Function library*
- *Defined Names*
- *Formula Auditing*
- *Calculation*

Function Library: Excel contains 461 functions and these are located in the Function Library Group. With the Function Library, you can learn and find a new formula from the formula categories such as Logical, Financial, Text, Math & Trig, etc.

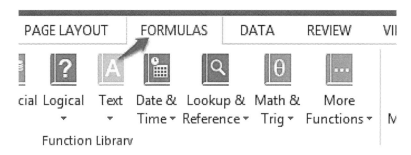

Defined Names: This option allows you to define the name of a cell. This feature allows you to view the named sections on the worksheet in the Name manager and also edit them to any desired defined name if you want

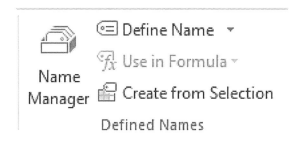

Formula Auditing: This option is used for checking and correcting formulas. This option has the following features;

- o **Trace Precedent:** This helps to know where the formula is based or located on the cell
- o **Trace Dependent:** This helps to check if the active cell is used by any formula
- o **Remove Arrow:** This is used to remove arrows from the cell
- o **Show Formula:** This shows the formula in the worksheet
- o **Error Checking:** This option checks the error in the formula on the worksheet
- o **Evaluate Formula**: This evaluates the formula step by step on the worksheet
- o **Watch Window**: This option allows you to monitor the values on all the cells within the window.

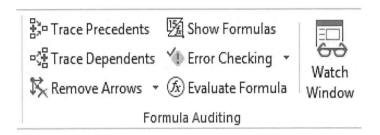

- • **Calculation:** This is the option that allows you to switch calculation from automatic to manual

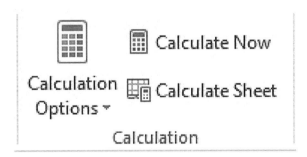

THE FORMULA BAR

The formula bar is a section in the Microsoft Excel worksheet where data or formulas entered into the worksheet appear in the active cell. With the formula bar, you can edit any data or formula typed into the active cell. Another name for the formula bar is the **Formula box.**

WHERE IS THE FORMULA BAR LOCATED IN MICROSOFT EXCEL?

The formula bar can be located above the spreadsheet. Check the picture below to see how the formula bar looks like and where it is located.

EXPANDING THE FORMULA BAR

There are two ways to expand the formula in Excel and they are:

Expanding the Formula Bar Horizontally: To expand the formula bar horizontally

- Move the mouse cursor in between the Name Box and the Formula Bar until the cursor becomes a horizontal double-ended arrow
- Left-click and drag the arrow to adjust the size

Expanding the Formula Bar Vertically: To expand the formula bar vertically,

- Move the mouse cursor to the bottom of the formula bar until the cursor becomes a horizontal double-ended arrow.
- Left-click and drag the arrow to adjust the size.

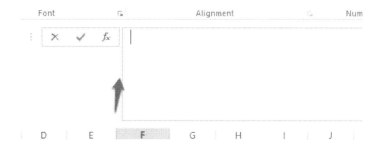

CONTRACTING THE FORMULA BAR

To contract the Formula bar, all you need is to locate the **Contract** or **Expand Toggle** at the right hand.

ENTERING AND EDITING DATA IN THE FORMULA BAR

To enter or edit any data into the formula bar:

- Select the cell you wish to input the data and start typing.
- As the data is being typed in the cell, automatically it appears in the formula bar.
- To accept any data entered, click the **Check Mark** on the formula bar or press **Enter**. To discard the data entered either click the **X** on the formula bar or press **Esc**

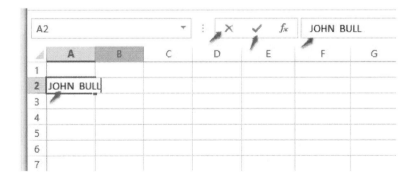

THE INSERT FUNCTION DIALOGUE BOX

This is a dialog box that is used to insert function to any data in a cell in the Excel worksheet. To use the Insert Function box

- Select the cell you wish to insert the function
- Click on the **Insert Function Dialog Box** and select a function
- Then press **Ok**

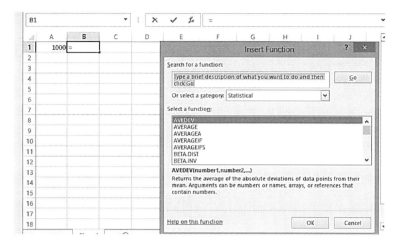

THE FUNCTION ARGUMENT DIALOG BOX

To use the **Function Argument Dialog Box,** you must have first used the **Insert Function Dialog Box.** The Function Argument shows the value that must be provided to get the function's result in the Excel worksheet.

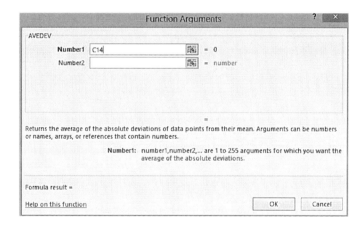

CONTROLLING THE DISPLAY OF THE FORMULA BAR

You can choose to control the display of the formula bar in your worksheet whether to make it visible or not. To do this, follow the steps below:

- From the **File tab**, go to **Option**
- At the left-hand side of the dialog box, click on **Advanced**
- Scroll downward to **Display** and select **Show formula bar**

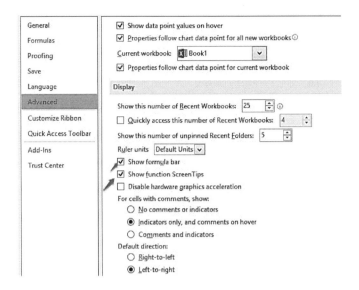

WHAT TYPE OF DATA DOES THE EXCEL FORMULA ACCEPT?

The Excel formula has certain data value it accepts and anything apart from all these may not work. Briefly, let's talk about these values

- **Constant:** These are numbers inputted directly into the formula. A good example is when you enter **=6+5** into a cell to get **11**

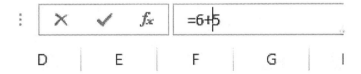

- **Operators:** These are symbols used to perform arithmetic operations (addition, subtraction, division, etc.), comparing values (greater than and less than) and joining values together (**&**) on Excel.

  For example, inputting **=6>4** into the formula returns the value to **TRUE** and this is because 6 is greater than 4

- **Cell References**: These are the values in a worksheet that refer you back to a single cell or range of cells. For Example, inputting A1+B1 in a cell shows that Excel adds the values in both cells in the formula

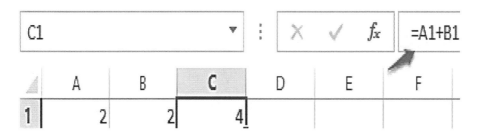

METHODS OF ENTERING AND EDITING OF FORMULAS

Here, we will be talking about how to enter formulas in Excel and also how to edit or make changes to any formulas.

METHODS OF ENTERING OR INSERTING FORMULAS

There are many ways to enter a formula into a cell and they include the following:

- **Simple Insertion:** This involves typing the formula into the cell or formula bar; the formula bar is located above the column headers. This always starts by typing an equality sign, accompanied by the name of the function, and then press **Enter**

- **The Insert Function:** Another way of entering a formula in Excel is through the Excel Insert Function dialogue box. To use this, go to the **Formulas tab** and select the **Insert function**. The Insert Function contains all the functions you need to use on the worksheet

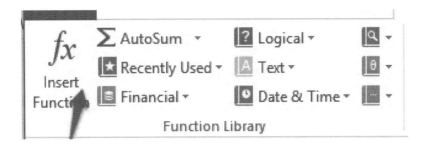

- **Selecting A Formula from One of the Groups in The Formula Tab:** You can enter formulas into your worksheet by selecting the formula from the groups of formula in the Formula tab. To locate a group of formula, move to the **Formula tab** and then select the preferred group from all other groups. In case you don't see your preference, you can click on **More function** options. These groups of the formula are found in the Formula Library

EDITING A FORMULA

Let's assume you need to edit a formula in your worksheet, there are three ways to go about it and they are listed below:

- **Editing Directly in The Formula Bar**: To edit any formula, go to the Formula to start the editing of the formula

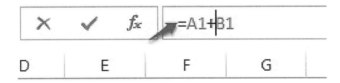

- **Double Clicking on The Formula Cell:** You can also edit any formula by clicking directly into the cell. By doing this, the cell is activated into an **Edit mode** where the formula can be edited

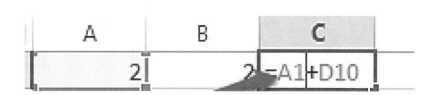

USING THE FORMULA OPERATORS

Formula operators are symbols that specify the operation to be carried out or accomplished in the Excel formula. The formula operators are divided into seven categories which are:

- Arithmetic
- Comparison
- Concatenation
- Logical
- Access
- the If
- the Alt operators.

Arithmetic Operators: These are operators that perform basic mathematical operations such as addition, subtraction, division or multiplication. These operators work with numbers. The different arithmetic operators are as follows in the table below:

ARITHMETIC OPERATOR	NUMBERS OF OPERANDS	ARITHMETIC FUNCTION	EXAMPLES
Plus sign +	2	Addition	3+5
Minus sign -	2	Subtraction	6-2
Minus sign -	1	Negation	-6
Asterisk *	2	Multiplication	3*7
Forward slash /	2	Division	4/2
Exponentiation ^	2	Raise the power of a value	4^2
Percent %	1	Divide by 100	45%

Comparison Operators: These operators compare two numbers with each other and they involve two input values and produce one output value. These operators involve greater than, less than, etc. They are listed in the table below:

COMPARISON OPERATOR	MEANING	EXAMPLE
Equal sign =	Equal to	5=5
Less than sign <	Less than	2<4
Greater than sign >	Greater than	5>3
Greater than or equal to sign>=	Greater than or equal to	67>=321
Less than or equal to sign =<	Less than or equal to	521=321
Not equal to sign <>	Not equal to	5<>7

Concatenation Operator: This operator joins or connects two or more texts or strings to produce a single text or string. The input values received by this operator are texts and if otherwise, they are automatically changed to texts.

OPERATOR	MEANING	EXAMPLE
Ampersand &	Connect or join two values to produce a single text	''In'' & ''put'' to form ''Input''

Logical Operators: There are three logical operations which are *And, Or, and Not*. They receive Boolean values as the values of their operands and they produce one Boolean value as their result or output. The logical operators are expressed in the table below:

LOGICAL OPERATOR	NUMBERS OF OPERANDS	MEANINGS	EXAMPLE
And	2	True if both input values are true	5<3 **and** amount <3
Or	2	True if one of the input value is true	7>5 **or** 4<7
Not	1	Reverses the value of its input value	**not** 5>6

Reference Operators: These operators join cells together for calculations and they are as follows:

REFERENCE OPERATOR	MEANING
(colon):	Range operator: This gives one reference to all the cells between two reference
comma '	Union operator: This joins multiple references into one reference
space	Intersection operator: This gives one reference to cells common to the two references.

- **Access Operators:** These consist of the Dot operator (.), the Index operator ([]), and the at operator (@).
- **The ''Alt'' Operator:** This operator is used to specify several alternative formulae that can be used in a cell
- **The ''if'' Operator:** The If operator is used to performing conditional calculations on the Excel worksheet.

ORDER OF FORMULA OPERATORS' PRECEDENCE

Formula operator precedence can be defined as the order in which the numeric base executes or carry out the operation in the formula. In the Excel worksheet, the operators are evaluated to execute calculations or workings in a specific order. For instance, Excel executes division before subtraction. The order of operators' formula is as follows:

- The member access operator (. [] and @)
- Negation (-1)
- Multiplication and division (* and /)
- Addition and subtraction (+ and -)
- The comparison operators (= < > <= >= < and >)
- Concatenation operator (&)
- Logical operator (not and or)
- The If operator
- The Alt operator

THE NESTED PARENTHESES

Nested parentheses are parentheses inside other parentheses. When there is a set of parentheses inside another, Excel evaluates the innermost set of parentheses first before the outer parentheses; = **((A2+B2) +(C2/D2) *E2**

Note that every open parenthesis must have a matching close parenthesis. In the course of adding parentheses to your formula, you can get confused and lost and that is why Excel helps to give the open parenthesis and matching close parentheses the same colour for easy and quick identification.

f_x | =((A1+B2)-(C2-D2))|

F	G	H

=((A1+B2)-(C2-D2))

WORKING WITH FUNCTIONS

As earlier said, a function is a predefined or pre-set formula. Functions give a quick and easy way to accomplish or execute a common task. There are a lot of calculations that cannot be done with formula except with functions.

WHY SHOULD YOU USE FUNCTIONS?

There are several reasons why you should use or get yourself acquainted with the use of Excel function. The following are the reasons:

- One of the benefits of the Excel function is that it helps to simplify your formula. For instance, you can add the value of C1 to C3 by using =SUM (C1:C3) rather than using =(C1+C2+C3).
- Function helps to execute calculations that cannot be done using the standard formula. For instance, there is no way you can get the highest or lowest number using the formula but with the function, you can use the **MAX** or **MIN** function.
- Function also helps to save time and reduce the stress of having to accomplish what you would have naturally done with a formula for long hours to be done in just a short period. For instance, using the LEFT function to bring out the left 8 characters in a cell; =LEFT(A1,10).

THE FUNCTION ARGUMENTS

Function arguments are the inputs or values needed by functions to perform or carry out calculations on the worksheet. For functions to calculate correctly, some information is needed which are known as the arguments.

To construct a function, the function name and arguments are required. When you need to use a function, enter the name of the function, open the parenthesis, followed by the argument to use, and lastly the close parenthesis; e.g., **AVERAGE (B2:C5)**

USING FUNCTIONS WITH NO ARGUMENTS

Some functions do not require the use of arguments to carry out their operations. These functions include RAND, TODAY, and NOW function. **Note** that even though these functions do not require the use of arguments, they still need to be used with the open and close parentheses; =**RAND** ()

USING FUNCTION WITH ONE OR MORE ARGUMENTS

There are some functions that require more than one argument to execute their operations. To separate the arguments in the function, a

comma is used. A very good example is the LARGE function. The LARGE function returns the largest number within the range of a cell. For instance, to get the fourth largest value in a range from A1 to A50, just type in the LARGE function on the formula bar

=LAREGE (A1:A3, 4)

USING FUNCTIONS WITH BOTH REQUIRED AND OPTIONAL ARGUMENT

Some functions do not only use their required arguments, they also come with optional arguments to execute their operations of which the NETWORKDAYS function is included.

The NETWORKDAYS function gives or returns the number of workdays between the start date and the end date. To get this result, you will need to use the required arguments which are the start date and the end date. And by implication, the answer will be 260 workdays from January 1, 2015 to December 31, 2015.

=NETWORKDAYS (''1/1/2015'',''12/31/2015'')

The optional arguments in the NETWORKDAYS Function allow you to exclude the range that contains the list of holiday dates. The function sees each date in the optional arguments as non-working days and thereby, returning the result to be 255 workdays from January 1, 2015, and December 31, 2015.

NETWORKDAYS (''1/1/2015'',''12/31/2015'', A1:A5)

LOCATING A FUNCTION'S ARGUMENTS

There are two ways of finding the required arguments of a function in a worksheet. They include the following:

- *The Function Dialogue Box*
- *Tooltip Windows in Excel*

- **The Excel Function Dialogue Boxes**: Every function in Excel has a dialogue box that contains or shows the list of the required and optional arguments. To open a function dialogue box, all you need to do is;
  - o Go to the Ribbon and click on the Formula tab
  - o Click on Insert Function and the function argument box will be displayed

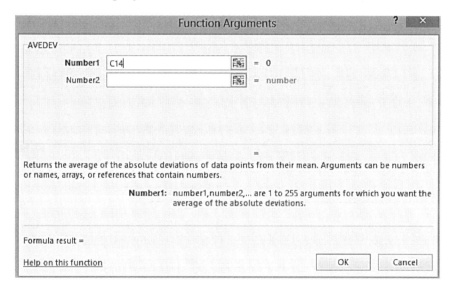

- **Tooltips**: Another way to find the function's arguments in Excel is through the Tooltips. To find the arguments;
  - o Select a cell and type the equal sign to notify the program that a formula is inputted
  - o Type the function's name with the open parenthesis: by doing this, the function name and its arguments are listed in the tooltips

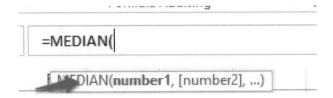

ERRORS IN FORMULAS AND FUNCTIONS

Of a truth, working with Excel functions and formulas can be difficult and time-consuming, especially when the formula or function returns an error in value instead of what you have in mind. Quickly, I will open your eyes to the seven errors that can occur while working with your functions and formulas and as well as the reason behind them.

#DIV/0! This error value implies that the formula is attempting to divide a value by zero. And mathematically, no number can be divided by zero. This can also occur when you are trying to divide an empty cell by zero.

#NAME? This error value means that the name used in a formula is not recognized by Excel as a valid object. This error can occur as a result of wrong spelling of function, sheet name, cell reference, or other syntax error.

#N/A: This error value means that the formula cannot give a valid or legitimate result. This error occurs when an inappropriate argument is used in a function. Also, this can happen when the lookup function does not a match.

#NULL! This error value implies that the formula uses an intersection of two ranges that do not relate or interact.

#NUM! This error value implies that there is a problem with a number in your formula most especially an invalid argument in math or trig function. For instance, when you are expected to give a positive number but you gave a negative number.

#REF! This error value connotes that the formula contains an invalid cell reference and this can be caused when a row or column to which the formula is referred is deleted or the formula uses a cell reference that does not exist.

#VALUE This error value implies that there is a wrong usage of data for operation by your formula.

DIFFERENCES BETWEEN AN EXCEL FORMULA AND FUNCTION

The Excel formulas and functions look-alike in so many ways and can be used interchangeably to perform the same operations. However, there is a lot of differences between them. Therefore, we will be stating some of the common differences:

- A **Formula** is a statement written by the users to calculate the value of data in a cell (A1*B2, C3*D4, etc. **WHILE** a **Function** is a piece of code already designed in the Excel worksheet to carry out a pre-defined operation on the Excel (SUM, AVERAGE, MIN, MAX, etc.).
- A **Formula** does not have a name **WHILE** every **Function** has a name.
- A **Formula** does not have a structure or syntax **WHILE Functions** have syntax.
- A **Formula** does not have a predefined parameter **WHILE** every **Function** has its predefined parameter for executing result.
- **Formulas** are mathematical equations WHILE **Function** uses words.

While using the Excel formula, keep the following in mind:
- Excel formulas must begin with an equal (=) sign. With this sign, Excel is able to identify it as a formula
- The answer to the formula is shown in the cell where the formula is entered.

USING CALCULATION OPERATORS IN EXCEL FORMULAS

Operators in Excel helps to identify or distinguish the type of calculation to be performed with the Formulas. There are four major types of calculation operators and they are as follows:

Arithmetic Operators: These are used to perform mathematical operations such as addition, subtraction, multiplication and division with numbers combined with them to produce a numeric result.

Arithmetic Operator	Meaning
+ (plus sign)	Addition
- (minus sign)	Subtraction
* (asterisk)	Multiplication
/ (forward slash)	Division
% (percent)	Percent
^ (caret)	Exponentiation

Comparison Operators: These are operators used to compare two values, therefore, giving a logical value. The following are the comparison operators

Comparison Operator	Meaning
=	Equal to
>	Greater than
<	Less than
>=	Greater than or equal to
<=	Less than or equal to
<>	Not equal to

Text Concatenation Operator: This uses the ampersand sign (&) to concatenate i.e., join one or more texts to form a single piece of text.

Reference Operators: These operators join cells together for calculations and they are as follows:

Reference Operator	Meaning
: (colon)	Range operator: This gives one reference to all the cells between two reference
, (comma)	Union operator: This joins multiple references into one reference
(space)	Intersection operator: This gives one reference to cells common to the two references.

MATHEMATICAL ORDER OF OPERATION IN EXCEL

There is an order of operation to follow when carrying out a mathematical calculation on Excel, especially arithmetic operation. Excel follows the general mathematical rules which are **Parenthesis, Exponents, Multiplication and Division**, and **Addition and Subtraction**. The following steps below show how they are applied;

- The values inside the parenthesis are calculated first.
- Secondly, the exponents are calculated.
- Then the multiplication or division is calculated.
- Lastly, the addition or subtraction is also calculated.

ARITHMETIC IN EXCEL

Here, we will be performing some basic arithmetic operations such as addition, subtraction, division, multiplication, etc.

The Plus Sign (+): This performs the addition of one or more cell

To add,

- Select the cell that will contain the formula
- Type in first, the equal to sign followed. by the first cell address with the **Plus sign** and lastly followed by the last cell address
- Then click on enter.

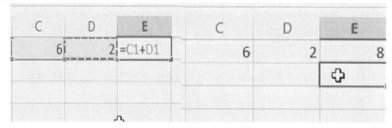

The Minus Sign (-): This is used for subtracting one cell from the other.

To subtract,

- Select the cell that will contain the formula

- Type in first, the equal to sign followed by the first cell address with the **Minus sign** and lastly followed by the last cell address
- Then click on enter.

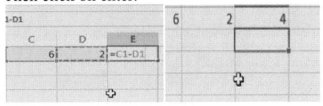

The Asterisk (*): This is used to perform multiplication between two or more cells.

To multiply,

- Select the cell that will contain the formula
- Type in first, the equal to sign followed by the first cell address with the **Asterisk sign** and lastly followed by the last cell address
- Then click on enter.

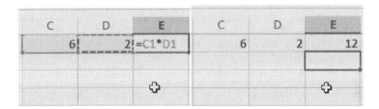

The Forward Slash (/): This is used for dividing

- Select the cell that will contain the formula
- Type in first, the equal to sign followed by the first cell address with the **Forward slash sign** and lastly followed by the last cell address
- Then click on enter.

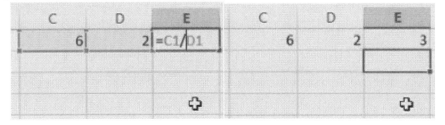

The Percent Sign (%): This divides numbers in the cell by 100

- Select the cell that will contain the formula
- Type in first, the equal to sign followed by the first cell address and followed by the **Percentage sign**
- Then click on enter.

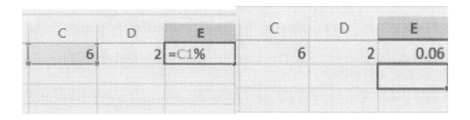

The Caret Sign (^): This is used to perform exponentiation

- Select the cell that will contain the formula
- Type in first, the equal to sign followed by the first cell address and followed by the **Caret sign**
- Then click on enter.

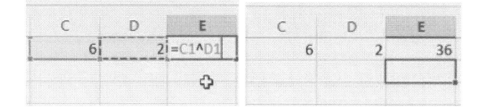

CHAPTER SIX

MUST KNOW EXCEL FORMULAS & FUNCTIONS

Since you have made it this far in this journey of learning more about Excel, there are certain formulas and functions in Excel you should be well acquainted with whether you are a pro or a rookie, it just doesn't matter. Therefore, we will be taking our time to discuss the basic formulas and functions that you need to know.

MATH FUNCTIONS

Math functions are functions that are used to perform arithmetic operations such as percentage of totals, addition, and basic business analysis.

THE SUM FUNCTION

The SUM function allows you to add or sum up the value of selected rows or columns.

=SUM (number1, [number2], …)

For reference purpose

To insert the SUM function

- In the cell, type the SUM function
- Go to the Function argument to select the cells into the cell range box
- Then click on Enter.

The SUM function uses the following arguments

=SUM (number1, [number2], [number3]……)

- **Number1(Required Argument):** This is the first value to sum
- **Number2 (Optional Argument):** This is the second value to sum
- **Number3 (Optional Argument):** This is the third value to sum

USING THE SUM FUNCTION

With the table, let's calculate the sum of the sales made from Monday to Friday using the SUM function

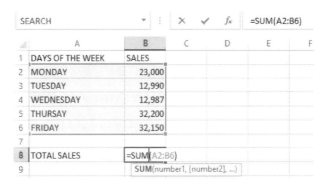

To calculate the sales from Monday to Friday using SUM, follow the steps below

- Select an empty cell and type in the function with the cell range to be summed up; =**SUM (A2:B6)**

- If you have followed the steps above, the total sales from Monday to Friday will be **113327**

NOTE: Keep this in mind while using the SUM function

- #VALUE! error occurs when the criteria supplied is more than 255 characters long
- SUM function ignores empty cells and cells with text values automatically
- The arguments provided can be constants, ranges, named ranges, or cell references
- Any argument that contains errors is returned as an error by the SUM function

THE SUMIF FUNCTION

The SUM function is one that sums up cells based on the criteria or condition provided. The Criteria or conditions are based on dates, numbers, and texts. This function makes use of logical operators such as <, >, etc. and wildcats (*,?)

The SUMIF function uses the following arguments

=SUMIF (range, criteria, [sum_range]

- **Range (Required Argument):** This is the range of cell that the criteria are applied against
- **Criteria (Required Argument):** This is what determines the cells to be summed up. Criteria arguments can be supplied in
  - A numerical value such as integer, decimal, or time
  - A text string such as Monday, East, Price, etc.
  - An expression e.g. >11, <3 etc.
- **Sum_range (Optional Argument):** This is the cell to sum up if there are other cells to sum up apart from the ones specified in the range argument

USING THE SUMIF FUNCTION

To have a clear picture of how the SUMIF function is used, let's calculate the sales made in January and also in USA

	A	B	C	D
1	MONTH	COUNTRY	SALES	
2	JAN	USA	23,000	
3	FEB	ENGLAND	12,990	
4	JAN	USA	12,987	
5	MARCH	FRANCE	32,200	
6	JAN	ITALY	32,150	
7	FEB	USA	33,212	
8	JAN	USA	12,900	

First of all, let's calculate the total sales made in Jan by following the steps below

- Select an empty cell, type in the function with the cell range to be summed up; =SUM (A2:A8

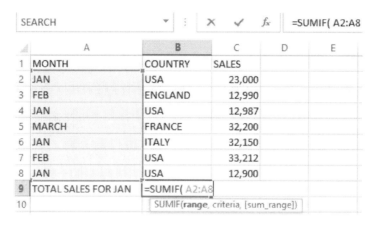

- Put in the criteria which is **Jan**; **SUM (A2:A8, "JAN",**

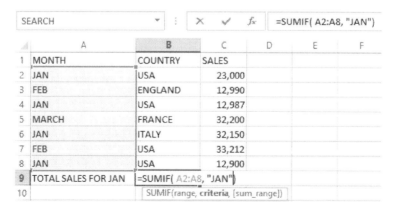

- Then put in the sum_range; **SUM (A2:A8, "JAN", C2;C8)**

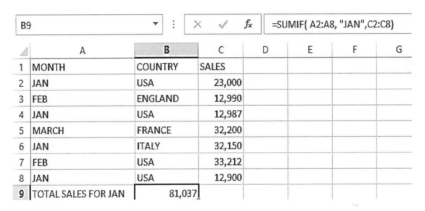

- The total sale of Jan is **81,037** and it is shown in the table below

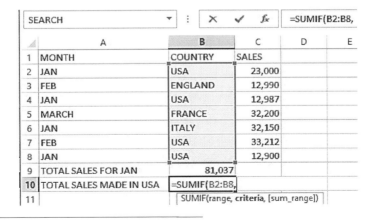

To get the total sales made in USA;

- Select an empty cell and type in the function with the cell range to be summed up; **=SUM(B2:B8**

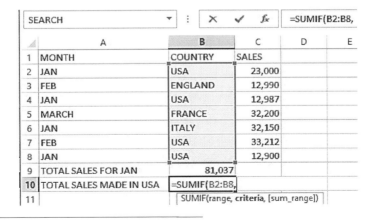

- Put in the criteria which are **USA**; **SUM(B2:B8 "USA"**

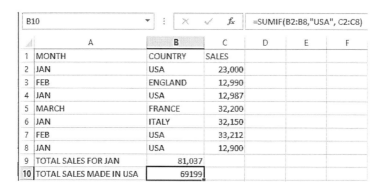

- Then put in the sum_range; **SUM(B2:B8, "USA", B2:B8)**

- The total sales made in USA is shown in the table below

NOTE: Keep this in mind when using the SUMIF FUNCTION

- VALUE! error occurs when the criteria supplied is more than 255 characters' long

- The cells in range will be summed automatically when the sum_range is omitted
- Text strings in criteria must be enclosed in double-quotes otherwise, it will not work
- The wildcards ? and * can be used in the SUMIF function

THE SUMIFS FUNCTION

The SUMIFS function is a function that is used to add cells that meet multiple criteria or conditions. The Criteria or conditions are based on dates, numbers, and texts. This function makes use of logical operators such as $<, >, \leq$ etc., and wildcards (*,?)

The SUMIFS FUNCTION uses the following arguments

SUMIFS (sum_range, criteria_range1, criteria1, [criteria_range2, criteria2] ...)

- **Sum_range:** This is the range to be summed up
- **Criteria_range1:** This is the range of cells that the criteria1 will be applied against
- **Criteria1:** This is used to determine the cells to be added
- **Criteria_range2:** This is the range of cells that the criteria2 will be applied against

USING THE SUMIFS FUNCTION

With the table below, let's calculate the total quantity of Apples supplied by Pete using the **SUMIFS** function

	A	B	C	D	E
	B11				
	A	B	C	D	E
1	Product	supplier	qty		
2	Cherries	John	200		
3	Bananas	Mike	350		
4	Apples	Pete	180		
5	Orange	Mike	400		
6	Apples	John	250		
7					
8	Product	Apple			
9	Supplier	Pete			
10	Qty				
11					

To calculate the total quantity of Apple that was supplied by Pete, follow the steps below

- Select an empty cell and type in the function with the cell range to be summed up; **=SUMIFS (C2:C6, A2:A6, "apples", B2:B6, "Pete")**

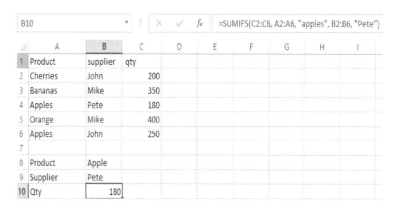

- After following the formula above, the total quantity of apples supplied will be **180**

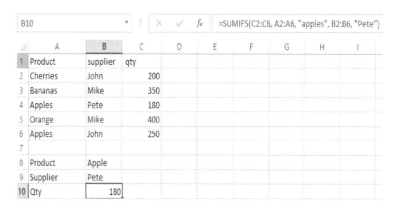

NOTE: Take note of the following when using the SUMIFS functions

- Text strings in criteria must be enclosed in double-quotes ("") e.g., "orange"
- The additional range must have the same number of rows and columns as sum_range.
- #VALUE error occurs when the supplied ranges do not match
- Cell references in criteria are not enclosed in quotes
- SUMIFS can be used on ranges and not on arrays

THE MOD FUNCTION

The MOD function is used to find the remainder of a number (dividend) that has been divided by another number (divisor).

The MOD function uses the following arguments:

- **Number (Required Argument):** This is the number you wish to find the remainder
- **Divisor (Required Argument):** This is the number by which we wish to divide the number

USING THE MOD FUNCTION

With the table below, find the remainder of cell A2 using the MOD function

	A	B	C	D
1	Number	Divisor	MOD FUNCTION	
2	23	2		
3	21	3		
4				
5				
6				

To find the remainder of A2, follow the steps below:

- Click on an empty cell, type in the function to be used, the number, and the divisor; =**MOD(A2, B2**

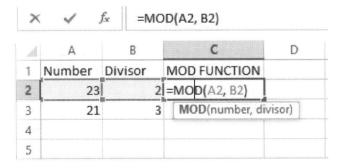

- The result of the above step is shown in the table below

	f_x	=MOD(A2, B2)

⊿	A	B	C
1	Number	Divisor	MOD FUNCTION
2	23	2	1
3	21	3	

NOTE: Things to keep in mind while using the MOD function:

- #DID/0! Error occurs when the divisor value is zero
- The MOD function will return a result in the same sign as the divisor

RANDBETWEEN FUNCTION

The RANDBETWEEN function is a function that returns a random integer as the numbers provided. This function recalculates each time the worksheet is opened or changed.

The RANDBETWEEN function uses the following arguments

=RANDBETWEEN (bottom, top)

- **Bottom: (Required Function):** This is the smallest integer in which the function will return in the range
- **Top (Required Function):** This is the largest integer in which the function will return in the range

USING THE RANDBETWEEN FUNCTION

To understand how the RANDBETWEEN function is being used, let examine the table below

	f_x	=RANDBETWEEN(A2, B2)

⊿	A	B	C	D
1	Bottom	Top	Result	
2	2	3	3	
3	3	10	4	
4	120	300	205	
5	32	121	102	

The table above shows that the RANDBETWEEN function has been applied; =RANDBETWEEN (A2, B2).

- When the calculations on the table are executed again, the worksheet changes its result as shown in the table below

		fx	=RANDBETWEEN(A2, B2)	
	A	B	C	D
1	Bottom	Top	Result	
2	2	3	2	
3	3	10	8	
4	120	300	181	
5	32	121	87	

NOTE: Few notes to keep in mind when using the RANDBETWEEN function

- RANDBETWEEN function returns a new value each time the worksheet is recalculated or changed.
- To stop the random number from changing when the worksheet is calculated, type the RANDBETWEEN function in the formula bar and then press F9 to change the formula into its result
- To generate a set of random numbers in multiple cells, select the cells, enter the RANDBETWEEN function and then press **Ctrl + Enter**

THE ROUND FUNCTION

The ROUND function is a function that rounds up a number to a specific number of digits. This function can either round up or down.

The ROUND function uses the following arguments

=ROUND(number, num_digits)

- **Number1 (Required Argument):** This is the number you want to round

- **Num_digits (Required Argument):** This is the number of digits to which you want to round the number

USING THE ROUND FUNCTION

Let's round 1844.123 to one decimal place, two decimal, nearest integer, nearest 10, nearest 100, and nearest 1000 using the ROUND function

- Round 1844.123 to one decimal place by entering **=ROUND(A1, 1)**

	A	B	C
1	1844.123	1844.1	
2			

=ROUND(A1,1)

- Round 1844.123 to two decimal place by entering **=ROUND(A1, 2)**

	A	B	C
1	1844.123	1844.12	
2			

=ROUND(A1,2)

- Round 1844.123 to the nearest integer by entering **=ROUND(A1, 0)**

B1   =ROUND(A1,0)

	A	B	C	D	E
1	1844.123	1844			
2					

- Round 1844.123 to the nearest 10 by entering **=ROUND(A1, -1)**

B1   =ROUND(A1, -1)

	A	B	C	D	E
1	1844.123	1840			
2					

- Round 1844.123 to the nearest 100 by entering =**ROUND(A1,- 2)**

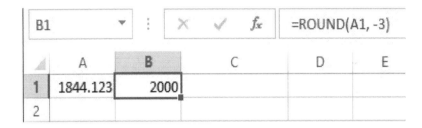

- Round 1844.123 to the nearest 1000 by entering =**ROUND(A1, - 3)**

THE ROUNDUP FUNCTION

The ROUNDUP function is a function that allows you to round up numbers from a certain number of decimal points.

The ROUNDUP function uses the following arguments

=**ROUNDUP(number, num_digits)**

- **Number1 (Required Argument):** This is the number you want to round up
- **Num_digits (Required Argument):** This is the number of digits to which you want to round the number

USING THE ROUNDUP FUNCTION

Let's round up 1233.345 to one decimal place, two decimal, nearest integer, nearest 10, nearest 100, and nearest 1000 using the ROUNDUP function

- Round up 1233.345 to one decimal place by entering **=ROUNDUP(A1, 1)**

	A	B	C	D	E
B1			f_x	=ROUNDUP(A1,1)	
1	1233.345	1233.4			
2					

- Round up 1233.345 to two decimal place by entering **=ROUNDUP(A1, 2)**

	A	B	C	D	E
B1			f_x	=ROUNDUP(A1,2)	
1	1233.345	1233.35			
2					

- Round up 1233.345 to the nearest integer by entering **=ROUNDUP(A1, 0)**

	A	B	C	D	E
B1			f_x	=ROUNDUP(A1,0)	
1	1233.345	1234			
2					

- Round up 1233.345 to the nearest 10 by entering **=ROUNDUP(A1, -1)**

	A	B	C	D	E
B1			f_x	=ROUNDUP(A1,-1)	
1	1233.345	1240			
2					

- Round up 1233.345 to the nearest 100 by entering **=ROUNDUP(A1, -2)**

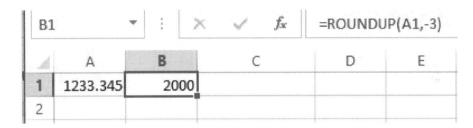

- Round up 1233.345 to the nearest 1000 by entering **=ROUNDUP(A1, -3)**

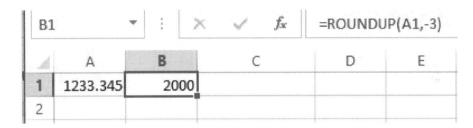

THE ROUNDDOWN FUNCTION

The ROUND DOWN function is a function that allows you to round down numbers from a certain number of decimal points.

The ROUND DOWN function uses the following arguments

=ROUNDUP(number, num_digits)

- **Number1 (Required Argument):** This is the number you want to round down
- **Num_digits (Required Argument):** This is the number of digits to which you want to round the number

USING THE ROUNDDOWN FUNCTION

Let's round up 1233.345 to one decimal place, two decimal, nearest integer, nearest 10, nearest 100, and nearest 1000 using the **ROUNDDOWN** function

- Round down 1233.345 to one decimal place by entering **=ROUNDDOWN(A1, 1)**

B1		▼	:	×	✓	f_x	=ROUNDDOWN(A1,1)	
	A		B		C		D	E
1	1233.345		1233.3					
2								

- Round down 1233.345 to two decimal place by entering **=ROUNDDOWN(A1, 2)**

B1		▼	:	×	✓	f_x	=ROUNDDOWN(A1,2)	
	A		B		C		D	E
1	1233.345		1233.34					
2								

- Round down 1233.345 to the nearest integer by entering **=ROUNDDOWN(A1, 0)**

B1		▼	:	×	✓	f_x	=ROUNDDOWN(A1,0)	
	A		B		C		D	E
1	1233.345		1233					
2								

- Round down 1233.345 to the nearest 10 by entering **=ROUNDDOWN(A1, -1)**

B1		▼	:	×	✓	f_x	=ROUNDDOWN(A1,-1)	
	A		B		C		D	E
1	1233.345		1230					
2								

- Round down 1233.345 to the nearest 100 by entering **=ROUNDDOWN(A1, -2)**

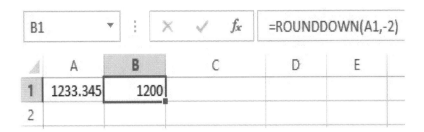

- Round up 1233.345 to the nearest 1000 by entering **=ROUNDUP(A1, -3)**

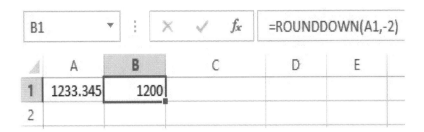

THE SORT FUNCTION

The Sort function is a function that is used to sort the content of a column in an ascending or descending order

The SORT function uses the following arguments

=SORT (array, [sort_index], [sort_order], [by col])

- **Array (Required argument)**: This is the range or array that contains the value to be sorted out
- **Sort_index (Optional Argument):** This specifies the row or column to sorted out
- **Sort _order (Optional Argument):** This is the number for sorting the cells; 1 for ascending and -1 for descending. If this part is omitted. It will sort automatically in ascending order
- **By_col (Optional Argument):** This specifies where the sorting is directed to; FALSE to sort by row and TRUE to sort by column.

USING THE SORT FUNCTION

Using the table below, arrange the cells in ascending order using the SORT formula

D2		
	A	B
1	Item	Qty.
2	Apples	38
3	Cherries	29
4	Grapes	31
5	Lemons	34
6	Oranges	36
7	Peaches	25
8	Pears	40

To sort in ascending order i.e., arranging from the smallest to the highest, follow the steps below

- Click into an empty cell and type in the function to be used (**=SORT**), the source array (**A2:B8**), the sort index (**2**), and sort_order (**1**). In summary, **=SORT(A2:B8, 2, 1)**

D2		=SORT(A2:B8, 2, 1)
	A	B
1	Item	Qty.
2	Apples	38
3	Cherries	29
4	Grapes	31
5	Lemons	34
6	Oranges	36
7	Peaches	25
8	Pears	40

- Click on Enter, and the data will be arranged in ascending order

D2			=SORT(A2:B8, 2, 1)	
	A	B	C	D	E
1	Item	Qty.		Item	Qty.
2	Apples	38		Peaches	25
3	Cherries	29		Cherries	29
4	Grapes	31		Grapes	31
5	Lemons	34		Lemons	34
6	Oranges	36		Oranges	36
7	Peaches	25		Apples	38
8	Pears	40		Pears	40

114

To sort in descending order, i.e., arranging from highest to the lowest

- Click into an empty cell and type in the function to be used (**=SORT**), the source array (**A2:B8**), the sort index **(2),** and sort_order **(1).** In summary =**SORT(A2:B8, 2,- 1)**

D2	▼	⋮	=SORT(A2:B8, 2, -1)

	A	B	C
1	Item	Qty.	
2	Apples	38	
3	Cherries	29	
4	Grapes	31	
5	Lemons	34	
6	Oranges	36	
7	Peaches	25	
8	Pears	40	

- Click on Enter, and the data will be arranged in descending order

D2	▼	⋮	=SORT(A2:B8, 2, -1)

	A	B	C	D	E
1	Item	Qty.		Item	Qty.
2	Apples	38		Pears	40
3	Cherries	29		Apples	38
4	Grapes	31		Oranges	36
5	Lemons	34		Lemons	34
6	Oranges	36		Grapes	31
7	Peaches	25		Cherries	29
8	Pears	40		Peaches	25

NOTE: Things to know about the SORT function

- By default, the SORT function sort values in ascending order using the first column
- The SORT function is only available in Microsoft 365 subscription
- The result is updated automatically as the source data is changing

CHAPTER SEVEN

STATISTICAL FUNCTIONS

The statistical functions are functions that apply mathematical processes or operations to a range of cells in a worksheet. The statistical functions were introduced from Excel 2013 and all later versions. Examples of statistical functions are COUNT, COUNTA, AVERAGE, etc.

THE COUNT FUNCTION

The COUNT function is a function that counts the number of cells that contain numbers and also counts the numbers of arguments that contain numbers.

The COUNT function uses the following arguments

=COUNT(value1, value2…)

- **Value1 (Required Argument)**: This is the cell range with which you wish to count the ones with numbers.
- **Value2, …(Optional Argument)**: Here, you can add up to additional 255 items, cell references, or ranges within which you wish to count numbers

USING THE COUNT FUNCTION

Using the table below, let's count the number of cells that have numbers using the COUNT function

B7					×	✓

▲	A	B	C
1	GOODS PURCHASED	PRICE	
2	JUG	450	
3	POTS	500	
4	CUTLERRIES	600	
5	SPOON	?	
6			

To know the cells that have numbers, using the COUNT function, follow the steps below

- Select an empty cell, type in the function name, and followed by the arguments; **=COUNT(A2:B5)**

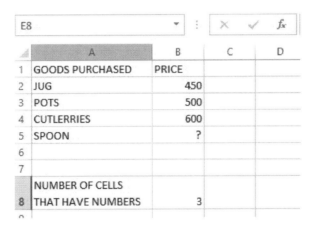

- Click on Enter and the result will be **3**

	A	B	C	D
1	GOODS PURCHASED	PRICE		
2	JUG	450		
3	POTS	500		
4	CUTLERRIES	600		
5	SPOON	?		
6				
7				
8	NUMBER OF CELLS THAT HAVE NUMBERS	3		

NOTE: Keep these in mind when using the COUNT function

- Argument with numbers, dates, or a text representing numbers are counted in the COUNT function
- Arguments with values or text errors are not counted by the COUNT function
- To count logical values, use the COUNTA function
- To count numbers based on criteria, use the COUNTAIF or IF function
- The COUNT function does not count logical value TRUE or FALSE

- When an argument is an array or reference, only the numbers in the reference or array are counted

THE COUNTIF FUNCTION

The COUNTIF function is used to count the number of cells that meet a certain criterion or condition. This can also be used to count cells that contain dates, numbers, and text. This function also supports the use of logical operators and wildcards.

The COUNTIF function has the following arguments

=COUNTIF(Range, criteria)

- **Range (Required Argument):** This indicates the range of cells that are to be counted.
- **Criteria (Required Argument):** This is the condition to be met by the cells provided in the worksheet. The criteria can be in the following:
    - A numerical value such as integer, decimal, time, or logical value
    - A text string such as Monday, East, Price and including wildcards such as asterisks and question mark

USING THE COUNTIF FUNCTION

With the table below, let's use the COUNTIF function to count how many times James' name appears on the list.

⊿	A	B	C	D
1	YEAR	NAMES		
2	2001	James		
3	2002	James		
4	2003	Peter		
5	2004	Jasmine		
6	2006	Gregg		

To get the number of times James' name appear on the list, follow the steps below

- Select an empty cell, type in the function name and the arguments to be used; =**COUNTIF(B2:B6, "James")**

| SEARCH | ▼ | : | × | ✓ | f_x | =COUNTIF(B2:B6, "James") |

▲	A	B	C	D	E	F
1	YEAR	NAMES				
2	2001	James	=COUNTIF(B2:B6, "James")			
3	2002	James	COUNTIF(range, criteria)			
4	2003	Peter				
5	2004	Jasmine				
6	2006	Gregg				

- Click on Enter and the result will be **2**

| C2 | ▼ | : | × | ✓ | f_x | =COUNTIF(B2:B6, "James") |

▲	A	B	C	D	E	F
1	YEAR	NAMES				
2	2001	James	2			
3	2002	James				
4	2003	Peter				
5	2004	Jasmine				
6	2006	Gregg				

NOTE: Take note of the following points when using the COUNTIF function

- When using the COUNTIF function, make sure the criteria argument is enclosed in quotes e.g., "James"
- When the provided criteria argument is a text string that is more than 255 characters in length, #VALUE ERROR occurs
- #VALUE error occurs when the formula is referring to a cell or range of cells in a closed workbook

THE COUNTIFS FUNCTION

The COUNTIFS function is a function used for counting cells that meet single or multiple conditions or criteria. Just like the COUNT, COUNTIF functions, the COUNTIFS function is used with criteria or conditions relating to numbers, dates, text, logical operators, and wildcards.

The COUNTIFS function has the following arguments

=COUNTIFS(criteria_range1,   criteria1,   [criteria_range2, criteria2]...)

- **Criteria_range1 (Required Argument):** This is the first range that would be evaluated with the related criteria
- **Critteria1 (Required Argument):** This is the criteria to be used on criteria_range1 and it may come in form of expression, numbers, cell reference, or a text that specifies what cells are to be counted. For instance, criteria can be expressed as 43, >23, D2, etc.
- **Criteria_range2, criteria2 (Optional Argument):** This contains the additional ranges and their related criteria. This function permits up to 127 range or criteria pairs. The criteria can be in the following:
  - A numerical value such as integer, decimal, time, or logical value
  - A text string such as Monday, East, Price and including wildcards such as asterisks and question mark

USING THE COUNTIFS FUNCTION

Using the table below, let's count the numbers of shoes that have red color

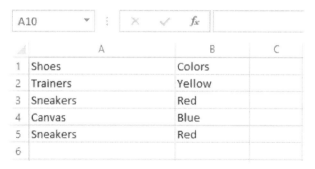

To get the number of shoes with red color on the list, follow the steps below:

- Select an empty cell, type in the function name and the arguments to be used; **=COUNTIFS(A2:A5, "sneakers", B2:B5, "red"**

| SEARCH | ▼ | : | ✕ | ✓ | ƒₓ | =COUNTIFS(A2:A5, "sneakers", B2:B5, "red") |

▲	A	B	C	D	E	F	G
1	Shoes	Colors	=COUNTIFS(A2:A5, "sneakers", B2:B5, "red")				
2	Trainers	Yellow	COUNTIFS(criteria range1, criteria1, [criteria_range2, crit				
3	Sneakers	Red					
4	Canvas	Blue					
5	Sneakers	Red					
6							

- Click on Enter and the result will be **2** as shown in the table below

| C1 | ▼ | : | ✕ | ✓ | ƒₓ | =COUNTIFS(A2:A5, "sneakers", B2:B5, "red") |

▲	A	B	C	D	E	F
1	Shoes	Colors	2			
2	Trainers	Yellow				
3	Sneakers	Red				
4	Canvas	Blue				
5	Sneakers	Red				

NOTE: Take note of the following when using the COUNTIFS FUNCTION

- The COUNTIFS function sees an empty cell as 0 when the criteria argument is a reference to an empty cell.
- #VALUE! error occurs when the criteria range arrays are not of the same length and also when the criteria arguments given are text strings that are greater than 255 characters long
- The use of the wildcard characters (question mark and asterisks) is made possible in criteria
- If the first cells meet their related criteria, the count is increased by 1 and if the second cells also meet their related criteria, the count is also increased by 1 and this continues until all the cells are evaluated

THE COUNTA FUNCTION

The COUNTA function is a function that returns the number of cells that are not empty within a range. The COUNTA function does not count empty cells. The COUNTA function can also be referred to as the **Excel COUNIF Not Blank** formula

The COUNTA function has the following arguments

=COUNTA(value1, [value2]

- **Value1 (Required Argument):** This is the argument indicating the values to be counted
- **Value2,…(Optional Argument):** This is the additional argument indicating the values to be counted with a maximum of 255 arguments

USING THE COUNTA FUNCTION

With the table below, let's count the number of cells that are not empty using the COUNTA function

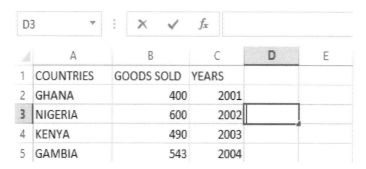

To get the number of cells that are not empty in the worksheet, follow the steps below

- Select an empty cell and type in the function name and its arguments; **=COUNTA(A1:C5)**

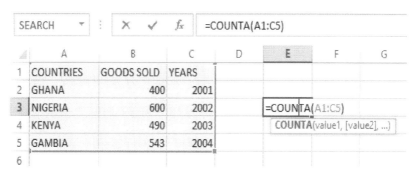

- Click on enter and the result will be 15 as shown in the table below

E3	▾	:	×	✓	f_x	=COUNTA(A1:C5)

◢	A	B	C	D	E	F
1	COUNTRIES	GOODS SOLD	YEARS			
2	GHANA	400	2001			
3	NIGERIA	600	2002		15	
4	KENYA	490	2003			
5	GAMBIA	543	2004			

NOTE: Keep these in mind when using the COUNTA function

- The COUNTA function does not count empty cells
- In case you don't want to count logical values, text, or error values, the COUNT function is to be used
- To count cells that meet certain criteria, use the COUNTIF or COUNTIFS function

THE COUNTBLANK FUNCTION

The COUNTBLANK is a function that returns the numbers of empty cells within a range of cells in a workbook

The COUNTA function has just one argument

=CONNTBLANK(range)

Range (Required Argument): This is the range at which the blank cells will be counted

USING THE COUNTABLANK FUNCTION

Let's count the number of cells that are blank in the table below using the COUNTBLANK function

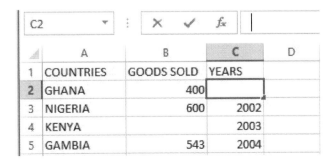

To count the blank cells using the COUNTBLANK function, follow the steps given below

- Select an empty cell, type in the function name and the arguments to be used; **=COUNTBLANK(A1:C5)**

	A	B	C	D	E
	SEARCH ▼ : ✕ ✓ *fx*		=COUNTBLANK(A1:C5)		
1	COUNTRIES	GOODS SOLD	YEARS		
2	GHANA	400			
3	NIGERIA	600	2002	=COUNTBLANK(A1:C5)	
4	KENYA		2003		
5	GAMBIA	543	2004		

- Click on enter and the result will be 2 as shown in the table below

	A	B	C	D	E
	D3 ▼ : ✕ ✓ *fx*		=COUNTBLANK(A1:C5)		
1	COUNTRIES	GOODS SOLD	YEARS		
2	GHANA	400			
3	NIGERIA	600	2002	2	
4	KENYA		2003		
5	GAMBIA	543	2004		

NOTE: Keep these in mind while using the COUNTA function

- The COUNTBLANK function does not count any cell that contains text, numbers, errors, etc.
- The COUNTBLANK function considers any formula blank when it returns an empty cell and thus, such a cell will be counted.
- Cells containing zero are not considered blank and will not be counted by the COUNTBLANK function

The AVERAGE Function

The AVERAGE function helps to calculate the arithmetic mean of a supplied set of arguments in a worksheet. The AVERAGE function can take up to 255 individual arguments which may include cell references, ranges, arrays, and constants.

The AVERAGE function uses the following arguments

- **Number1 (Required Argument):** This is the first number of a cell reference or range one wishes to find the average.
- **Number2 (Optional Argument):** These are additional numbers, cell references, or ranges one wishes to find the average with up to a maximum of 255 characters to be inputted.

USING THE AVERAGE FUNCTION

Find the arithmetic mean of the goods sold in the table given below, using the AVERAGE function

D16	▼	⋮	×	✓	ƒx	

◢	A	B	C	D
1	COUNTRIES	GOODS SOLD		
2	GHANA	400		
3	NIGERIA	600		
4	KENYA	698		
5	GAMBIA	543		
6				

To find the average of the goods sold using the AVERAGE function, follow the steps given below

- Select an empty cell, type in the function name and its arguments; **=AVERAGE(B2:B5)**

SEARCH	▼	⋮	×	✓	ƒx	=AVERAGE(E

◢	A	B	C	D
1	COUNTRIES	GOODS SOLD		
2	GHANA	400		
3	NIGERIA	600		
4	KENYA	698		
5	GAMBIA	543		
6		=AVERAGE(B2:B5)		

- Click on enter and the result will be 560.25 as shown in the table below

NOTE: Keep this in mind when using the AVERAGE function

- The AVERAGE function ignores empty cells
- The AVERAGE function ignores a cell reference argument that contains text, logical values. Cells with the value of zero are however counted
- The cell reference arguments must contain numbers
- To count logical values and text representation of numbers as part of the calculation, use the **AVERAGE** function
- To calculate the average of any value that meet certain condition or criteria, use the AVERAGE IF or AVERAGE IFS function

THE AVERAGEIF FUNCTION

The AVERAGEIF function is a function that is used to calculate the average of cells that meet a given criterion or condition. The AVERAGEIF function criteria include the use of logical operators (<,>, <>, =) and wildcards (*,?).

The AVERAGEIF function uses the following argument for its operations

=AVERAGEIF(range, criteria,[average_range])

- **Range (Required Argument):** This is the range of cell or cells to average and these cells may include numbers or names, arrays or references that contain numbers
- **Criteria (Required Argument):** The criteria are what determines how the cells will be average and it can come in form of a number, expression, cell reference, or texts. E.g., 13, <14 etc.

- **Average_range (Optional Range):** This is the actual or real range of cells to be averaged. When this is omitted, the function makes use of the given range

USING THE AVERAGEIF FUNCTION

Using the table given below, let's find out the average sales of cakes

B12		⌄	⋮	✕	✓	*fx*	

◢	A	B	C	D
1	Goods	Sales		
2	Cakes	200		
3	Chocolate	300		
4	Vanilla	345		
5	Cakes	564		
6	Chocolate	232		
7				

To calculate the average sales of cakes using the AVERAGEIF function, follow the procedures given below

- Select an empty cell, type in the function name and its arguments; **= AVERAGEIF(A2:A6, "chocolate", B2:B6)**

SEARCH	⌄	⋮	✕	✓	*fx*	=AVERAGEIF(A2:A6, "chocolate", B2:B6)

◢	A	B	C	D	E	F	G
1	Goods	Sales					
2	Cakes	200					
3	Chocolate	300					
4	Vanilla	345					
5	Cakes	564					
6	Chocolate	232					
7		=AVERAGEIF(A2:A6, "chocolate", B2:B6)					
8		AVERAGEIF(**range**, criteria, [average_range])					

- Click on enter and the result will be **266** as shown in the table below

| B7 | ▼ | : | × | ✓ | fx | =AVERAGEIF(A2:A6, "chocolate", B2:B6) |

	A	B	C	D	E	F	G
1	Goods	Sales					
2	Cakes	200					
3	Chocolate	300					
4	Vanilla	345					
5	Cakes	564					
6	Chocolate	232					
7		266					

NOTE: Keep the following in mind when using the AVERAGEIF function

- #DVD! error takes place when
    - No cell in the range meets the criteria given
    - The range is blank or is a text value
- AVERAGEIF function treats a cell as zero when the criteria are given is empty
- The AVERAGEIF function ignores cells that contain TRUE or FALSE
- Wildcards such as asterisk and question mark can be used in criteria

THE AVERAGEIFS FUNCTION

The AVERAGEIFS function is a function that calculates the average (arithmetic mean) of the numbers in a given range of cells that meet more than one criterion. The AVERAGEIFS function also uses logical operators (<,>, <>) and wildcards (*?) as its criteria. This function was first introduced in Excel 2007.

The AVERAGEIFS uses the following argument for its operation
**=AVERAGEIFS(average_range, criteria_range1
criteria1,,[criteria_range2, criteria2), ...)**
- **Average_range (Required Argument):** This is the range of one or more cells to be average and the argument include names or numbers, arrays or references that contain numbers

- **Criteria_range1: (Required Argument):** This is the first range to be evaluated
- **Criteria_range2 (Optional Argument:** This is the second range to be evaluated it can be up to 127 ranges and related criteria
- **Criteria2 (Optional Argument):** This also determines how the cells will be averages and be up to 127 criteria in form of a number, cell reference, expression, or a text indicating which cells are to be averaged. This is used against critera_range2.

USING THE AVERGAEIFS FUNCTION

Using the table, let's find out the average salary of males that work full time using the AVERAGEIFS function

	A	B	C	D	E
1					
2		Name	Gender	Position	Salary
3		Jenny Davies	Female	Full Time	£17,883.00
4		Kevin Matthews	Male	Part Time	£15,966.00
5		Chris Sandford	Female	Part Time	£17,930.00
6		Peter Charkiw	Male	Full Time	£23,614.00
7		Paul Jones	Male	Full Time	£24,579.00

To find the average salary of males that work full time using the AVERAGEIFS functions, follow the steps below

- Select an empty cell and type in the function name and its arguments; = **AVERAGEIFS(E3:E7, C3:C7, "Male", D3:D7, "Full Time")**

	A	B	C	D	E	F	G	H	I
1									
2		Name	Gender	Position	Salary				
3		Jenny Davies	Female	Full Time	£17,883.00				
4		Kevin Matthews	Male	Part Time	£15,966.00				
5		Chris Sandford	Female	Part Time	£17,930.00				
6		Peter Charkiw	Male	Full Time	£23,614.00				
7		Paul Jones	Male	Full Time	£24,579.00				
8					=averageifs(E3:E7,C3:C7,"Male",D3:D7,"Full Time")				

- Click on enter and the result will be **£24,096.50** as shown in the table below

	A	B	C	D	E	F	G
1							
2		Name	Gender	Position	Salary		
3		Jenny Davies	Female	Full Time	£17,883.00		
4		Kevin Matthews	Male	Part Time	£15,966.00		
5		Chris Sandford	Female	Part Time	£17,930.00		
6		Peter Charkiw	Male	Full Time	£23,614.00		
7		Paul Jones	Male	Full Time	£24,579.00		
8					£24,096.50		

NOTE: Keep this in mind when using the AVERAGEIFS function

- The AVERAGEIFS function treats any cell as zero value when the criteria range is empty
- In the AVERAGEIFS function, all the criteria_range must be the same size and shape as the sum_range
- When a number or date is used together with a logical operator in the AVERAGEIFS' criteria, they must be enclosed in a double quote e.g., ">4/23/2018"
- In the AVERAGEIFS function, cells in a range that contains TRUE are evaluated as a 1 and the ones that contain FALSE are evaluated as zero
- #DIV0! Error occurs
  - When the argument average_range is blank or is a text value
  - When the average_range cannot be interpreted into numerical values
  - When all the criteria or conditions are not met
- The use of wildcards such as asterisks and question mark are allowed as criteria in the function

THE MIN FUNCTION

The MIN function returns the minimum or smallest number in a given set of values or arguments. The MIN function ignores numbers, texts, and logical values as well as text values

The MIN function uses the following argument

=MIN (number1, [number2],…)

- **Number1 (Required Argument):** This is the range of a cell or cells where the lowest number will be returned from
- **Number2 (Optional Argument):** Here, up to 255 numbers can be accepted

USING THE MIN FUNCTION

With the table given below, find the minimum number using the MIN function

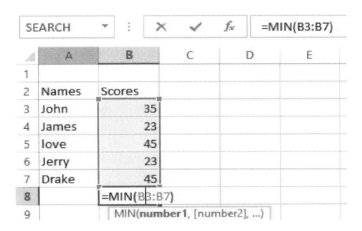

To find the minimum number using the MIN function, follow the steps below:

- Select an empty cell, type in the function name and its arguments; **=MIN(B3:B7)**

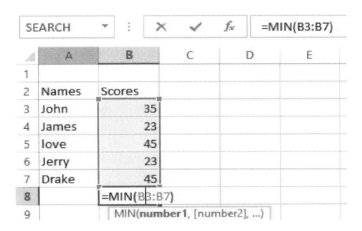

- Click on enter and the result will be **23** as shown in the table below

	A	B	C	D	E
1					
2	Names	Scores			
3	John	35			
4	James	23			
5	love	45			
6	Jerry	23			
7	Drake	45			
8		23			

B8 ... f_x =MIN(B3:B7)

NOTE: Keep the following when using the MIN function

- When values provided into the MIN function are not numbers, VALUE! error occurs
- To use the logical values and text representation of numbers in a calculation, use the MINA function
- The arguments in the MIN function can be number or names, array or reference that contain numbers
- Empty cells, logical values, or text are ignored in the MIN function
- When an argument contains error values and text that cannot be interpreted, they cause errors to occur
- The MIN function returns any argument without numbers as 0

THE MAX FUNCTION

The MIN function returns the maximum or largest number in a given set of values or arguments. The MAX function ignores numbers, texts, and logical values as well as text values

The MAX function uses the following argument

=MAX(number1, [number2],...)

- **Number1 (Required Argument):** This is the range of a cell or cells where the highest number will be returned from
- **Number2(Optional Argument):** Here, up to 255 numbers can be accepted

USING THE MAX FUNCTION

With the table given below, find the minimum number using the MAX function

	A	B	C	D
1				
2	Names	Scores		
3	John	35		
4	James	23		
5	love	45		
6	Jerry	23		
7	Drake	45		

B12

To find the minimum number using the MAX function, follow the steps below

- Select an empty cell and type in the function name and its arguments; **=MAX(B3:B7)**

SEARCH — =MAX(B3:B7)

	A	B	C	D	E
1					
2	Names	Scores			
3	John	35			
4	James	23			
5	love	45			
6	Jerry	23			
7	Drake	45			
8		=MAX(B3:B7)			

- Click on enter and the result will be **45** as shown in the table below

B8 — =MAX(B3:B7)

	A	B	C	D	E
1					
2	Names	Scores			
3	John	35			
4	James	23			
5	love	45			
6	Jerry	23			
7	Drake	45			
8		45			

133

NOTE: Keep these in mind when using the MAX function

- When values provided into the MAX function are not numbers, VALUE! error occurs
- The MAX function returns any argument without numbers as 0
- To use the logical values and text representation of numbers in a calculation, use the MAXA function
- The arguments in the MAX function can be number or names, array or reference that contain numbers
- Empty cells, logical values, or text are ignored in the MAX function
- When an argument contains error values and text that cannot be interpreted, they cause errors to occur

THE MEDIAN FUNCTION

The MEDIAN function calculates the middle value of a given set of numbers. For instance, the MEDIAN function returns 3 in the =MEDIAN (1, 2,3,4,5). The MEDIAN function contains the following arguments

=MEDIUM (number1, [number2],…)

- **Number1 (Required Argument)**: This is the argument that contains the range of one or more cells that we wish to calculate or find the median.
- **Numnber2 (Optional Argument)** This can contain up to 255 numbers that we may wish to find the median

USING THE MEDIAN FUNCTION

With the table given below, let's calculate the median of the numeric data using the MEDIAN function

	A	B	C	D	E
1					
2	Names	Scores			
3	John	35			
4	James	23			
5	love	45			
6	Jerry	23			
7	Drake	45			

To calculate the median of the numeric values in the table, follow the steps given below

- Select an empty cell, type in the function name and its arguments; **=MAX(B3:B7)**

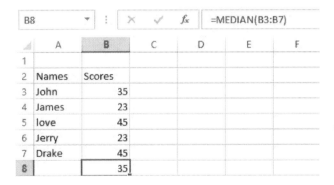

- Click on enter and the result will be **35** as shown in the table below

NOTE: Keep these in mind when using the MEDIAN function

- When an argument contains error values and text that cannot be interpreted, they cause errors to occur
- The arguments in the MEDIAN function can be number or names, array or reference that contain numbers
- Empty cells, logical values, or text are ignored in the MEDIAN function
- When there is an even number of values in the table, the average of the two middle number is returned.

CHAPTER EIGHT

THE FINANCIAL FUNCTION

Excel financial functions are designed to carry out varieties of financial operations such as calculation of yield, interest rates, internal rate of return, investment valuations, asset depreciation, etc. The functions are not available in earlier versions of Excel but from Excel 2013 and all later versions. The most commonly used financial functions in Excel are as follows:

THE PV FUNCTION

The PV function which stands for **Present Value** is a function designed to calculate the present value of an investment or loan which is based on a constant interest rate. The PV function can be used with periodic, constant payments e.g mortgage and other loans or a future value (investment goal)

The PV function uses the following arguments for its operations

=PV(rate, nper,pmt, [fv], [type])

- **Rate (Required Argument):** This is the interest rate per the compounding period. For instance, a loan with a 14% annual interest rate and monthly required payment will have monthly interest of 1.2% rate i.e 14/12= 1.2%
- **Nper(Required Argument)**: This is the number of the total payments made to clear the loans. For instance, If the loan year is 4 years, then the monthly payment period will be 48 months
- **Pmt (Required Argument)**: This is the payment that is done per period and it remains constant until the end of the investment or loan
- **Fv (Optional Argument):** This is the investment's future value when the payment period is over. In case there is input for this, Excel returns the value by default to 0
- **Type (Optional Argument):** This is used to indicate when the payment periods are issued and due. When 0 is inputted, the payment period is at the end of the period and when 1 is inputted, the payment period is at the beginning of the month.

USING THE PV FUNCTION

From the table below, we have an annuity that makes periodic payments of $500.00 with a 3.5 annual interest rate. The annuity will make payments for 6 years every month. Using the PV function, find the present value

B10		⊠ ✓ ƒx	
◢	A	B	C
1			
2	Annual Interest Rate	3.50%	
3	Periodic Payment	500	
4	Numbers of Periods (Monthly)	72	
5	Compounding Periods per Year	12	
6	Present Value		

To find the present value of the table above using the PV function

- Select an empty cell, type in the function and its argument **=PV(B2/B5,B4,B3,0,0)**

SEARCH		⊠ ✓ ƒx	=PV(B2/B5,B4,B3,0,0)		
◢	A	B	C	D
1				
2	Annual Interest Rate	3.50%		
3	Periodic Payment	500		
4	Numbers of Periods (Monthly)	72		
5	Compounding Periods per Year	12		
6	Present Value	=PV(B2/B5,B4,B3,0,0)		
7		PV(rate, nper, pmt, [fv], [type])		

- Click on enter and the present value will be -£32,428.79 as shown in the table below

C3		⊠ ✓ ƒx		
◢	A	B	C	D
1				
2	Annual Interest Rate	3.50%		
3	Periodic Payment	500		
4	Numbers of Periods (Monthly)	72		
5	Compounding Periods per Year	12		
6	Present Value	-£32,428.79		

NOTE: Keep these in mind while using the PV function

- When the arguments given are non-numeric, the PV function returns a #VALUE! error
- In the PV function, the annual interest rate cannot be converted to a periodic interest rate.

THE FV FUNCTION

The FV function is a function that is designed to help calculate the **future value** of an investment or loan with a periodic constant payment and a constant interest rate.

The FV function uses the following arguments to execute its operation

=FV(rate, nper,pmt, [pv], [type])

- **Rate (Required Argument):** This is the interest rate per the compounding period.
- **Nper (Required Argument):** This is the total period of payment made for a lifetime
- **Pmt (Optional Argument):** This indicates the payment per period. In case this argument is omitted, the PV argument must be provided
- **PV (Optional Argument):** This indicates the present value of the investment or loan. In case the PV argument is omitted, the Pmt argument must be provided
- **Type (Optional Argument):** This is used to indicate when the payment periods are made whether at the start or end of the year. When 0 is inputted, the payment period is at the end of the period and when 1 is inputted, the payment period is at the beginning of the month.

USING THE FV FUNCTION

Using the information in the table below, let's calculate the future value using the FV function

B8	▾	:	×	✓	fx	

	A	B	C	D
1				
2	Present Value	20,000		
3	Interest rate	5%		
4	Term(Year)	14		
5	Compounding periods per year	12		
6	Future Value			
7				

To find the future value of the table above using the FV function

- Select an empty cell and type in the function and its argument **=FV(B3/B5,B4*B5,0,-B2)**

SEARCH	▾	:	×	✓	fx	=FV(B3/B5,B4*B5,0,-B2)	

	A	B	C	D	E
1					
2	Present Value	20,000			
3	Interest rate	5%			
4	Term(Year)	14			
5	Compounding periods per year	12			
6	Future Value	=FV(B3/B5,B4*B5,0,-B2)			
7		FV(**rate**, nper, pmt, [pv], [type])			

- Click on enter and the future value will be £40,216.52 as shown in the table below

A8	▾	:	×	✓	fx	

	A	B	C	D
1				
2	Present Value	20,000		
3	Interest rate	5%		
4	Term(Year)	14		
5	Compounding periods per year	12		
6	Future Value	£40,216.52		
7				

NOTE: keep the following in mind when using the FV function

- When the argument is given is non-numeric #VALUE! error
- The payment value will be negative when the pmt argument is for the cash going out of a business

THE NPV FUNCTION

The NPV function is a function that is used to calculate the **net present value** of an investment by making use of discount rate and a series of future cash flows

The NPV function uses the following arguments for its operations

=NPV(rate,value1,[value2],...)

- **Rate (Required Argument):** This is the discount rate over the length of a period
- **Value1(Required Argument):** This is the first value that represents a series of payments and income. The negative payments connote outgoing payments while the positive payments connote incoming payments
- **Value2 (Optional Argument):** This is the second value that represents a series of payments and income

USING THE NPV FUNCTION

Given the table below, let's calculate the net present value using the NPV function

	A	B	C	D	E
4	1	200			
5	2	300			
6	3	400			
7	4	500			
8	5	600			
9	Required return	15%			
10					

B10

To calculate the net present value;

- Select an empty cell, type in the function and its argument **=NPV(B9,B3:B8)**

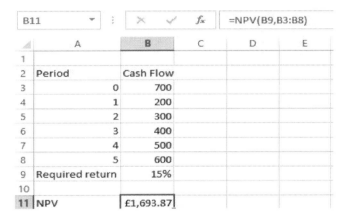

- Click on enter and the net present value will be £1,693.87 as shown in the table below

	A	B	C	D	E
1					
2	Period	Cash Flow			
3	0	700			
4	1	200			
5	2	300			
6	3	400			
7	4	500			
8	5	600			
9	Required return	15%			
10					
11	NPV	£1,693.87			

B11 — fx =NPV(B9,B3:B8)

NOTE: Keep these in mind when using the NPV function

- Arguments must be numerical or a function with a numerical output. Other forms of input will be returned as an error
- In the NPV function, arrays with numerical values are evaluated and all other values are ignored.
- For the series of cash flow, the input order is important
- With the NPV function, there is an assumption that payments are spaced on equal periodic payments

- The NPV function and the IRR(Internal Rate of Return) are related to each other

THE PMT FUNCTION

The PMT function is a function that helps to calculate the **total payment** that is needed to pay up a loan or an investment with a fixed interest rate over a given period

The PMT function uses the following arguments for its operations

PMT(rate, nper, pv, [fv], [type])

- **Rate (Required Argument):** This is the interest rate for the loan
- **Nper (Required Argument):** This is the total number of payments to be made for the loan taken
- **PV (Required Argument):** This is the present value or the total amount that a series of future payment is worth now and this is also known as the principal
- **FV (Optional Argument):** This is the future value or the cash balance you wish to attain or get to after the last payment has been made. If the FV is omitted, it is assumed to be zero
- **Type (Optional Argument):** This indicates when payments are due. If it is omitted, it defaults to 0 and payments are due at the end of the month. When 1 is used in the argument, payments are due at the beginning of the period

USING THE PMT FUNCTION

Using the table below, let assume we need to invest for three years and we will receive £85,000 with an interest rate of 3.5% per year in which the payment will be made at the start of each month and with a future value of 0

	A	B	C	D	E
1					
2	Rate of Interest	3.50%			
3	Nper	36			
4	PV	85,000			
5	FV	0			
6					
7	PMT				

To calculate the PMT;

- Select an empty cell, type in the function and its argument **=PMT(B2/12,B3,B4,B5)**

| SEARCH | ▾ | : | ✕ | ✓ | fx | =PMT(B2/12,B3,B4,B5) |

▲	A	B	C	D	E
1					
2	Rate of Interest	3.50%			
3	Nper	36			
4	PV	85,000			
5	FV	0			
6					
7	PMT	=PMT(B2/12,B3,B4,B5)			
8		PMT(rate, nper, pv, [fv], [type])			

- Click on enter and the net present value will be -£2,490.87 as shown in the table below

| B7 | ▾ | : | ✕ | ✓ | fx | =PMT(B2/12,B3,B4,B5) |

▲	A	B	C	D	E
1					
2	Rate of Interest	3.50%			
3	Nper	36			
4	PV	85,000			
5	FV	0			
6					
7	PMT	-£2,490.68			

NOTE: Keep these in mind when using the PMT function

- #VALUE! occurs when the arguments provided is non-numeric
- #NUM! error occurs when the given rate is less than or equal to -1
- #NUM! error also occurs when given nper is equal to 0
- When calculating monthly or quarterly payment using the PMT function, convert the annual interest rates to months or quarters

- To find the total amount that was paid for the duration of the loan, multiply the PMT as calculated by nper

THE SLN FUNCTION

The SLN function helps to calculate the depreciation of an asset using a straight-line depreciation method for one period of time

The SLN function uses the following arguments to perform its operations

=SLN(cost, salvage, life)

- **Cost (Required Argument):** This is the initial cost of an asset
- **Salvage (Required Argument):** This is the value at the end of the depreciation which is also known as the salvage value of the asset
- **Life(Required Argument):** This is the number of periods at which the asset depreciates and this can also be called useful life of the asset.

USING THE SLN FUNCTION

From the table below, let calculate the depreciation of an asset given the cost of the asset to be £55,000, the salvage value to be £8,500, and the useful life to be 10 years

| B7 | ▼ | ⋮ | ✕ | ✓ | *fx* | |

◢	A	B	C	D	E
1					
2					
3	Cost of the asset	55,000			
4	Salvage value	8,500			
5	Useful life	10			
6					

To find the depreciation of the asset in the table below

- Select an empty cell, type in the function and its argument **=SLN(B3,B4,B5)**

| SEARCH | ▼ | : | ✕ | ✓ | *fx* | =SLN(B3,B4,B5) |

	A	B	C	D	E
1					
2					
3	Cost of the asset	55,000			
4	Salvage value	8,500			
5	Useful life	10			
6	SLN	=SLN(B3,B4,B5)			
7		SLN(**cost**, salvage, life)			

- Click on enter and the depreciation value of the asset will be £4,650.00 as shown in the table below

| B7 | ▼ | : | ✕ | ✓ | *fx* | |

	A	B	C	D	E
1					
2					
3	Cost of the asset	55,000			
4	Salvage value	8,500			
5	Useful life	10			
6	SLN	£4,650.00			
7					

NOTE: Observe the following when using the SLN function

- #DIV/0! error occurs when the arguments that are given is equal to zero
- #VALUE! error occurs when the arguments that are given are non-numeric

The SYD Function

The SYD function is a function that helps to calculate the sum of years depreciation of an asset over a specific period in the lifetime of the asset. This function is centered on the cost of the asset, the salvage value, and the number of periods the asset depreciated

The SYD function uses the following arguments to carry out its operation

=SYD(cost, salvage, life, per)

- **Cost (Required Argument):** This is the initial cost of an asset
- **Salvage (Required Argument):** This is the value at the end of the depreciation which is also known as the salvage value of the asset
- **Life (Required Argument):** This is the number of periods at which the asset depreciates and this can also be called useful life of the asset.
- **Per (Required Argument):** This is the period in which the depreciation will be calculated for

USING THE SYD FUNCTION

Assuming we want to calculate the depreciation of an asset with an initial cost of £400,000 with a salvage cost of £6,000 after 8 years with a period of 3 years to calculate the depreciation

B6	▼	:	✕	✓	*fx*	

◢	A	B	C	D	E
1					
2	Initilal cost	400,000			
3	Salvage value	6,000			
4	Life	8			
5	Period	3			
6					

To calculate the sum of years' depreciation of the asset given in the table above

- Select an empty cell, type in the function and its argument **=SYD(B2,B3,B4,B5)**

| SEARCH | ▼ | ⋮ | ✕ | ✓ | *fx* | =SYD(B2,B3,B4,B5) |

◢	A	B	C	D	E
1					
2	Initilal cost	400,000			
3	Salvage value	6,000			
4	Life	8			
5	Period	3			
6	SYD	=SYD(B2,B3,B4,B5)			
7		SYD(cost, salvage, life, per)			

- Click on enter and the sum years of the depreciation value of the asset will be £65,666.67 as shown in the table below

| B6 | ▼ | ⋮ | ✕ | ✓ | *fx* | =SYD(B2,B3,B4,B5) |

◢	A	B	C	D	E
1					
2	Initilal cost	400,000			
3	Salvage value	6,000			
4	Life	8			
5	Period	3			
6	SYD	£65,666.67			

NOTE: Observe the following when using the SYD function

- When inputting *life* and *per* arguments, they must be in the same units of time e.g., days, months, and years
- When the arguments given are non-numeric, it returns a #VALUE! error
- #NUM! error occurs due to the following reasons
  - When the salvage argument supplied is less than zero
  - When the life or per argument provided is less than or equal to zero
  - When the per argument provided or supplied is greater than the life argument supplied in the formula

THE DB FUNCTION

The DB function is a function that calculates the depreciation of an asset using the fixed declining balance method for a specified period.

The DB function uses the following arguments to execute its operations

=DB(cost, salvage, life, period,[month)

- **Cost (Required Argument):** This is the initial cost of an asset
- **Salvage (Required Argument):** This is the value at the end of the depreciation which is also known as the salvage value of the asset
- **Life (Required Argument):** This is the number of periods at which the asset depreciates and this can also be called useful life of the asset.
- **Period (Required Argument):** This is the period in which the depreciation will be calculated for
- **Month (Optional Argument):** This indicates how many months of the year are used in the calculation of the first period of depreciation. If this is omitted, the function defaults the value to 12.

USING THE DB FUNCTION

Let's calculate the depreciation of an asset with an initial cost of £200,000 with the salvage value of £8,000 after 5 years with a period of 2 years and 4 months in the first year

B8		:	X	✓	f_x	

▲	A	B	C	D	E
1					
2	Initial Cost	200,000			
3	Salvage value	8,000			
4	Life	5			
5	Period	2			
6	Month	4			
7					

To find the depreciation value using the DB function

- Select an empty cell, type in the function and its argument **=DB(B2,B3,B4,B5,B6)**

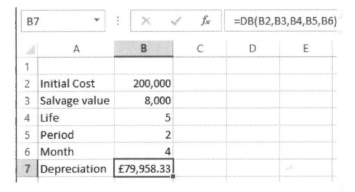

- Click on enter and the depreciation value of the asset will be £79,958.33 as shown in the table below

NOTE: Keep these in mind when using the DB function

- #VALUE error occurs when the argument supplied is non-numeric
- #NUM! error occurs due to the following reasons
- When the given cost or salvage is less than zero
- When the life or period argument provided is less than or equal to zero
- When the month argument provided is less than or equal to zero is greater than 12
- When the period argument provided is greater than the life argument and when the month argument is omitted
- When the period provided is greater than life +1

THE DDB FUNCTION

The DDB function is a function that calculates the depreciation of an asset for a specific period using the double-declining balance method or any other method that is specified by changing the factor argument

The DDB function uses the following arguments

=DDB (cost, salvage, life, period, [factor})

- **Cost (Required Argument):** This is the initial cost of an asset
- **Salvage (Required Argument):** This is the value at the end of the depreciation which is also known as the salvage value of the asset
- **Life (Required Argument):** This is the number of periods at which the asset depreciates and this can also be called useful life of the asset.
- **Period (Required Argument):** This is the period where the depreciation of the asset will be calculated.
- **Factor (Optional Argument):** This is the rate at which the balance declines. If the factor is omitted, it defaults to 2.

USING THE DDB FUNCTION

Let's calculate the depreciation of an asset with an initial cost of £300,000 with the salvage value of £5,000 after 5 years with a period of 2 years. Use the DBB function to calculate the depreciation by a factor of 1.

B10	▼	:	×	✓	fx	
◢	A		B	C	D	E
1						
2						
3	Initial Cost		300,000			
4	Salvage Value		5,000			
5	Life		5			
6	Period		2			
7	Factor		1			
8						

To calculate depreciation using the DDB

- Select an empty cell, type in the function and its argument **=DDB(B3,B4,B5,B6,B7)**

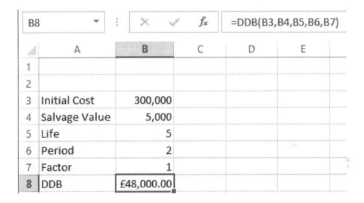

- Click on enter and the depreciation value of the asset will be £48,000.00 as shown in the table below

	A	B	C	D	E
1					
2					
3	Initial Cost	300,000			
4	Salvage Value	5,000			
5	Life	5			
6	Period	2			
7	Factor	1			
8	DDB	£48,000.00			

NOTE: Keep the following in mind when using the DDB function

- #VALUE! error occurs when the argument provided in the function is non-numeric
- #NUM! error occurs due to the following reasons
  o When the value of the coat and that of salvage is less than 0
  o When the value of the life of the asset is less than or equal to zero
  o When the period argument is less than or equal to 0 or greater than the life value
  o When the factor argument is less than 1

THE SEARCH FUNCTION

The SEARCH Function locates or finds the position of a substring within a string. This is just like locating the position of **S** in the word **JOURNALISM.** The SEARCH function in this case is insensitive, that is, it doesn't mind whether the text to find is in capital letter or small letter

The syntax for SEARCH function is =SEARCH (find text, within text, [start_num]

- find text= The text to find
- within text= The text to search from
- start_num = Where to start the search for the text within the text.

Let's get practical with the SEARCH function

Example 1

Search for the position T in cell A1 in the table below

To search for the position of T in cell A1

- Go to cell B2 to type =**SEARCH ("T", A1,1)** and press **Enter**

The position of T in cell A1 is 3

Example 2

Search for the position MAN in cell C1 in the table below

C6		▾	:	✕	✓	*fx*				▾

◢	A	B	C	D	E	F	G	H	▲
1	INTERGRATION	LIFE	EMANCIPATION						
2									
3									
4									

To search for the position of MAN in cell D2

- Go to cell D2 to type **=SEARCH("MAN",C1,1)** and press **Enter**

D1		▾	:	✕	✓	*fx*	=SEARCH("MAN",C1,1)

◢	A	B	C	D	E	F	G	H
1	INTERGRATION	LIFE	EMANCIPATION	2				
2								
3								
4								

The position of MAN in cell C1 is 3

THE FIND FUNCTION

Just like the SEARCH Function, the FIND Function also locates or finds the position of a substring within a string. The SEARCH function in this case is sensitive i.e., it observes the capital and small letter before searching for a text therefore, searching for the exact text.

The syntax for FIND function is =FIND (find text, within text, [start_num]

- find text= The text to find
- within text= The text to search from
- start_num = Where to start the search for the text within the text.

Example 1

Find the position of GROWTH In cell B2 in the table below

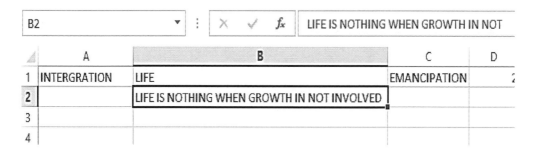

To find the position of GROWTH in cell B2

- Go to cell C2 to type =**FIND ("GROWTH", B2,1)** and press **Enter**

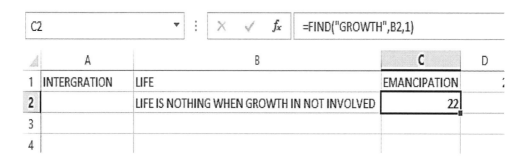

The position of GROWTH in cell B2 is 22.

CHAPTER NINE

LOGICAL FUNCTIONS

Logical functions are the functions that provide decision-making tools that allow you to look at the content of a cell, execute a calculation, and then test the result against a required value. The logical function is also used to test if a situation is true or false and these results can be used to display information and execute all kinds of calculations. Examples of the logical functions are IF, NOT, OR, IFS, etc.

THE IF FUNCTION

The IF function is a function that tests a given condition and returns one value for a TRUE result and another value for a FALSE result. This function allows you to make a logical comparison between a value and what you expect.

The IF function uses the following arguments

=IF (Logical_text,[Value_if_true],[Value_if_false])

- **Logical_text (Required Argument):** This is the value or logical expression that are to be tested and evaluated as either TRUE or FALSE
- **Value_if_true (Optional Argument):** This is the value that will be returned if the logical test evaluates to TRUE
- **Value_if_false (Optional Argument):** This is the value that will be returned if the logical test evaluates to FALSE

While using this function, the following logical operators can be used

- Equal to (=)
- Greater than (>)
- Greater than or equal to (≥)
- Less than (<)
- Less than or equal to (≤)
- Not equal (≠)

USING THE IF FUNCTION

In the table below, we want to test if the values in the cells are greater than 500 or not, if it is true, the value will be returned stating **Yes** and if it is false, the value will be returned stating **No**

	A	B	C	D
C6				
1	Price	Result		
2	400			
3	800			
4	212			
5	454			
6	789			

- To check if cell A2 is greater than 500, type in =IF(A2>500," Yes", "No")

=IF(A2>500,"Yes", "No")

	A	B	C	D	E	F	G
1	Price	Result					
2		400 =IF(A2>500,"Yes", "No")					
3		800 IF(logical_test, [value_if_true], [value_if_false])					
4		212					
5		454					
6		789					

- Click on enter and the return value will be **No**

FILE   HOME   INSERT   PAGE LAYOUT   FORMULAS   DATA   REVIEW

B2 =IF(A2>500,"Yes", "No")

	A	B	C	D	E	F	G
1	Price	Result					
2		400 No					
3		800					
4		212					
5		454					
6		789					

156

- Use the steps above to get the value of A3 to B6; **=IF(A3>500,"
Yes", "No"), =IF(A4>500," Yes", "No"), =IF(A5>500," Yes",
"No"), =IF(A6>500," Yes", "No")** respectively

	A	B	C	D
			C13	
1	Price	Result		
2	400	No		
3	800	Yes		
4	212	No		
5	454	No		
6	789	Yes		

NOTE: Keep these in mind when using the IF functions:

- The IF function works if the logical_test returns a numeric value.
- The IF function treats any non-zero values as TRUE and zero value as FALSE
- #VALUE! occurs when the logical_test argument cannot be evaluated to be TRUE or FALSE
- The IF function evaluates every element of the array when any of the arguments is supplied to the function as an array
- To count condition, use the COUNTIF and COUNTIFS functions
- To add up conditions, use the SUMIF and SUMIFS functions

THE NESTED IF FUNCTION

The Nested IF function means one IF function located inside another nest IF function thereby allowing you to test multiple criteria and increasing the number of possible outcomes. You can get the same result with the nested IF function when used individually with just the IF function. Now let's use the Nested IF function in the table below to check the prices that are greater or lesser than 500

	A	B	C	D
				D4
1	Price	Result		
2	400			
3	800			
4	323			
5	454			
6	2323			

- To use the Nested IF to get the value that is greater 500, type in the function in an empty cell; **=IF(A2>500, "Yes", "No" =IF(A3>500, "Yes", "No "=IF(A4>500, "Yes", "No" =IF(A5>500, "Yes", "No") =IF(A6>500, "Yes", "No"))))** and then click enter

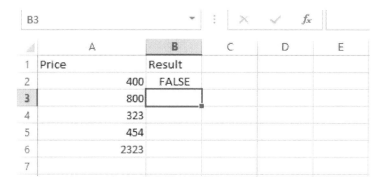

- You will get the value of the first cell referenced

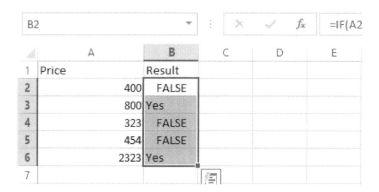

- To get the values of the remaining cells, use the fill handle to drag the function to reflect on the other cells.

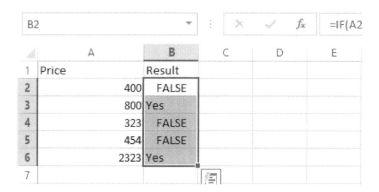

NOTE: When using the Nested IF functions, take note of the following:

- The Nested IF function involves a lot of thinking and accuracy when building so that the logic can calculate correctly with the condition given to the very end.
- The Nested IF functions can be confusing at times, especially when there are a lot of IF functions to be nested

THE IFS FUNCTION

The IFS function is a function that is used as a substitute to the nested IF function. This function checks whether one or more conditions or criteria are met and returns the values that correspond to or meet the first TRUE condition

The IFS function uses the following for its operations

=IFS (Logical_test1, value1[logical_test2, value2] …, [logical_test127, value127])

- **Logical_test1 (Required Argument):** This is a condition that Excel uses to evaluate whether a value is TRUE or FALSE
- **Value1 (Required Argument):** This is when the logical_test 1 is true. Other logical values are optional.

USING THE IFS FUNCTION

Let's use the IFS function to assign grades to the marks of students given in the table below

	A	B	C	D	E
1					
2	Marks	Grade			
3	80				
4	75				
5	70				
6	65				
7	60				
8	55				

B3 · fx

To assign grades to the marks above;

- Select an empty cell and type in the function name and its arguments; **=IFS(A3>75,"A", A3>70, "B", A3>65, "C", A3>60, "D", A3>55, "E", A3>50, "F")**

- To get the values of the remaining cells, use the fill handle to drag the function to reflect on the other cells.

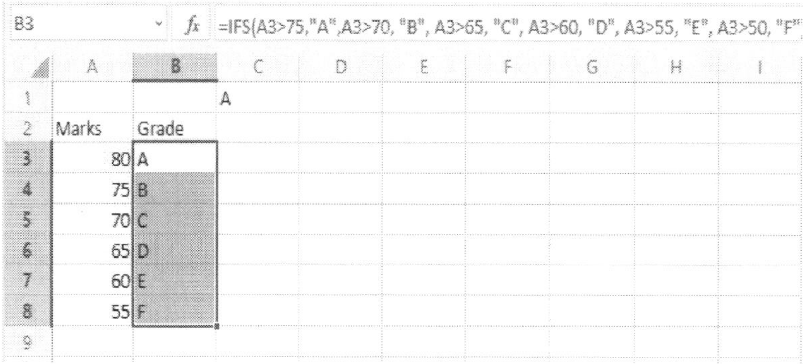

NOTE: Keep these in mind when using the IFS function

- #N/A error occurs when there are no TRUE conditions found by the IFS function
- When the logical_test argument resolves to a value other than TRUE or FALSE, #VALUE! error occurs

The IFFEROR Function

The IFFEROR function is a function that is used to custom result when a formula generates an error. The IFERROR is to trap and manage errors without using more complicating nested IF statements.

The IFERROR uses the following arguments

160

=IFFERROR (value, value_if_error)

- **Value (Required Argument):** This is a value or expression that is checked or tested for error
- **Value_if_error (Required Argument):** This is the value that will be returned when an error is found in the formula

USING THE IFERROR FORMULAS

With the table given below, let's use the IFFEROR function to remove the errors and put in a customized message "invalid data"

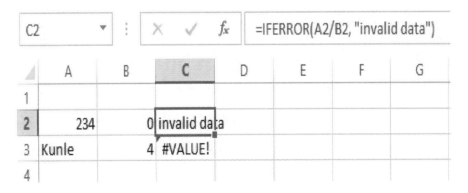

To change the error in cell C2

- Select an empty cell and type in the function name and its arguments; **=IFERROR (A2/B2, "invalid data")**

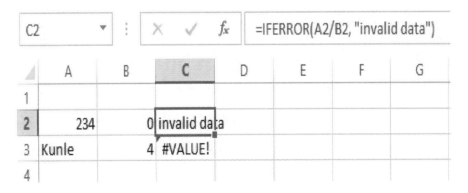

To change the error in cell C3

- Select an empty cell and type in the function name and its arguments; **=IFERROR (A3/B3, "invalid data")**

C3			✕ ✓ ƒx	=IFERROR(A3/B3, "invalid data")			
	A	B	C	D	E	F	G
1							
2	234		0 invalid data				
3	Kunle		4 invalid data				

NOTE: Keep these in mind when using the IFERROR FUNCTION

- When the value or value_if_error is an empty cell, the IFERROR function treats it as an empty string value
- The IFFEROR returns an array of results for each cell in the range specified in the value if the value is an array formula

THE AND FUNCTION

The AND function is a function that is used to determine if the conditions given in a data set are TRUE and when any of the conditions is not met, it returns a FALSE value e.g., B1 is greater than 50 and less than 100

The AND function uses the following arguments to execute

=AND (logical1, [logical2},)

- **Logical1 (Required Argument):** This is the first condition or logical value to be evaluated
- **Logical2 (Optional Argument):** This is the second condition or logical value to be evaluated

USING THE AND FUNCTION

Using the table given below, let's examine if cell A2 is greater than 67 and less than cell A3 using the AND function to return TRUE or FALSE value depending on the result.

	A	B	C	D
1				
2	23			
3	56			

To get the result of the table above;

- Select an empty cell and type in the function name and its arguments; =**AND(A2>67, A2<A3)**

	A	B	C	D
1				
2	23	FALSE		
3	56			
4				

`=AND(A2>67,A2<A3)`

- The AND function returns FALSE in the table above because one of the conditions given in the data set was not met i.e. A2 is not greater than 67
- When the conditions given in a dataset are met, the AND function will return TRUE as shown in the table below

	A	B	C	D
1				
2	23	TRUE		
3	56			
4				

`=AND(A2>20,A2<A3)`

NOTE: Keep the following in mind when using the AND function

- When there is no logical value found or created during the evaluation, the AND function returns a VALUE! error
- The AND function ignores test values and empty cell provided as arguments
- The AND function can contain 255 conditions
- The AND function returns TRUE when all the conditions are met

THE OR FUNCTION

The OR function is a function that returns TRUE if any of the conditions are TRUE and returns FALSE if all conditions are false. Unlike the AND function, when one of all the conditions is false, it will be returned as FALSE.

The OR function uses the following arguments

=OR (logical1, [logical2},...)

- **Logical1 (Required Argument):** This is the first condition or logical value to evaluate.
- **Logical (Required Argument):** The second condition or logical value to evaluate

USING THE OR FUNCTION

let's examine if cell A2 is greater than 30, B2 is less than 50 and B3 is equal to 45 using the OR function to return TRUE or FALSE value depending on the result.

	A	B	C	D	E
1					
2	45	32			
3	3	3			
4					
5					

To get the result of the table above;

- Select an empty cell and type in the function name and its arguments; =OR(A2>30,B2<50, B3=45)

=OR(A2>30,B2<50, B3=45)

	A	B	C	D	E	F	G
1							
2	45	32	=OR(A2>30,B2<50, B3=45)				
3	3	3	OR(logical1, [logical2], [logical3], [logical4], ...)				
4							
5							

- Click on enter and the result will be returned as FALSE as shown in the table below

=OR(A2>30,B2<50, B3=45)

	A	B	C	D	E
1					
2	45	32	TRUE		
3	3	3			
4					

NOTE: Keep the following in mind when using the OR function

- When any of the logical_test cannot be interpreted as numeric or logical values, the function returns a #VALUE! error
- This function ignores text values or empty cells supplied in the arguments
- The function can contain 255 conditions in total
- This function can also be used together with the AND function depending on the arguments

CHAPTER TEN

LOOKUP AND REFERENCE FUNCTIONS

The Lookup functions are used for retrieving information from a list of data or tables and used on the worksheet or workbook. Examples of the lookup functions are HLOOK UP, VLOOK UP, etc.

The Reference functions return information about cell references as text values such as the entire address, row, and column. Examples of these functions are ADDRESS function, ROW function, etc. Now let's talk about the lookup and reference functions and how they can be applied to the worksheet.

THE VLOOKUP FUNCTION

The VLOOKUP function in which the V means **Vertical** is a quick way to lookup up a piece of information in the first column of a table or dataset and extracting or returning some corresponding data or information in the same row from another column of the data set or table.

The VLOOKUP function uses the following arguments to execute its operation:

=VLOOKUP (lookup_value, table_array, col_index_num, [range_lookup])

- **Lookup_value (required argument):** This is the value to look up for in the first column of the table or dataset
- **Table_array (required argument):** This is the data array that is to be searched by the lookup value in the left part of the column
- **Col_index_num (required argument):** This is the column number or integer in the table array where the matching value must be returned.
- **Range_lookup (optional argument):** This part of the function specifies if you want the VLOOK to find an exact match or the appropriate match. The argument is set to either TRUE or FALSE. TRUE stands for appropriate match and if not found, the next largest value is returned. FALSE on its stands for exact match and if not found, it returns as error #N/A

USING THE VLOOKUP FUNCTION

Let's look at the example below; this is a table containing 4 fruits and their prices. With the VLOOKUP function, let's find out the price of yam in the table

	A	B	C	D	E
1	GOOD TABLE				
2					
3					
4	FRUIT	IN STOCK	PRICE $		
5	Grapes	Yes	23		
6	Yam	Yes	54		
7	Bananas	No	78		
8	Orange	Yes	54		
9					
10					
11	FRUIT	PRICE			
12	YAM				

To find the price of yam in the table above using the VLOOKUP function, follow the steps below:

- Select an empty cell and type in the function to be used with the **lookup_value** i.e., the cell that contains the information to lookup for. The lookup cell here is A12 which contains **Yam =VLOOKUP (A12**

			fx	=VLOOKUP(A12			
	A	B	C	D	E	F	G
1	GOOD TABLE						
2							
3							
4	FRUIT	IN STOCK	PRICE $				
5	Grapes	Yes	23				
6	Yam	Yes	54				
7	Bananas	No	78				
8	Orange	Yes	54				
9							
10							
11	FRUIT	PRICE					
12	YAM	=VLOOKUP(A12					
13		VLOOKUP(lookup_value, table_array, col_index_num, [range_lookup])					

- Select the table where the data is to be searched from by inputting the **table_array**: =VLOOKUP (A12, A4:C8

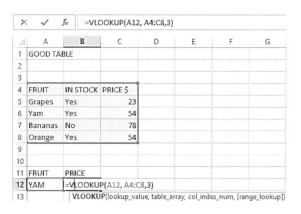

- Tell Excel the column that contains the data you want the VLOOKUP to use as output by inputting the **col_index_num** which is **3: =VLOOKUP (A12, A4:C8,3**

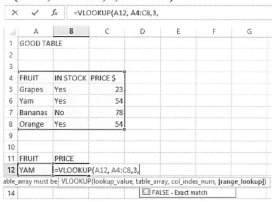

- The final step which is optional is to tell Excel if you are looking for an appropriate match or exact match by inputting either TRUE or FALSE; **=VLOOKUP (A12, A4:C8,3, FALSE) or =VLOOKUP (A12, A4:C8,3, TRUE)**

- If you have followed the steps above, the result of your operation using the VLOOKUP function with the table must be **54**

	fx		=VLOOKUP(A12, A4:C8,3,FALSE)		
	A	B	C	D	E
1	GOOD TABLE				
2					
3					
4	FRUIT	IN STOCK	PRICE $		
5	Grapes	Yes	23		
6	Yam	Yes	54		
7	Bananas	No	78		
8	Orange	Yes	54		
9					
10					
11	FRUIT	PRICE			
12	YAM	54			

NOTE: When using the VLOOKUP function, keep the following in mind:

- When the range lookup is not used, the VLOOKUP function will not permit a non-exact match, rather it will use an exact match if it does exist.
- If the dataset contains duplicate values, the VLOOKUP function will only pick the first one
- The VLOOKUP function is not case-sensitive i.e., it works with both upper case and higher case characters
- This function permits the use of wildcards such as asterisks, question marks, and tilde
- #N/A! error occurs when the VLOOKUP function cannot find a match to the given lookup value
- #VALUE! error can occur due to two reasons
  - When the col_index_num argument is less than one or not even seen as a numeric value
  - If the range_lookup value argument is not seen or recognized as one of the logical values TRUE or FALSE
- #REF! error can occur when the col_index_num argument is bigger than the number of columns in the given table_array or when the formula used in the table to reference a cell does not exist.

THE HLOOKUP FUNCTION

The HLOOKUP function in which the H means Horizontal is a tool that is used to lookup for a value or a piece of information in the top row of a table array or dataset and then return the value or information in the same column from another row specified in the table array or dataset.

The HLOOKUP function uses the following arguments to execute its operation

=HLOOKUP (lookup_value, table_array, row_index_num, [range_lookup])

- **Lookup_value (required argument):** This is the value to look up for in the first row of the table or dataset
- **Table_array (required argument):** This is the data array that is to be searched by the lookup value in the left part of the column
- **Row_index_num (required argument):** This is the row number or integer in the table array where the matching value must be returned.
- **Range_lookup (optional argument):** This part of the function specifies if you want the VLOOK to find an exact match or the appropriate match. The argument is set to either TRUE or FALSE. TRUE stands for appropriate match and if not found, the next largest value is returned. FALSE on its own stands for exact match and if not found, it returns back as error #N/A

USING THE HLOOKUP FUNCTION

With the table below, let's find out the score of Joy in Mathematics using the HLOOKUP function

	A	B	C	D	E
	STUDENT SCORES	JOY	LOVETH	JOHN	ADE X
	MATHEMATICS	59	45	68	98
	ENGLISH	69	78	43	76
	ECONOMICS	34	56	65	89
	PHE	23	89	24	97
	THE TOTAL SCORE OF JOY IN MATHEMATICS				

To find the total score of Joy in Mathematics, follow the steps below

- Select an empty cell and type in the function to be used with the **lookup_value** i.e., the cell that contains the information to lookup for. The lookup cell here is B1 which carries the name **Joy;** =**HLOOKUP (B1**

	fx	=HLOOKUP(B1					
	A	B	C	D	E	F	G
1	STUDENT SCORES	JOY	LOVETH	JOHN	ADE X		
2	MATHEMATICS	59	45	68	98		
3	ENGLISH	69	78	43	76		
4	ECONOMICS	34	56	65	89		
5	PHE	23	89	24	97		
6							
7	THE TOTAL SCORE OF JOY IN MATHEMATICS	=HLOOKUP(B1					
8		HLOOKUP(**lookup_value**, table_array, row_index_num, [range_lookup])					

- Select the table where the data is to be searched from by inputting the **table_array**: =**HLOOKUP (B1, A1:E5**

	fx	=HLOOKUP(B1, A1:E5					
	A	B	C	D	E	F	G
1	STUDENT SCORES	JOY	LOVETH	JOHN	ADE X		
2	MATHEMATICS	59	45	68	98		
3	ENGLISH	69	78	43	76		
4	ECONOMICS	34	56	65	89		
5	PHE	23	89	24	97		
6							
7	THE TOTAL SCORE OF JOY IN MATHEMATICS	=HLOOKUP(B1, A1:E5					
8		HLOOKUP(lookup_value, **table_array**, row_index_num, [range_lookup])					

- Tell Excel the row that contains the data you want the HLOOKUP to use as output by inputting the **row_index_num** which is **2:** =**HLOOKUP (B1, A1:E5, 3**

	fx	=HLOOKUP(B1, A1:E5,2					
	A	B	C	D	E	F	G
1	STUDENT SCORES	JOY	LOVETH	JOHN	ADE X		
2	MATHEMATICS	59	45	68	98		
3	ENGLISH	69	78	43	76		
4	ECONOMICS	34	56	65	89		
5	PHE	23	89	24	97		
6							
7	THE TOTAL SCORE OF JOY IN MATHEMATICS	=HLOOKUP(B1, A1:E5,2					
8		HLOOKUP(lookup_value, table_array, **row_index_num**, [range_lookup])					

- The final step which is optional is to tell Excel if you are looking for an appropriate match or exact match by inputting either TRUE or FALSE; = **HLOOKUP (B1, A1:E5,3, FALSE) or =HLOOKUP (B1, A1:E5,3, TRUE)**

	X	✓	f_x	=HLOOKUP(B1, A1:E5, 2, FALSE)			
	A	B	C	D	E	F	G
1	STUDENT SCORES	JOY	LOVETH	JOHN	ADE X		
2	MATHEMATICS	59	45	68	98		
3	ENGLISH	69	78	43	76		
4	ECONOMICS	34	56	65	89		
5	PHE	23	89	24	97		
6							
7	THE TOTAL SCORE OF JOY IN MATHEMATICS	=HLOOKUP(B1, A1:E5,2, FALSE)					
8		HLOOKUP(lookup_value, table_array, row_index_num, [range_lookup])					

- If you have followed the steps above, the result of your operation using the VLOOKUP function with the table must be **59**

	X	✓	f_x					
	A	B	C	D	E	F	G	H
1	STUDENT SCORES	JOY	LOVETH	JOHN	ADE X			
2	MATHEMATICS	59	45	68	98			
3	ENGLISH	69	78	43	76			
4	ECONOMICS	34	56	65	89			
5	PHE	23	89	24	97			
6								
7	THE TOTAL SCORE OF JOY IN MATHEMATICS	59						

NOTE: When using the HLOOKUP functions, ensure to keep these in mind

- Just like the VLOOKUP, the HLOOKUP function is also case insensitive
- It also supports wildcard characters such as asterisks and question mark
- #N/A! error occurs when the range_lookup is FALSE and the HLOOKUP function is not able to find the lookup_value in the range
- #REF! error occurs when the row_index_num is greater than the number of columns in table_array

- #VALUE! error surfaces when the row_index_num is lesser than 1
- HLOOKUP function will only return one value and this is always the first value that matches the lookup value

THE CHOOSE FUNCTION

The CHOOSE function is a tool that uses an index number provided to return a value from the list of value arguments.

The CHOOSE function uses the following arguments to execute its operation

=CHOOSE (index_num, value1, [value2] …)

- **Index_num (required argument):** This is an integer that specifies the position of the value to return. This must contain any number between 1 and 254, formula, or a reference to a cell ranging between 1 and 254
- **Value1, Value2…** This is a list that ranges from 1 and 254 values from which the CHOOSE function is to look from. The value 1 is required while others are optional. These values can come in form of numbers, text values, formulas, cell references, or defined names.

USING THE CHOOSE FUNCTION

With the table below, let's return the second value from a list using the CHOOSE function

B2			✕	✓	fx	
	A	B	C	D	E	
1	Names of students					
2	Joy					
3	Loveth					
4	Jasmine					
5	Anita					

To return the second value in the list;

- Select an empty cell and type in the function name and its arguments; **=CHOOSE (3, A2, A3, A4, A5)**

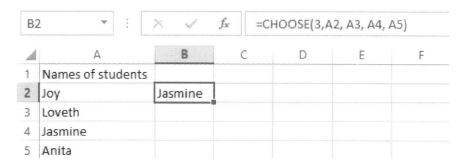

- Click on Enter and the function will return the third value as **Jasmine** as shown in the table below

NOTE: Keep these in mind when using the CHOOSE function:

- When the text values in an argument are not enclosed in quotes and are not invalid cell reference, it returns #NAME? error
- #VALUE! error occurs when the index_num provided is less than 1 or greater than the given number of values or when the index_num argument is non-numeric

THE MATCH FUNCTION

The MATCH function is a tool that is used to look up a value within a range and then returns the relative position of that value within that range.

The MATCH function uses the following arguments for its operations

=MATCH (lookup_value, lookup_array, [match_type])

- **Lookup_value (Required Argument):** This is the value to be looked up
- **Lookup_array (Required Argument):** This is the data array where the value will be looked up from
- **Match_type (Optional Argument):** This argument indicates how the Lookup_value with values in lookup_array are matched together.

Match_type	Behaviour
1 or omitted	This match_type finds the largest value that is less or equal to the lookup_value. When this argument is used, the lookup_array must be in ascending order.
0	This match_type finds the first value that is equal to the lookup_value. when this argument is used, the lookup_array can be ordered anyhow
-1	This match_type finds the smallest value that is greater than or equal to the lookup_value. When this argument is used, the lookup_array must be in descending

USING THE MATCH FUNCTION

With the table below, let's find the value of Apple

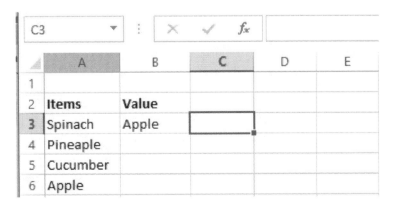

To find the value of Apple;

- Select an empty cell and type in the function name and its arguments; =**MATCH (B3, A3:A6,0)**

- Click on Enter and the function will return the value of Apple to be 4 as shown in the table below

NOTE: keep the following in mind when using the MATCH function

- The MATCH function is case insensitive i.e., it does not distinguish between lowercase and uppercase letters when looking up the values in the dataset
- When the MATCH function cannot find a match for the lookup_value, #N/A! error is returned
- The Function allows for appropriate and exact matching and also the use of wildcards for partial matches

THE TRANSPOSE FUNCTION

The TRANSPOSE function is a tool that is used to change the orientation of a given range or array; TRANSPOSE changes a vertical range to horizontal range and vice versa.

The TRANSPOSE function uses just an argument

=TRANSPOSE (array)

The array argument contains the range of cells to be transposed. When an array is transposed, the first row becomes the first column of the new array and the second row also becomes the second column of the new array and it continues like that.

USING THE TRANSPOSE FUNCTION

With the example below, let's change the orientation display of the array from vertical portrait to horizontal portrait using the TRANSPOSE function

	A	B	C	D
1	MONDAY	45		
2	TUESDAY	78		
3	WEDNESDAY	98		
4	THURSDAY	65		
5	FRIDAY	98		

B6

To do this, follow the procedures below:

- The first thing to do is to select some blank cells. Ensure that the cells selected are the same as the numbers of the original set of the cell but in the other direction

C10

	A	B	C	D	E	F	G
1	MONDAY	45					
2	TUESDAY	78					
3	WEDNESDAY	98					
4	THURSDAY	65					
5	FRIDAY	98					
6							
7							
8							
9							
10							
11							

- In the selected blanks cells, type =**TRANSPOSE**

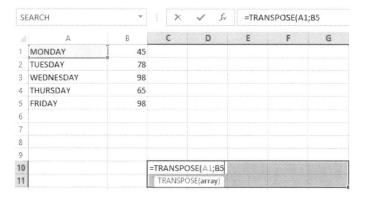

- Type in the range of the original set of cells in the TRANSPOSE function; =**TRANSPOSE (A1:B5)**

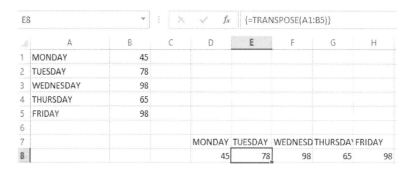

- Finally, press **CTRL+SHIF+ENTER,** then the cell range will be transposed

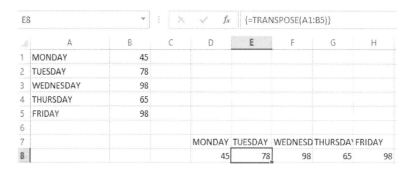

NOTE: Observe the following points in mind when using the TRANSPOSE function:

- The TRANSPOSE function being an array function does not permit changing any part of the array it returns. However, you can still edit

178

the TRANSPOSE function by selecting the entire range used with the function and then make any corrections. When this is done, press **Ctrl +Shift +Enter** to save the changes made.

- The TRANSPOSE location range must have the same numbers of rows and columns as the original set of cells
- The TRANSPOSE formula must be inputted as an array formula by pressing **Ctrl +Shift +Enter.**

THE FORMULATEXTS FUNCTION

The FORMULATEXT function is used to get a formula in a text form from a given reference or referred cell. With the FORMULATEXT function, you can extract a formula as a text from a cell. This function was first introduced in MS Excel 2013.

The FORMULATEXT function uses just one argument

= FORMULATEXT (reference)

- **Reference (Required argument):** This is the reference to the cell or range of cells you want the formula as texts.

USING THE FORMULATEXT FUNCTION

With the table below, let's use the FORMULATEXT function to check the formula used to find the total score of Joy in mathematics

	A	B	C	D	E
C15				*fx*	
1	STUDENT SCORES	JOY	LOVETH	JOHN	ADE X
2	MATHEMATICS	59	45	68	98
3	ENGLISH	69	78	43	76
4	ECONOMICS	34	56	65	89
5	PHE	23	89	24	97
6					
7	THE TOTAL SCORE OF JOY IN MATHEMATICS	59			

To check the formula used, using the FORMULATEXT, follow the steps below:

- Select an empty cell and type in the function =**FORMULATEXT**

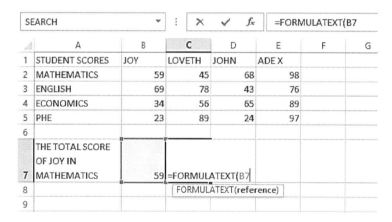

- Type the reference which is **B7** to the function; =**FORMULATEXT(B7)**

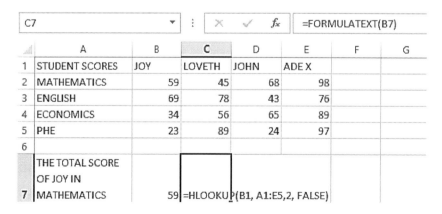

- Finally, click on enter and the formula used in the table will be displayed for you to see

	A	B	C	D	E	F	G
1	STUDENT SCORES	JOY	LOVETH	JOHN	ADE X		
2	MATHEMATICS	59	45	68	98		
3	ENGLISH	69	78	43	76		
4	ECONOMICS	34	56	65	89		
5	PHE	23	89	24	97		
6							
7	THE TOTAL SCORE OF JOY IN MATHEMATICS	59	=HLOOKUP(B1, A1:E5,2, FALSE)				

NOTE: Keep the following points in mind when using the FORMULATEXT function:

- #VALUE error occurs when invalid data types are used as inputs
- The N/A error can occur due to the following reasons:
  - When you use the FORMULATEXT on a cell that does not contain a formula
  - When a reference argument is to another workbook that is not open.
  - When the formula input in the cell is longer than 8192 characters
  - When the worksheet cannot be opened because it is protected
- VBA is needed in an older version of Excel to use the formula in the cell
- The Reference argument can be used in another worksheet or workbook

THE COLUMN FUNCTION

The column function returns the column number of a given cell reference in a worksheet. It helps to give or provide the column number of a given cell reference

The COLUMN function uses one argument

= COLUMN (reference)

- **Reference (Optional Argument):** This is the cell or range for which to find the column number

USING THE COLUMN FUNCTION

In the table below, we will be using the COLUMN function to find out the column numbers of the targeted cells A4, B3, and C4

To find the column number of cell A4

- Click on a blank cell and then type the function and the cell reference you wish to know its column number =**COLUMN(A4)**

- Click on Enter and the column number will be displayed

To find the column number of cell B3

- Click on a blank cell and then type the function and the cell reference you wish to know its column number =**COLUMN(B4)**

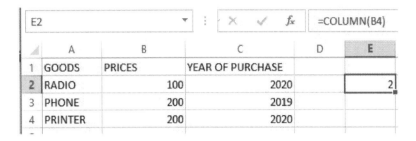

- Click on Enter and the column number will be displayed

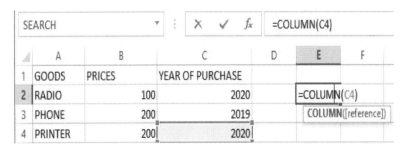

To find the column number of cell C1;

- Click on a blank cell and then type the function and the cell reference you wish to know its column number =**COLUMN(C4)**

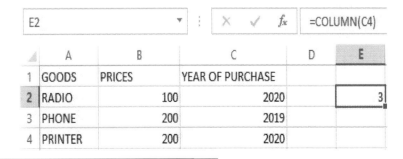

- Click on Enter and the column number will be displayed

When you use the COLUMN function without specifying the reference, the function will automatically pick the column number of the cell it is inserted into =**COLUMN ()**

	A	B	C	D	E
1	GOODS	PRICES	YEAR OF PURCHASE		
2	RADIO	100	2020		5
3	PHONE	200	2019		
4	PRINTER	200	2020		

(Formula bar: E2 — =COLUMN())

NOTE: Keep the following points in mind while using the COLUMN function

- The COLUMN function cannot include more than one cell reference or address
- The cell reference in a COLUMN function can be a single cell or a range of cells
- The reference argument in the COLUMN function is optional

THE ROW FUNCTION

The ROWS function returns the row number of a given cell reference in a worksheet. This function helps to look up and give the number of rows in a dataset or table. For instance, the formula =ROW(C6) returns 6 since C5 is the fifth row in the worksheet. To use the ROW function, all you need is to select the cell reference of the row number you wish to know.

The ROWS function uses an argument

=**ROWS (reference)**

- **Reference (Optional Argument):** This is the cell or range of cells to find the row numbers

USING THE ROW FUNCTION

In the table below, we will be using the ROWS function to find out the row numbers of the targeted cells A3, B4 and C3

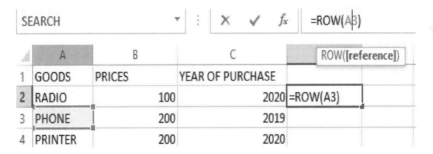

	A	B	C	D
			A10	
1	GOODS	PRICES	YEAR OF PURCHASE	
2	RADIO	100	2020	
3	PHONE	200	2019	
4	PRINTER	200	2020	
5				
6				

To find the row number of cell A3;

- Click on a blank cell, type the function and the cell reference you wish to know its row number **=ROW(A3)**

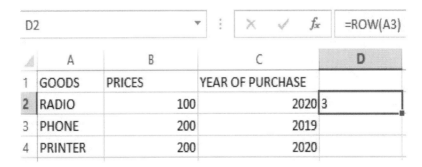

- Click on Enter and the column number will be displayed

To find the row number of cell B4;

- Click on a blank cell and then type the function and the cell reference you wish to know its column number **=ROW(B4)**

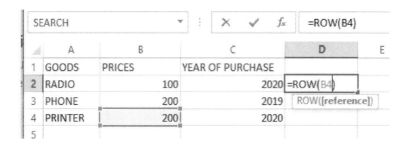

- Click on Enter and the column number will be displayed

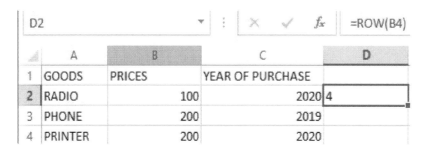

To find the row number of cell **C3;**

- Click on a blank cell and then type the function and the cell reference you wish to know its column number =**ROW(C3)**

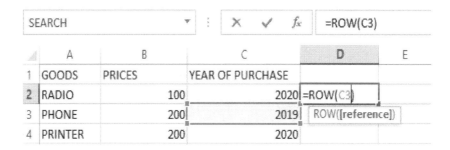

- Click on Enter and the column number will be displayed

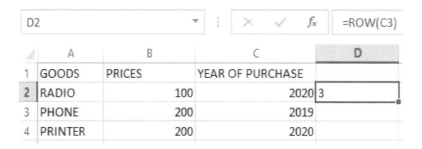

Just like the COLUMN function, you can also use the ROW function without specifying the reference. The function automatically picks the row number of the cell it is inserted into =**ROW ()**

D2				:	×	✓	f_x	=ROW()

▲	A	B	C	D
1	GOODS	PRICES	YEAR OF PURCHASE	
2	RADIO	100	2020	2
3	PHONE	200	2019	
4	PRINTER	200	2020	

NOTE: Keep the following points in mind while using the COLUMN function

- The ROW function cannot include more than one cell reference or address
- The cell reference in a ROW function can be a single cell or a range of cells
- The reference argument in the COLUMN function is optional
- If the reference in the ROW function is entered as an array, the ROW function returns the row of numbers of all the rows in that array

THE INDEX FUNCTION

The INDEX function returns a value or a reference to a value within a table based on the intersection of rows and columns within the dataset or table. The INDEX function is mostly used with the MATCH function and can also be used in the replacement of VLOOKUP. There are two formats for the INDEX function

- Array Format
- Reference Format

THE ARRAY FORMAT OF THE INDEX FUNCTION

The array format of the INDEX function is used to return the value of a specific cell or an array of cells.

The array format of the INDEX functions takes the following arguments:

=INDEX (array, row_num, [col_num]

- **Array (Required Argument):** This is the specific array or range of cells to look up From.
- **Row_num (Required Argument):** This indicates the row number of the specified array from which to return a value from. When this argument is set to zero or blank, all rows in the array will default to zero or blank.
- **Column_num (Optional Argument):** This indicates the row number of the specified array from which to return a value from. When this argument is set to zero or blank, all columns in the array will default to zero or blank.

USING THE ARRAY FORMAT OF THE INDEX FUNCTION

From the table below, we will use the array format of the INDEX function to find out the numbers of goals scored by LOVETH

	A	B	C
	NAME OF PLAYERS	POSITION	GOALS SCORED
1			
2	FAVOUR	1	34
3	JOY	2	21
4	LOVETH	3	11
5	LILIAN	4	10
6			
7	NUMBER OF GOALS SCORED BY LOVETH		

To find out the total number of scores by LOVETH, follow the steps below:

- Select an empty cell and type in the function to be used with the **array** i.e., the specified range of cells which are A2:C5=**INDEX (A2:C5**

- Put in the row and column number alongside the array; **INDEX (A2:C5,3,3)**

- If you have followed the steps above, the result of your operation using the array format of the INDEX function with the table will be **11**

	A	B	C
1	NAME OF PLAYERS	POSITION	GOALS SCORED
2	FAVOUR	1	34
3	JOY	2	21
4	LOVETH	3	11
5	LILIAN	4	10
6			
7	NUMBER OF GOALS SCORED BY LOVETH	11	

THE REFERENCE FORMAT OF THE INDEX FUNCTION

The reference format of the INDEX function returns the reference of the cell when the row_num and col_num are intersected.

The reference format of the INDEX functions takes the following arguments:

=INDEX((reference,row_num,[column_num],[area_num])

- **Reference (Required Argument):** This is a reference to one or more cells. When multiple areas are inputted into the function, each is separated by commas e.g. (A1:B2, D5:E6)
- **Row_num (Required Argument):** This indicates the row number of the specified reference from which to return a value from. When this argument is set to zero or blank, all rows in the array will default to zero or blank.
- **Col_num (Optional Argument):** This indicates the col number of the specified reference from which to return a value from. When this argument is set to zero or blank, all columns in the array will default to zero or blank.
- **Area_num (Optional Argument):** When the reference supplied is a multiple range, the area_num specifies the range in reference from which to return the intersection of row_num and column_num

USING THE REFERENCE FORMAT OF THE INDEX FUNCTION

From the table below, we will be using the reference format of the INDEX function to find out the price of mango

C12				
	A	B	C	D
1	FRUIT	PRICE $	NUMBERS	
2	ORANGE	23	20	
3	MANGO	12	11	
4	BANANA	25	10	
5	PEARS	21	9	
6	CASHEWS	20	8	
7	ALMONDS	35	12	
8	LEMON	45	7	
9	GUAVA	34	4	
10	CHERRY	30	2	

To find out the price of mango in the table, follow the steps below:

- Select an empty cell and type in the function to be used with the reference i.e., the specified range of cells which is A2:C10=**INDEX (A2:C10**

	A	B	C	D	E	F
1	FRUIT	PRICE $	NUMBERS			
2	ORANGE	23	20			
3	MANGO	12	11			
4	BANANA	25	10			
5	PEARS	21	9			
6	CASHEWS	20	8			
7	ALMONDS	35	12			
8	LEMON	45	7			
9	GUAVA	34	4			
10	CHERRY	30	2			
11						
12	The price of mango	=INDEX(A2:C10				
13		INDEX(**array**, row_num, [column_num])				
14		INDEX(**reference**, row_num, [column_num], [area_num])				

- Put in the row and column number alongside the reference; **INDEX (A2:C10,2,2,1)**

	A	B	C	D	E	F
1	FRUIT	PRICE $	NUMBERS			
2	ORANGE	23	20			
3	MANGO	12	11			
4	BANANA	25	10			
5	PEARS	21	9			
6	CASHEWS	20	8			
7	ALMONDS	35	12			
8	LEMON	45	7			
9	GUAVA	34	4			
10	CHERRY	30	2			
11						
12	The price of mango	=INDEX(A2:C10,2,2,1)				
13		INDEX(array, row_num, [column_num])				
14		INDEX(reference, row_num, [column_num], [**area_num**])				

- If you have followed the steps above, the result of your operation using the reference format of the INDEX function with the table will be **12**

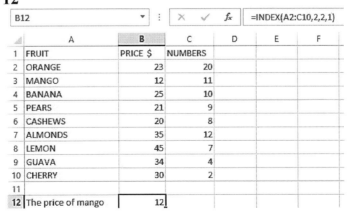

	A	B	C	D	E	F
1	FRUIT	PRICE $	NUMBERS			
2	ORANGE	23	20			
3	MANGO	12	11			
4	BANANA	25	10			
5	PEARS	21	9			
6	CASHEWS	20	8			
7	ALMONDS	35	12			
8	LEMON	45	7			
9	GUAVA	34	4			
10	CHERRY	30	2			
11						
12	The price of mango	12				

NOTE: Keep these in mind when using the array and reference format of the INDEX function:

- The INDEX function returns the value in the cell at the intersection of row_num and column_num when both the rows_num and column_num arguments are used.
- When the row_num or column_num is set to 0, the INDEX function automatically returns the array of values for the entire column or row.
- #VALUE! error occurs when the given row_num, col_num or area_num arguments are non-numeric
- #REF! error occurs:
    - When the row_num argument given is greater than the number of rows in the given range
    - When the col_num argument given is greater than the number of columns provided in the range
    - When the area_num argument is more than the number of areas provided in the range given.

CHAPTER ELEVEN

TEXT FUNCTIONS

One of the most important functions in excel is the text function. The Text functions are used when the data you are working on has too many texts. In this chapter, we will be talking about some text functions and how they can be used and applied to the Excel worksheet.

THE FIND FUNCTION

The FIND function is used to return the position of a particular text string or subtext string within a given text string. When this text string is not found, the FIND function returns a #VALUE error

The FIND function has the following arguments

=FIND(find_text, within_text [start_num])

- **Find_text (Required Argument):** This is the text string to find or search for
- **Within_text (Required Argument)**: This is where the text string will be searched from
- **Start_num (Optional Argument):** This indicates the position in the within_text where the search should begin from. When this is not applied, it will start the search at the start of the within_text string i.e., it will take on the default value of 1.

USING THE FIND FUNCTION

Using the table below, let's find the position of
  i.   a
 ii.   the
iii.   love

	A	B	C
1			
2	The boy is up to the task		
3	Life is the accumulation of time		
4	Love is a beautiful thing		
5			

To find the position of "a" in cell A2

- Select an empty cell, type in the function and its argument =**FIND("a", A2, 1)**

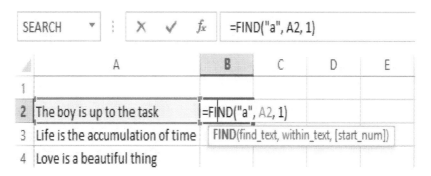

- Click on enter and the result will be 23 as shown in the table below

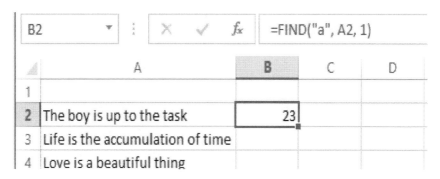

To find the position of "the" in cell A3

- Select an empty cell, input the function alongside with the arguments; =**FIND("the", A3,** 1)

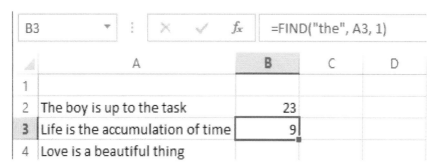

- Click on enter and the result will be 9 as shown in the table below

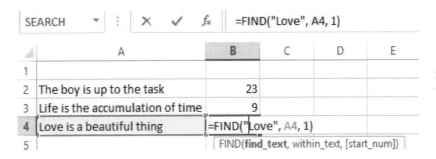

To find the position of Love in cell A4

- Select an empty cell and type in the function and its argument **=FIND("Love", A4, 1)**

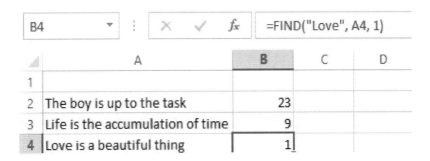

- Click on enter and the result will be 1 as shown in the table below

	A	B	C	D
1				
2	The boy is up to the task	23		
3	Life is the accumulation of time	9		
4	Love is a beautiful thing	1		

NOTE: Keep this in mind when using the FIND function

- The FIND function returns the location of the first instance of find_text in within_text
- #VALUE error occurs when the find_text is not found in within_text
- The FIND function is case sensitive and it does not support the use of wildcards

- The start_num is optional and when omitted, it defaults to 1
- The FIND function returns the location as the number of characters from the start of within_text.
- To search without case sensitivity, use the SEARCH function.
- To use the wildcards, use the SEARCH function

CONCATENATE FUNCTION

The CONCATENATE function is a function that allows for the joining of two or more strings to form a single string.

The CONCATENATE function uses the following arguments to carry out its operations

=CONCATENATE(text1, [text2],...)

- **Text1 (Required Argument)**: This is the first item to join and it can be in form of a text value, cell reference, or a number
- **Text2 (Required Argument)**: This is the next item to be joined with the first item. This can be up to 255 items with up to 8192 characters

USING THE CONCATENATE FUNCTION IN EXCEL

With the table below, we will be using the CONCATENATE to join some text strings into a single text string

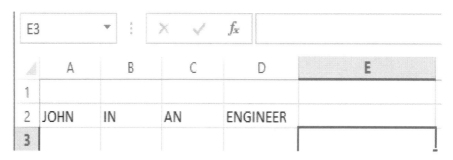

To join the texts in the table together using the CONCATENATE function

- Select an empty cell, type in the function and its argument **=CONCATENATE(A2, B2, C2, D2)**

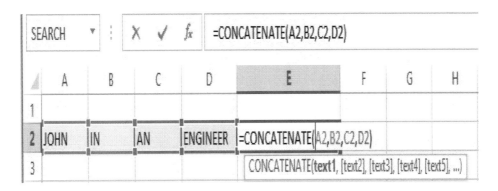

- Click on enter and the texts will be joined to form a single text string as shown in the table below

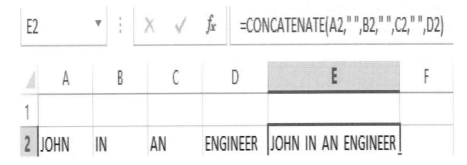

ADDING SPACE, COMMA, QUOTATION MARK, HYPHEN USING THE CONCATENATE FUNCTION

- To concatenate the text strings with space, add two double quotes in the middle of each text string

E2	▼	:	X	✓	fx	=CONCATENATE(A2," ",B2," ",C2," ",D2)

	A	B	C	D	E	F
1						
2	JOHN	IN	AN	ENGINEER	JOHN IN AN ENGINEER	

- To concatenate text strings with a comma, add two double quotes with a comma in between the two double quotes in the middle of each text string

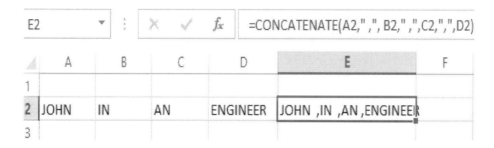

- To concatenate text strings with a quotation mark, add a comma with four double quotes before the text strings and also close it with the four double quotes

- To concatenate text strings with a hyphen, add two double quotes with a minus sign in between in the middle of each text string

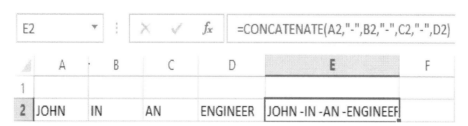

NOTE: Keep the following in mind when using the CONCATENATE function

- In the CONCATENATE function, numbers don't need to be in quotation mark
- The CONCATENATE function converts numbers to text when they are joined
- The CONCATENATE function does not recognize arrays
- #NAME! error occurs when a quotation is missing from a text argument

- When one of the CONCATENATE function's argument is invalid, #VALUE! error occurs

THE TEXTJOIN FUNCTION

The TEXTJOIN function is a function that joins or combines from multiple cells or ranges with a delimiter that is used to separate each value. This is introduced in MS Excel 2016.

The TEXTJOIN function uses the following arguments for its operations

=TEXTJOIN(delimiter,ignore_empty, text1,[text2], ...

- **Delimiter (Required Argument):** This is the text string that can be either empty or with one or more characters enclosed by double quotes or a reference to a valid text string. The most common delimiters used are comma or a space separator
- **Ignore_empty (Required Argument)**: This argument determines whether empty cells are included in the resulting string. Empty cells will be ignored if the argument is TRUE and empty cells will be included if it FALSE.
- **Text1(Required Argument):** This argument contains the text you wish to join together
- **Text2(Optional Required)** This is the argument additional texts you wish to be joined together

USING THE TEXTJOIN FUNCTION

Using the table below, join the texts together using the TEXTJOIN function

B25		f_x		
	A	B	C	D
1				
2	Monday			
3	Tuesday			
4	Wednesday			
5	Thursday			
6	Friday			

To join the texts in the table using the TEXTJOIN FUNCTION

199

- Select an empty cell type in the function and its argument **=TEXTJOIN(",", TRUE, A2, A3, A4, A5, A6)**
- Click on enter and the texts will be joined to form a single text string as shown in the table below

B2		fx	=TEXTJOIN(", ", TRUE, A2, A3, A4, A5, A6)		
	A	B	C	D	E	F
1						
2	Monday	Monday , Tuesday, Wednesday, Thursday, Friday				
3	Tuesday					
4	Wednesday					
5	Thursday					
6	Friday					

NOTE: Keep the following in mind when using the TEXTJOIN function

- #VALUE! error occurs when the resulting string exceeds the cell value limit which is 32767
- The TEXTJOIN function can take in 252 text arguments
- The TEXTJOIN function accepts delimeter
- When an older version of Excel that doesn't support this function is used, #NAME? error occurs
- #NULL! error occurs when we forget to put the comma between the text string we wish to join
- The TEXTJOIN function allows the users to use cell ranges instead of using individual cell references

TRIM FUNCTION

The TRIM function is used to remove extra spaces from a text, leaving only a single space between words and with no space character at the start or end of the text.

The TRIM function uses the following arguments for its operations

=TRIM(text)

- **Text (Required Argument):** This is the text you wish to remove the spaces from

USING THE TRIM FUNCTION

Remove the spaces in the texts in the table below using the TRIM function

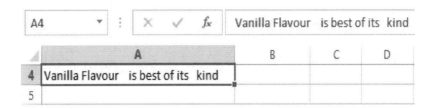

To remove the space from the text in the table;

- Select an empty cell and type in the function and its argument **=TEXTJOIN(",", TRUE, A2, A3, A4, A5, A6)**

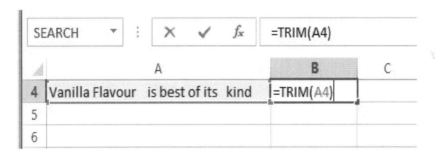

- Click on enter and the texts will be joined to form a single text string as shown in the table below

NOTE: Keep the following in mind when using the TRIM function

- TRIM function only removes extra spaces from text and leave just a single space in the texts
- TRIM function is useful for cleaning up text that comes from other applications or environment
- The TRIM function removes the ASCII space character from the text

THE UPPER FUNCTION

The UPPER function is one of the Excel Text function that changes texts to capital letters(UPPERCASE) without having any effect on the punctuations and numbers

This function has just one argument which is =**UPPER(Text)**

- **Text (Required Argument):** This is the text you wish to change to UPPERCASE. It can be a text string or a cell reference

USING THE UPPER FUNCTION

Convert the characters in the table to capital letters using the UPPER function

To convert text strings using the UPPER function:

- Select an empty cell, type in the function and its argument =**UPPER(A2)**

- Click on enter and the text strings will be converted to capital letters as shown in the table below

| B2 | ▼ | : | × | ✓ | f_x | =UPPER(A2) |

⬜	A	B	C	D	E
1					
2	all that glitters is not gold	ALL THAT GLITTERS IS NOT GOLD			
3					

NOTE: Keep these in mind while using the UPPER function

- The UPPER function does not affect the numbers and punctuation characters
- All text characters are converted to uppercase

THE LOWER FUNCTION

The LOWER function is a function that converts text characters to lowercase and this can be a text string or cell reference

This function has just one argument which is =**LOWER(Text)**

- **Text (Required Argument):** This is the text you wish to change to lowercase. It can be a text string or a cell reference

USING THE LOWER FUNCTION

Convert the characters in the table to lower case using the LOWER function

| A2 | ▼ | : | × | ✓ | f_x | all that glitters is not gold |

⬜	A	B	C	D	E
1					
2	all that glitters is not gold				
3					

To convert text strings using the LOWER function:

- Select an empty cell, type in the function and its argument =**LOWER(A2)**

- Click on enter and the text strings will be converted to lower case as shown in the table below

NOTE: Keep these in mind while using the LOWER function

- The LOWER function does not affect the numbers and punctuation characters
- All text characters are converted to lowercase

THE PROPER FUNCTION

The PROPER function is a function that changes texts or characters into a proper case. The first letter of each text string is written in upper case and the remaining words that precede are in lower case

The PROPER function uses just an argument which is =**PROPER(Text)**

- **Text (Required Argument):** This is the text you wish to change to a proper case. It can be a text string or a cell reference

USING THE PROPER FUNCTION

Change the text strings in the table to a proper case using the PROPER function

| A2 | ▼ | : | × | ✓ | *fx* | all that glitters is not gold |

◢	A	B	C	D	E
1					
2	all that glitters is not gold				
3					

To convert the text strings to proper case

- Select an empty cell and type in the function and its argument **=PROPER(A2)**

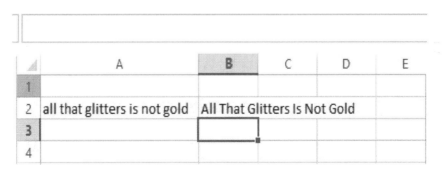

```
=PROPER(A2
```

◢	A	B	C	D	E
1					
2	all that glitters is not gold	=PROPER(A2			
3		PROPER(**text**)			
4					

- Click on enter and the text strings will be converted to a proper case as shown in the table below

◢	A	B	C	D	E
1					
2	all that glitters is not gold	All That Glitters Is Not Gold			
3					
4					

NOTE: Keep these in mind while using the PROPER function

- In the PROPER function, the first letter of each text string is converted to an upper case while the remaining words are changed into lower case
- The PROPER function does not affect numbers and punctuations

LEN FUNCTION

The LEN function is a function that returns or counts the numbers of characters in a text string excluding the number formatting

The LEN function uses an argument

=LEN(text)

- **Text (Required Argument):** This is the text you wish to find or calculate its length

USING THE LEN FUNCTION

With the table below, find the numbers of characters using the LEN function

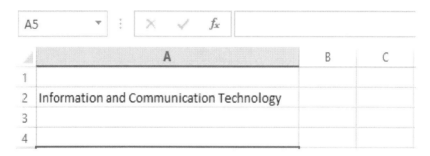

To find the numbers of characters;

- Select an empty cell, input the function with arguments to be used=**LEN(A2)**

- Click on enter and the number of text strings will be 41 as shown in the table below

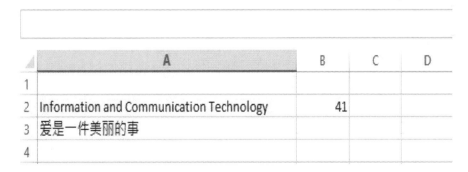

	A	B	C	D
1				
2	Information and Communication Technology	41		
3				
4				

THE LENB FUNCTION

The LENB function is a function that returns the number of bytes used in representing characters in a text string.

Just like the LEN function, the LENB function uses one argument

=LEN(text)

- **Text (Required Argument):** This is the length you wish to find or calculate the length of a text string.

USING THE LENB FUNCTION

With the table below, find the length of the text strings in cell A3 using the LENB function

	A	B	C	D
1				
2	Information and Communication Technology	41		
3	爱是一件美丽的事			
4				

To calculate the length of characters in the text strings;

- Select an empty cell, type in the function and its argument **=LENB(A3)**

207

```
=LENB(A3)
```

	A	B	C
1			
2	Information and Communication Technology	41	
3	爱是一件美丽的事	=LENB(A3)	
4		LENB(text)	

- Click on enter and the number of text strings will be 8 as shown in the table below

```
=LENB(A3)
```

	A	B	C
1			
2	Information and Communication Technology	41	
3	爱是一件美丽的事	8	
4			

NOTE: Keep these in mind when using the LEN and LENB function

- Spaces are counted as characters
- The number of formatting is not included

MID Function

The MID function is a function that is used to extract a specified number of characters from the middle of the text string given.

The MID function uses the following arguments to execute its operation

=MID(text,start_num,num_chars)

- **Text (Required Argument): This is the original text to extract from**
- **Start_num (Required Argument):** This specifies or indicates the position of the first character you wish to extract the text
- **Num_chars (Required Argument):** This is used to indicate the numbers of characters to be extracted from the texts

USING THE MID FUNCTION

Extract a specified number of characters from the middle using the MID function from the table below

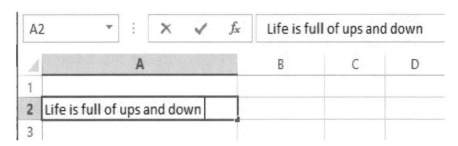

To get the specified number of characters from the middle using the MID function

- Select an empty cell, type in the function and its argument =MID(**A2, 9,5**)

SEARCH	▼	⋮	✕	✓	fx	=MID(A2, 9,5)

◢	A	B	C	D	E
1					
2	Life is full of ups and down	=MID(A2, 9,5)			
3		MID(**text**, start_num, num_chars)			

- Click on enter and the number of characters extracted from the middle will be shown in the table below

B2	▼	⋮	✕	✓	fx	=MID(A2, 9,5)

◢	A	B	C	D
1				
2	Life is full of ups and down	full		
3				

NOTE: Take note of the following when using the MID function

- #VALUE! error occurs when the num_chars is less than 0 and when the given start_num argument is less than 1

- When the MID function is used on a date, it will return the middle characters of the number that indicates that date.
- In the MID function, the number formatting is not included as a part of the string and it will not be extracted or counted
- While using the MID function, the user must specify the last parameter otherwise it will take 0 by default

THE MIDB FUNCTION

The MIDB function is a function that is used to extract a specified number of bytes from the middle of the text string given. The MID function

The MID function uses the following arguments to execute its operation

=MID B(text,start_num,num_bytes)

- **Text (Required Argument):** This is the original text to extract from
- **Start_num (Required Argument):** This specifies or indicates the position of the first character you wish to extract the text
- **Num_bytes (Required Argument):** This indicates the numbers of characters to be extracted from the texts in bytes

USING THE MIDB FUNCTION

Extract a specified number of texts in bytes from the middle using the MIDB function from the table below

To return the specified number of text in bytes from the middle using the MIDB function

- Select an empty cell, type in the function and its argument **=MIDB(A3,3,4)**

- Click on enter and the number of characters extracted from the middle will be shown in the table below

LEFT FUNCTION

The LEFT function returns a specified number of characters from the start of a text string. This function extracts characters from the left-hand side of the text.

The LEFT function uses the following arguments to execute

=LEFT(text,[num_chars])

- **Text (Required Argument):** This is the original text to extract from
- **Nun_chars (Optional Argument):** This is used to indicate the numbers of characters to be extracted from the given texts

USING THE LEFT FUNCTION

From the table below, let's extract some characters using the LEFT function

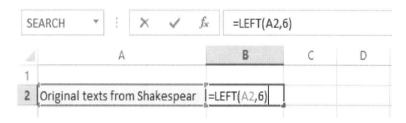

To extract the characters from the given text string using the LEFT function

- Select an empty cell and type in the function and its argument **=LEFT(A2,6)**

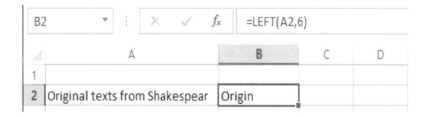

- Click on enter and the number of characters extracted from the left will be shown in the table below

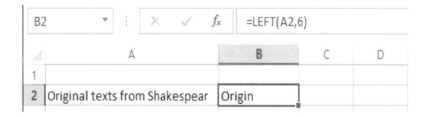

THE LEFTB FUNCTION

The LEFTB function returns the left portion of a text string based on a specified number of bytes.

The LEFTB function uses the following arguments to execute its operation

=LEFTB(text,[num_bytes])

- **Text (Required Argument):** This is the text string you wish to extract from

- **Num_bytes (Optional Argument):** This indicates the numbers of characters to be extracted from the texts in bytes

USING THE LEFTB FUNCTION

Extract a specified number of texts in bytes from the left using the LEFTB function from the table below

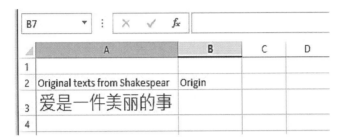

To return the specified number of text in bytes from the left using the LEFTB function

- Select an empty cell, type in the function and its argument =LEFTB**(A2,6)**

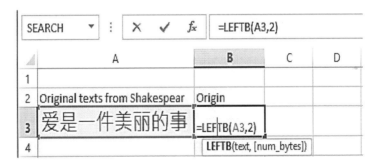

- Click on enter and the number of characters extracted from the left based on bytes will be shown in the table below

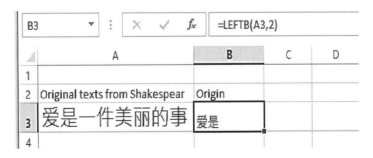

NOTE: Keep the following in mind when using the LEFT and LEFTB functions

- #VALUE! error occurs when the given num_chars or num_bytes arguments is less than 0
- When the LEFT or LEFTB function is used on a date, the start character of the number that indicates the date will be returned
- If the num_chars or num_bytes is omitted, it defaults to 0

THE RIGHT FUNCTION

The RIGHT function returns a specified number of characters from the end of a text string. This function extracts characters from the right-hand side of the text.

The RIGHT function uses the following arguments to execute

=RIGHT(text,[num_chars])

- **Text (Required Argument):** This is the original text to extract from
- **Nun_chars (Optional Argument):** This is used to indicate the numbers of characters to be extracted from the given texts

USING THE RIGHT FUNCTION

With the table below, let's find some characters using the RIGHT function

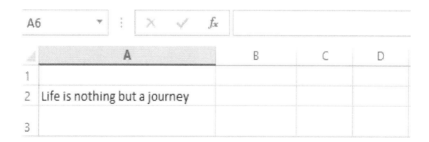

To find the character in the text string fusing the RIGHT function

- Select an empty cell and type in the function and its argument **=LEFTB(A2,4)**

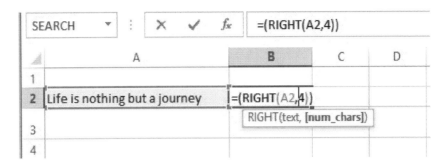

- Click on enter and the number of characters extracted from the right will be shown in the table below

THE RIGHTB FUNCTION

The RIGHTB function returns the right portion of a text string based on a specified number of bytes.

The RIGHTB function uses the following arguments to execute its operation

=RIGHTB(text,[num_bytes])

- **Text (Required Argument):** This is the text string you wish to extract from
- **Num_bytes (Optional Argument):** This indicates the numbers of characters to be extracted from the texts in bytes

USING THE RIGHTB FUNCTION

With the table given below, find some text characters using the RIGHTB function

To find the characters at the right portion of the text string using the RIGHTB function,

- Select an empty cell, type in the function and its argument =RIGHTB**(A3,3)**

- Click on enter and the number of characters extracted from the right will be shown in the table below

NOTE: Keep these in mind when using the RIGHT and RIGHTB function

- #VALUE! error occurs when the given num_chars or num_bytes arguments is less than 0

- If the num_chars or num_bytes is omitted, it defaults to 0
- When the RIGHT or RIGHTB function is used on a date, the start character of the number that indicates the date will be returned

CHAPTER TWELVE

DATE AND TIME FUNCTION

Here in this chapter, we will be discussing the date and time functions that are available in Excel and how they can be used. But before that, let me briefly explain the date format.

THE DATE FORMAT

A date is a number and just like a percentage format, it can be customized to any format of your choice. In Excel, a date is the number of days since 01/01/1900 which is the first date in excel. When you insert a date in a cell, it displays in the format dd/mm/yy.

However, there are two ways of displaying the date and they are

- Short Date
- Long Date

To locate these options on your Excel, go to the **Number Format** drop-down on the **Home menu** and then click on it

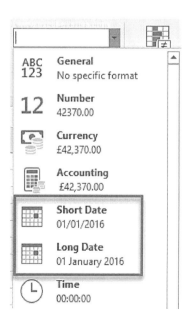

The date can be in different formats such as

- 01/01/2021
- Jan 2021
- Fri, 1 Jan 2021

DATA PARAMETER

A date has the following parameters

- d for the day
- m for the month
- y for the year

CUSTOMIZING A DATE

To customize a date on Excel, you have to open the dialog box. To open the dialog box

- Go to the **Home tab** and click on **More number** formats at the bottom of the format dropdown
- In the dialog box, select the **Custom** in the Category list and write the date format code in the **Type**

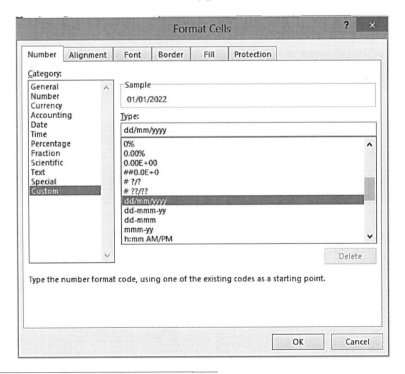

THE DAY FUNCTION

The DAY function returns the day of the date and the result is displayed in form of a serial number. The day is given as an integer from 1 to 31.

The DAY function uses this argument

=DAY (Serial_number)

- **Serial_number (Required Argument):** This is the day of the date one is trying to find. The date can be provided to the DAY function in form of serial numbers, date values from other Excel functions, and references to a cell containing dates

USING THE DAY FUNCTION

Using the table below, let's find the day in the date using the DAY function

	A	B	C	D	E
1					
2	05/03/21				
3	09 April 2021				
4					
5					

To find the day in the dates in cell A2 from the table above

- Select an empty cell, type in the function name and its arguments; **=DAY(A2)**
- Click on enter and the result will be **5** as shown in the table below

	A	B	C	D	E
1					
2	05/03/21	5			
3	09 April 2021				
4					
5					

To find the day in the dates in cell A3 from the table above;

- Select an empty cell, type in the function name and the argument to be used; **=DAY(A3)**
- Click on enter and the result will be **9** as shown in the table below

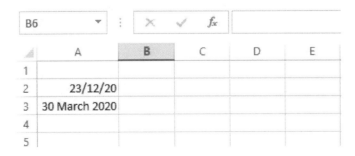

THE MONTH FUNCTION

The MONTH function returns the month of a date that is represented by a serial number. The month is given as an integer from 1 to 12.

The MONTH function uses an argument to execute its operation

=MONTH (serial_number)

- **Serial_number (Required Argument):** This is the date you wish to return the month of. The date can be a serial number, a reference to cells containing dates and date value from the Excel function.

USING THE MONTH FUNCTION

Using the table below, let's find the months in the date using the MONTH function

To find the month in the dates in cell A2 from the table above

- Select an empty cell, type in the function name and its arguments; **=MONTH(A2)**
- Click on enter and the result will be **12** as shown in the table below

B2	▾	⋮	✕	✓	*fx*	=MONTH(A2)

◢	A	B	C	D	E
1					
2	23/12/20	12			
3	30 March 2020				
4					
5					

To find the month in the dates in cell A3 from the table above

- Select an empty cell, type in the function name and its arguments; **=MONTH(A3)**
- Click on enter and the result will be **30** as shown in the table below

B3	▾	⋮	✕	✓	*fx*	=DAY(A3)

◢	A	B	C	D	E
1					
2	23/12/20	12			
3	30 March 2020	30			
4					
5					

THE YEAR FUNCTION

This is a function that is used for calculating the year number from a given date by returning an integer that is a four-digit number. For instance, if you use this function on a date e.g., 11/11/2021, it will return the year to be 2021.

The YEAR function uses an argument

=YEAR(serial_number)

- **Serial_number (Required Argument): This is the date you wish to return** the year. The date can be a serial number, a reference to cells containing dates and date value from the Excel function

USING THE YEAR FUNCTION

Using the table below, let's find the months in the date using the **YEAR** function

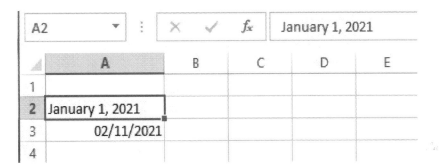

To find the year in the dates in cell A2 from the table above

- Select an empty cell, type in the function name and its arguments; **=YEAR(A2)**
- Click on enter and the result will be **2021** as shown in the table below

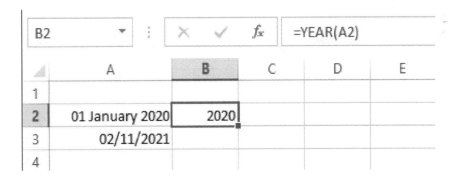

To find the year in the dates in cell A3 from the table above

- Select an empty cell, type in the function name and its arguments; **=YEAR(A3)**
- Click on enter and the result will be **2021** as shown in the table below

B3		:	×	✓	f_x	=YEAR(A3)	

▲	A	B	C	D	E
1					
2	01 January 2020	2020			
3	02/11/2021	2021			
4					

NOTE: Keep the following in mind when using the DAY, MONTH, AND YEAR FUNCTION

- The values returned by the DAY, MONTH, AND YEAR FUNCTION are always in Gregorian values not minding the display format of the date value supplied
- For the DAY, MONTH and YEAR function work correctly, the date must be entered using the DATE (year, month, and day) function

THE DATE FUNCTION

The DATE function is a function that creates a valid date from an individual year, month, and day components

The DATE function uses the following arguments

=DATE(year, month, day)

- **Year (Required Argument):** This is the number representing the year ranging from one to four digits.
- **Month (Required Argument):** This is the number representing the month which can be either positive or negative ranging from 1 to 12 (January to December).
- **Day (Required Argument):** This is the number representing the days of the month from 1 To 31

USING THE DATE FUNCTION

Using the table below, let's find the date using the DATE function

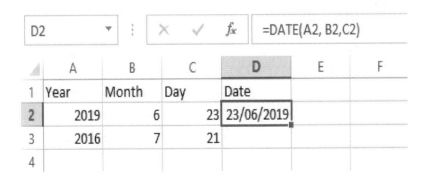

	A	B	C	D	E
1	Year	Month	Day	Date	
2	2019	6	23		
3	2016	7	21		
4					

To find the date in cell A2:C2

- Select an empty cell, type in the function, and followed by the arguments; **=DATE(A2,B2,C2)**

=DATE(A2, B2, C2)

	A	B	C	D	E	F
1	Year	Month	Day	Date		
2	2019	6	23	=DATE(A2, B2, C2)		
3	2016	7	21			

- Click on enter and the result will be **23/062019** as shown in the table below

=DATE(A2, B2,C2)

	A	B	C	D	E	F
1	Year	Month	Day	Date		
2	2019	6	23	23/06/2019		
3	2016	7	21			
4						

To find the date in cell A3:C3

- Select an empty cell, type in the function name and its arguments; **=DATE(A3,B3,C3)**

- Click on enter and the result will be **23/062019** as shown in the table below

NOTE: Keep these in mind when using the DATE function

- When any of the provided arguments is < 0 or ≥ 10000, #NUM! error is returned.
- When any of the provided arguments is non-numeric, #VALUE! error is returned.
- While using the DATE function, the result can be in serial numbers. However, this can be changed to date format

THE DATEDIF FUNCTION

The DATEDIF function is a function that calculates the number of days, months, and years between two dates. This function returns the numerical value that indicates the number of days, months, and years between two dates.

The DATEDIF function uses the following arguments to execute its operations

=DATEDIF(start_date, end_date, unit)

- **Start_date (Required Argument):** This is the initial date of the period or the starting date of the value of the period
- **End_date (Required Argument):** This connotes the ending date of the value of the period
- **Unit (Required Argument):** This indicates the time unit where we want the information

Unit	Returns
"Y"	The difference in complete years
"M"	The difference in complete months
"D"	The difference in complete days
"MD"	The difference in days, ignoring months and years.
"YM"	The difference in months, ignoring the years
"YD"	The difference in days, ignoring the years

USING THE DATEDIF FUNCTION

With the table, let's use the DATEDIF to find numbers of years and months between two dates

A12		:	×	✓	f_x	

	A	B	C	D
1	Start Date	End Date	Unit	
2	12/09/2017	11/10/2018	Y	
3	23/05/2019	22/12/2020	M	
4				

To find the difference in years between the start date (A2) and the end date (B2)

- Select an empty cell, type in the function name and its arguments; **=DATEDIF(A2,B2, "y")**

SEARCH	▼	⋮	✕	✓	*fx*	=DATEDIF(A2, B2, "Y")	

◢	A	B	C	D	E
1	Start Date	End Date	Unit		
2	12/09/2017	11/10/2018	Y	=DATEDIF(A2, B2, "Y")	
3	23/05/2019	22/12/2020	M	DATEDIF()	
4					

- Click on enter and the result will be **1** as shown in the table below

D2	▼	⋮	✕	✓	*fx*	=DATEDIF(A2, B2, "Y")	

◢	A	B	C	D	E	F
1	Start Date	End Date	Unit			
2	12/09/2017	11/10/2018	Y	1		
3	23/05/2019	22/12/2020	M			
4						

To find the difference in months between the start date (A3) and the end date (B3)

- Select an empty cell, type in the function name and the arguments to be used; **=DATEDIF(A3,B3, "M")**

SEARCH	▼	⋮	✕	✓	*fx*	=DATEDIF(A3,B3, "M")	

◢	A	B	C	D	E	F
1	Start Date	End Date	Unit			
2	12/09/2017	11/10/2018	Y	1		
3	23/05/2019	22/12/2020	M	=DATEDIF(A3,B3, "M")		
4				DATEDIF()		

- Click on enter and the result will be **18** as shown in the table below

D3	▼	⋮	✕	✓	*fx*	=DATEDIF(A3,B3, "M")	

◢	A	B	C	D	E	F
1	Start Date	End Date	Unit			
2	12/09/2017	11/10/2018	Y	1		
3	23/05/2019	22/12/2020	M	18		
4						

NOTE: Observe the following when using the DATEDIF function

- When the start_date is greater than the end_date, #NUM! error is returned
- When the date argument provided is invalid, the #VALUE error is returned

THE DAYS FUNCTION

The DAYS function is a date and time function that is used for returning the number of days between two dates. The DAYS FUNCTION was first introduced in Excel 2013

The DAYS function uses the following arguments to perform its operations

=DAYS (end_date, start_date)

- **The end_date and start_date (Required Arguments):** These are the two dates between which you want to know the number of days.

USING THE DAYS FUNCTION

Using the table below, let's find the number of days between the two dates using the DAYS function

	A	B	C	D	E
1					
2	12 July 2020	23 September 2020			
3					
4					

To find the number of days in the dates in cell A2 and B2 from the table above

- Select an empty cell, type in the function name and its arguments; **=DAY(B2,A2)**

`=DAYS(B2,A2)`

	A	B	C	D	E
1					
2	12 July 2020	23 September 2020	=DAYS(B2,A2)		
3			DAYS(end_date, start_date)		
4					
5					

- Click on enter and the result will be **73** as shown in the table below

	A	B	C	D	E
1					
2	12 July 2020	23 September 2020	73		
3					
4					
5					

NOTE: Keep these in mind when using the DAYS function

- When both date arguments are numbers, the DAYS function uses EndDate and StartDate to calculate the number of days between both dates
- When any of the arguments is in text, the argument is treated as DATEVALUE (date_text). In this instance, the integer date is returned instead of the time component.
- #NUM! error occurs when the numeric data given for the date argument is outside the range of the valid dates
- #VALUE! error value occurs when the date arguments are strings that cannot be parsed
- #NAME? error occurs when the syntax used in the formula is incorrect.

THE EDATE FUNCTION

The EDATE function is a function used to add or subtract a specified number of months to date (the start date) and returns as serial date as the result.

The EDATE function uses the following arguments for its operations

=EDATE(start_date, months)

- **Start_date (Required Argument):** This is the starting date to use in the calculation. To enter dates in the date format, use the DATE function or other formulas or functions. For instance, use DATE (2021, 5, 24) for May 24, 2021. When dates are entered as text, the function returns error,
- **Month (Required Arguments):** This is the number of months before or after the start_date. A positive value produces a future date while a negative value produces a past date.

USING THE EDATE FUNCTION

With the table below, calculate the date using the EDATE function

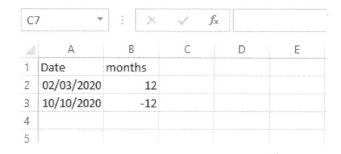

To calculate the value of A2

- Select an empty cell and type in the function name and its arguments; **=EDATE(A2,B2)**
- Click on enter and the result will be **44257** as shown in the table below

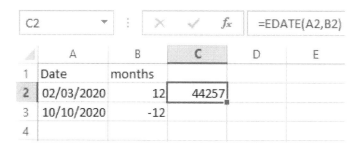

To calculate the value of A3

- Select an empty cell, type in the function name and its arguments; **=EDATE(A3,B3)**
- Click on enter and the result will be **43748** as shown in the table below

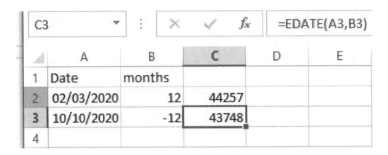

You can change the dates from serial numbers to the normal date format. To achieve this,

- Go to the **Home tab** and click on **More number** formats at the bottom of the format dropdown
- In the dialog box, select the **Date** and click on the date format you want

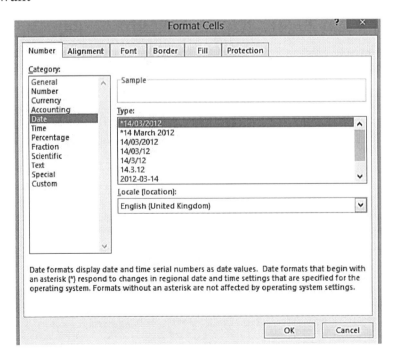

- If you follow the instructions given above, your result will be displayed as shown in the table below

C5	▼	:	× ✓ fx		
◢	A	B	C	D	E
1	Date	months			
2	02/03/2020	12	02/03/21		
3	10/10/2020	-12	10/10/19		
4					

NOTE: Keep these in mind when using the EDATE function

- When the date to be returned from the calculation is not a valid number, #NUM! error occurs
- #VALUE error occurs when the start_date provided is not a valid date or when any of the arguments provided is non-numeric

THE DATEVALUE FUNCTION

The DATEVALUE function is a function that converts date stored in a text format to a serial number that Excel recognizes as its date format. The DATEVALUE is most useful when you have a worksheet containing dates in a text format that need to be filtered, sorted out, or formatted as dates or used in the date calculation

The DATEVALUE function uses the following argument for its operations

= DATEVALUE(date_text)

- **Date_text (Required Argument):** This is the text that indicates a date in the Excel format, or a reference to a cell indicating a date in the Excel date format.

USING THE DATEVALUE FUNCTION

With the table below, let's convert the date in text format to Excel date

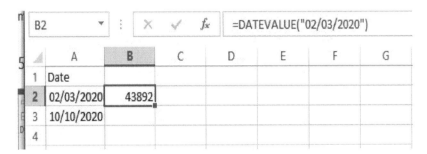

To change cell A2 to Excel date format

- Select an empty cell, type in the function name and its arguments; **=EDATE("02/03/2021")**
- Click on enter and the result will be **43892** as shown in the table below

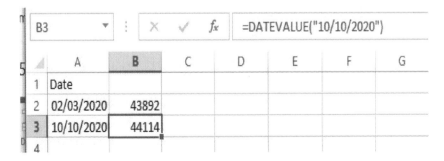

To change cell A3 to Excel date format

- Select an empty cell, type in the function name and its arguments; **=EDATE(("10/10/2021")**
- Click on enter and the result will be **44114** as shown in the table below

To convert date from serial numbers to date format, you can refer to the steps given in the EDATE function

NOTE: Keep this in mind when using the DATEVALUE function

- When the start_date is greater than the end_date, NUM! error will occur]
- When the value of the date_text argument falls out of the range of January! 1990 and December 31, 1996

THE NETWORKDAYS FUNCTION

The NETWORKDAYS function is a function that is used for calculating the numbers of working days between two dates in Excel. By default, the NETWORKDAYS function excludes weekends i.e., Saturday and Sunday. Not only that, this function allows you to skip a list of holidays as provided in the worksheet as dates.

The NETWORKDAYS function uses the following arguments

=NETWORKDAYS(start_date, end_date, [holidays])

- **Start_date (Required Argument)**: This is the date that indicates the start date
- **End_date (Required Argument):** This is the date that indicates the end date
- **Holidays (Optional Argument):** This indicates the list of holidays that should be excluded from the workdays

USING THE WORKDAYS FUNCTION

Using the table below, let's find the number of working days using the NETWORKDAYS function

	B7	▾	:	✕	✓	*fx*	

	A	B	C	D	E
1	Start Date	End Start		Holidays	
2	01/10/2020	01/01/2021		01/10/2020	
3				25/12/2020	
4				01/01/2021	

To find the number of working days

- Select an empty cell and type in the function name and its arguments; **=EDATE(("10/10/2021")**

SEARCH		× ✓ fx	=NETWORKDAYS(A2,B2,D2:D4)		
	A	B	C	D	E
1	Start Date	End Start		Holidays	
2	01/10/2020	01/01/2021		01/10/2020	
3				25/12/2020	
4				01/01/2021	
5					
6	WORKDAYS	=NETWORKDAYS(A2,B2,D2:D4)			
7		NETWORKDAYS(start_date, end_date, [holidays])			
8					

- Click on enter and the result will be **43** as shown in the table below

B6		× ✓ fx	=NETWORKDAYS(A2,B2,D2:D4)		
	A	B	C	D	E
1	Start Date	End Start		Holidays	
2	01/10/2020	01/01/2021		01/10/2020	
3				25/12/2020	
4				01/01/2021	
5					
6	WORKDAYS	64			

NOTE: Few points to observe when using the NETWORKDAYS function

- A negative value is returned when the start date is later than the end date
- The NETWORDAYS function must include both the start date and end date when calculating the workdays.
- When any of the provided arguments is not a valid date, #VALUE! error occurs
- To use weekends apart from Saturday and Sunday, use the NETWORKDAYS.INTL function
- The NETWORKDAYS function calculates workdays ignoring any time values

THE NOW FUNCTION

The NOW function is a function that is used to show the current date and time in an Excel worksheet. This function uses no argument and requires empty parentheses.

=NOW()

USING THE NOW FUNCTION

Let's use the NOW function to find the current date and time. To do this

- Select an empty cell and type in the function name and its arguments; **=NOW()**

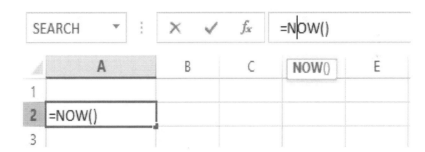

- Click on enter and the current date and time will be displayed

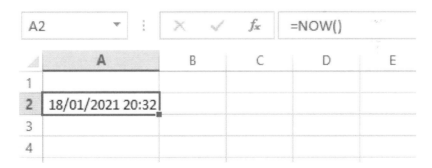

NOTE: Observe the following when using the NOW function

- When the provided serial number is not a valid Excel time, it returns a #VALUE! error
- To display date only, format the cell with a date format that only displays the date or

THE TODAY FUNCTION

The TODAY function is a function that returns the current date in an Excel worksheet. This updates from time to time whenever the worksheet is opened or changed by the user. This function uses no argument

=TODAY()

USING THE TODAY FUNCTION

- When you use the TODAY function. It gives you the current date; **=TODAY()**

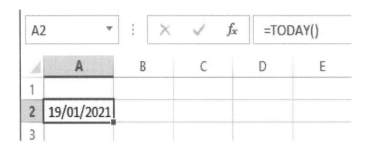

- When you use the add 15 days to the TODAY function, it adds 15 days to the current date; **=TODAY()+15**

A2	▾	⋮	✕	✓	*fx*	=TODAY()+15	
◢	A	B	C	D	E		
1							
2	03/02/2021						
3							

- When you use the WORKDAY function with TOADY function, it adds 30 workdays to today's date; **=WORKDAY(TODAY()30)**

A2	▾	⋮	✕	✓	*fx*	=WORKDAY(TODAY(),30)	
◢	A	B	C	D	E	F
1						
2	02/03/2021					
3						

When you add the MONTH function to the TODAY function, it will return the current month of the year (1-12). Now that we are in January, the result will be returned to 1; =**MONTH(TODAY())**

A2	▼	:	✕	✓	*fx*	=MONTH(TODAY())

	A	B	C	D	E	F
1						
2	1					
3						

NOTE: keep the following in mind when using the TODAY function

- In case you don't want the date to change, enter the current date using the keyboard shortcut; **Ctrl + ;**
- To get the current date and time, use the NOW function

THE TIME FUNCTION

The TIME function is a function that is used to create time using individual hour, minute, and second components

The TIME function uses the following arguments for its operations

=**TIME(hour, minute, second)**

- **Hour (Required Argument):** This time value can start from zero (0) to 32767 indicating the hour. When the value exceeds 23, it will be divided by 24 and the remainder will be treated as the hour value.
- **Minute (Required Argument):** This also starts from 0 to 32767 indicating the minutes. When the value is greater than 59, it will be converted to hours and minutes.
- **Second (Required Argument):** This ranges from 0 to 32767 indicating second. When the value is greater than 59, it will be converted to hours, minutes, and seconds.

USING THE TIME FUNCTION

From the table, let's use the TIME function to extract the date

	A	B	C	D	E
1	Hour	Minute	Second		
2	4	23	23		
3	12	34	2		
4					

To extract the time in cell **A2:C3**

- Select an empty cell, type in the function name and its arguments; **=TIME(A2,B2,C2)**

=TIME(A2,B2,C2)

	A	B	C	D	E	F
1	Hour	Minute	Second			
2	4	23	23	=TIME(A2,B2,C2)		
3	12	34	2	TIME(hour, minute, second)		
4						

- Click on enter and the time will be extracted to be **4:23 AM** as shown in the table below

=TIME(A2,B2,C2)

	A	B	C	D
1	Hour	Minute	Second	
2	4	23	23	4:23 AM
3	12	34	2	
4				

To extract the time in cell A3:B3

- Select an empty cell, type in the function name and its arguments; **=TIME(A2,B2,C2)**

	A	B	C	D	E	F
1	Hour	Minute	Second			
2	4	23	23	4:23 AM		
3	12	34	2	=TIME(A3,B3,C3)		
4				TIME(hour, minute, second)		

- Click on enter and the time will be extracted to be **4:23 AM** as shown in the table below

=TIME(A3,B3,C3)

	A	B	C	D	E
1	Hour	Minute	Second		
2	4	23	23	4:23 AM	
3	12	34	2	12:34 PM	

NOTE: Keep these in mind when using the TIME function

- When the hour arguments provided are evaluated to a negative number, #NUM! error is returned
- When any of the arguments provided is non-numeric, #VALUE! error is returned

CHAPTER THIRTEEN

THE EXCEL POWER QUERY

WHAT IS POWER QUERY?

Power query is a business intelligence tool in Excel that allows you to extract or import data from different sources, transform them and reshape the data and produced the desired result on the worksheet.

WHERE IS THE POWER QUERY LOCATED?

The **Power Query** is an add-in. This is downloaded and installed in Excel 2010 and 2013 which appears as a new tab in the ribbon tagged as Power Query. In Excel 2016, 2019, Office 365, and Excel 2021, the Power Query comes automatically with them and it is found in the Data tab as q group names Get & Transform

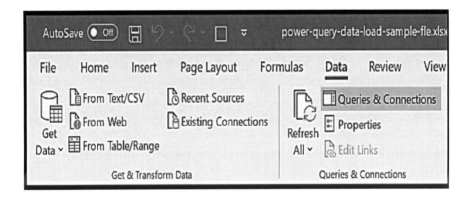

What Can Power Query Do?

The Power Query can do the following operations:

- To import data from multiple log files.
- To create a custom view over data.
- To carry out data cleansing operation.
- To gather data into Power Pivot from new data sources such as Facebook, XML, etc.
- To search and connect data from a large variety of sources.
- To merge and redefine data sources to match your data analyses criteria or requirements.

SOURCES OF POWER QUERY DATA

You can get data for the Power Query in the sources below;

- Excel or CSV file
- Text File
- Web Page
- XML file
- Folder
- SQL Server database
- Microsoft Azure SQL Database
- Access database
- Active Directory
- Microsoft Exchange
- SharePoint List
- Hadoop File (HDFS) etc.

IMPORTING DATA SOURCE USING POWER QUERY

Here, I will be showing you how to import data source using the Power Query. Most importantly, how to import data from Excel workbook, CVS, or text file.

IMPORTING A SINGLE DATA SOURCE FROM THE WORKBOOK

- From the **Data tab**, go to **Data** and select **Get Data**.
- Then go to **File** and select Workbook.

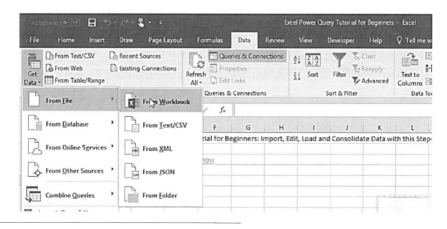

- In the **Import Data dialog box**, select the workbook and double click on it.

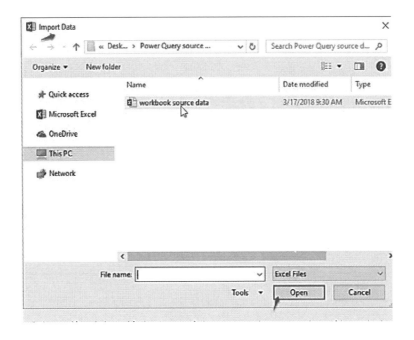

- In the **Navigation dialog box**, click on the data source you wish to work with.
- Then click on **Load**

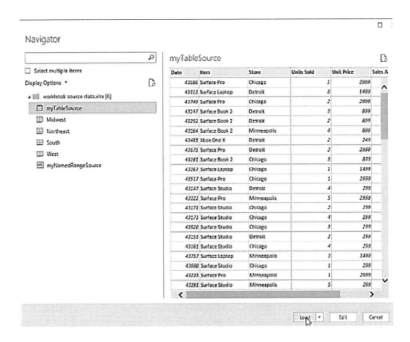

IMPORTING DATA FROM MULTIPLE DATA SOURCES IN A WORKBOOK

- From the **Data tab**, go to **Data** and select **Get Data**.
- Then go to **File** and select Workbook.

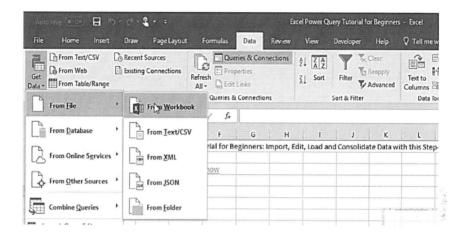

- In the **Import Data dialog box**, select the workbook and double click on it.

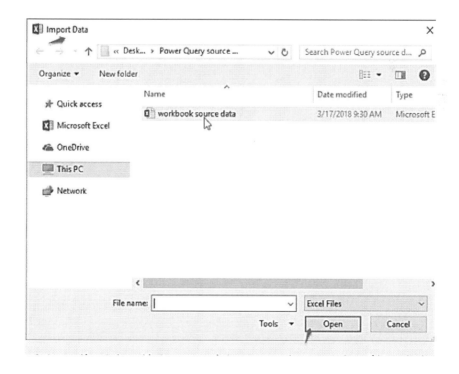

- In the **Navigation dialog box**, click on Select **multiple items**
- Then click on **Load**

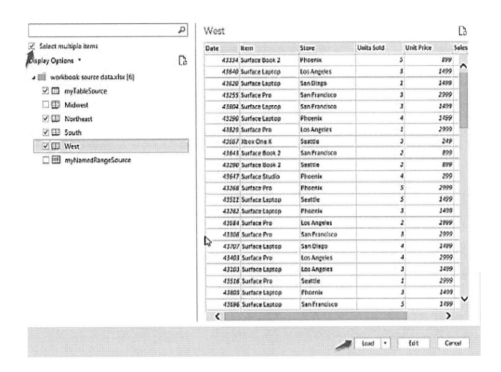

IMPORTING DATA FROM A CSV FILE

- From the **Data tab**, go to **Data** and select **Get Data**.
- Then go to **File** and select **Text/CVS**

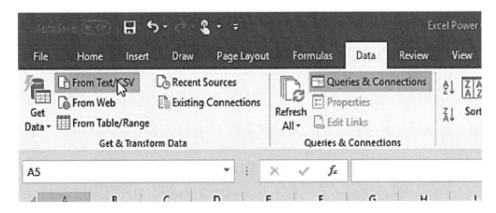

- In the **Import Data dialog box**, select the **CVS File** and click on **Import**

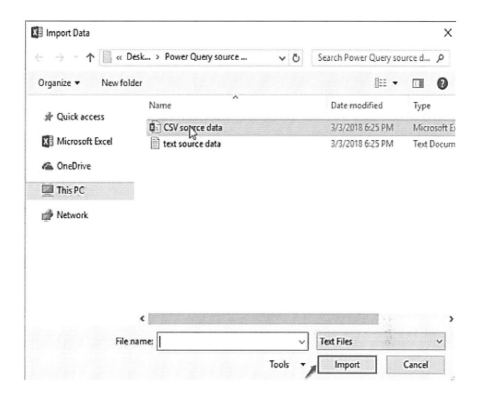

- In the dialog box named CSV file, click on **Load**

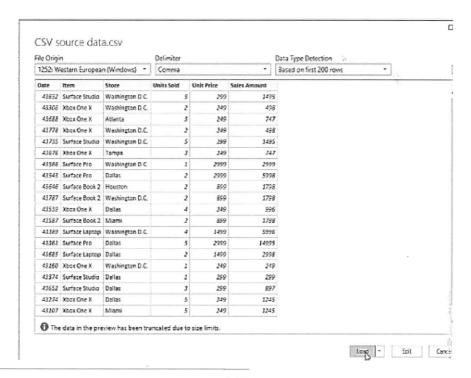

IMPORTING DATA FROM A TEXT FILE

- From the **Data tab**, go to **Data** and select **Get Data**.
- Then go to **File** and select **Text/CVS**

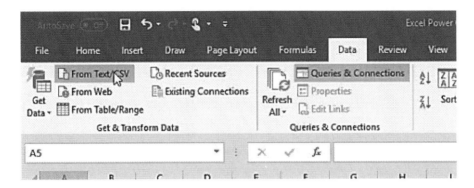

- In the **Import Data dialog box**, select the **Text File** and click on **Import**

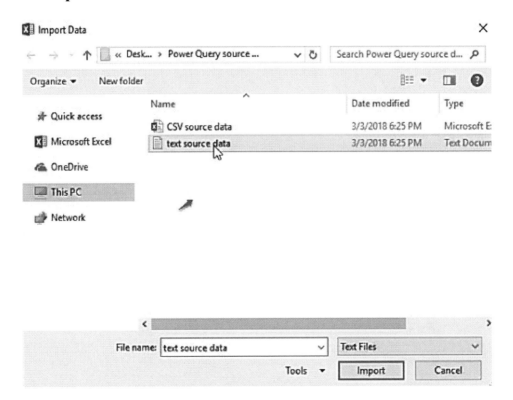

- In the dialog box named Text file, click on **Load**

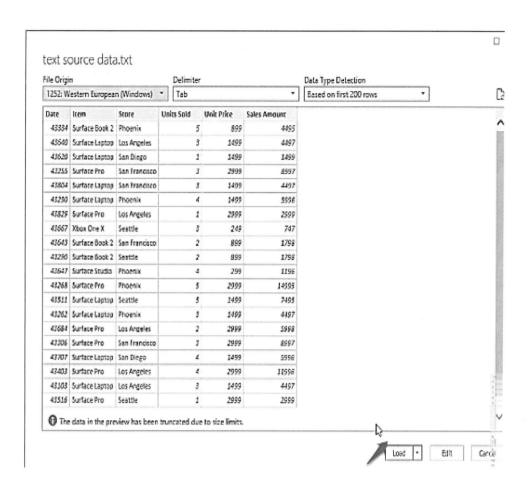

POWER QUERY EDITOR

The power Query Editor displays when you want to load, edit, and create a new query. The Query Editor when displayed has 4 main divisions; The Ribbon, Formula bar, Preview pane, and Query Setting task pane. The operation is done above such as importing data from Text File, CSV, etc. are done in the Power Query Editor.

To launch the Query Editor;

- Move to the Data **tab**, Select Data, and select **Get Data**.
- Then launch the **Query Editor**.

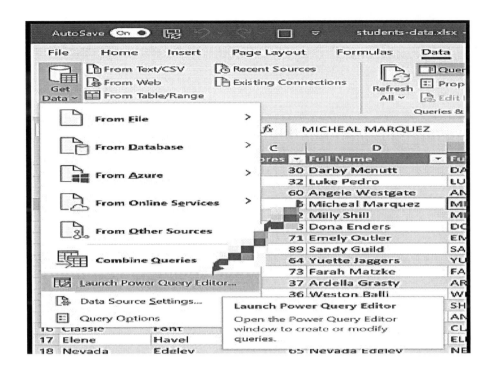

CHAPTER FOURTEEN

EXCEL SHORTCUTS, TIPS & TRICKS

Imagine there is a shortcut to getting to a particular place in just 5 minutes and initially, the journey should cost you not less than an hour, I am sure you will opt-in for that shortcuts. To make the use of Excel especially that of 2021 easier, faster, and convenient to use, we will be taking ourselves to learn some tips and tricks which will come in handy as you begin to get yourself more accustomed to the use of this app.

EXCEL SHORTCUTS

EDITING SHORTCUTS

Keys	Functions
F2	To edit cell
Ctrl + C	To copy
Ctrl + V	To paste
Ctrl + X	To cut
Ctrl + D	To fill down
Ctrl + R	To fill right
Alt+ E+ S	Paste special
F3	To paste the name into a formula
F4	Toggle reference
Alt +Enter	To start another new line within the same old cell
Shift + F2	To insert or edit a cell comment
Shift + F10	To display a shortcut menu
Ctrl + F3	To define the name of a cell
Ctrl + Shift + A	To insert arguments names with parentheses for a function after typing a function name in a formula
Alt + I + R	To insert a row
Alt + I + C	To insert a column

FORMATTING SHORTCUTS

Keys	Functions
Ctrl + B	To bolden
Ctrl + I	For italics
Ctrl + Z	To undo
Ctrl + Y	To repeat the last action
Ctrl + A	To select all cells
Ctrl + 1	To display or bring up the format cell menu
Ctrl + Shift + !	For number formatting
Ctrl + Shift + %	For percent format
Ctrl + Shift + #	For date format
Alt + h	To increase decimal
Alt + h+ 9	To decrease decimal
Alt + h + 6	To increase indent

NAVIGATION SHORTCUTS

Keys	Functions
Arrow	To move from one cell to the next
F5	Go to
Ctrl + Home	Go to cell 1
Home	To go to the beginning of a row
Shift + Arrow	To select the adjacent cell
Shift + Spacebar	To select an entire row
Ctrl + Spacebar	To select an entire column
Ctrl + Shift + Home	To select all to the start of the sheet
Ctrl+ Shift + End	To select all to the last used cell of the sheet
Ctrl + Shift + Arrow	To select the end of the last used row/column
Ctrl + Arrow	To select the last used cell in rows/columns

PageUp	To move the screen up
PageDown	To move the screen down
Alt + PageUp	To move the screen to the left
Alt+ PageDown	To move the screen to the right
Ctrl + PageUP/Down	To move the next or previous worksheet
Ctrl + Tab	To move to the next worksheet while on the spreadsheet
Tab	To move to the next cell

FILE SHORTCUTS

Keys	Functions
Ctrl + N	New
Ctrl + O	To open
Ctrl + S	To save workbook
F12	Save As
Ctrl + P	Print
Ctrl + F2	To open the preview print window
Ctrl + Tab	To move to the next workbook
Ctrl + F4	To close a file
Alt + F4	To close all open Excel files

PASTE SPECIAL SHORTCUTS

Keys	Functions
Ctrl + Alt + V+T	Paste Special formats
Ctrl + Alt + V+V	Paste Special values
Ctrl + Alt + V+F	Paste Special formulas
Ctrl + Alt + V+ C	Paste Special comments

RIBBON SHORTCUTS

Keys	Functions
Alt	To show ribbon accelerator keys
Ctrl + F1	To show or hide the ribbon

CLEAR SHORTCUTS

Keys	Functions
Delete	To clear cell data
Alt+ h + e + f	To clear cell format
Alt+ h + e + m	To clear cell comments
Alt+ h + e + a	To clear all data formats and comments

SELECTION SHORTCUTS

Keys	Functions
Shift + Arrow	To select a cell range
Ctrl + Shift + Arrows	To highlight a contiguous range
Shift + PageUp	To extend selection up one screen
Shift + PageDown	To extend selection down one screen
Alt + Shift + PageUp	To extend selection left one screen
Alt + Shift + PageDown	To extend selection right one screen
Ctrl + A	Select or highlight all

DATA EDITING SHORTCUT

Keys	Functions
Ctrl + D	To fill down from cell above
Ctrl + R	To fill right from cell left
Ctrl + F	To find and replace
F5 + Alt + s +o	To show all constants
F5 + Alt + s +c	To highlight the cell with comments

DATA EDITING (INSIDE A CELL) SHORTCUTS

Keys	Functions
F2	To edit the active cell
Enter	To confirm a change in a cell before opting out of that cell
Esc	To cancel a cell entry before opting out of that cell
Alt + Enter	To insert a line break within a cell
Shift + Left/Right	To highlight within a cell
Ctrl + Shift + Left/Right	To highlight contiguous items
Home	To move to the beginning of the cell contents
End	To move to the end of a cell content
Backspace	To delete a character from left
Delete	To delete a character from the right
Tab	To accept autocomplete suggestion
Ctrl + PageUp/Down + Arrows	For referencing a cell from another worksheet

OTHER SHORTCUTS

Keys	Functions
Ctrl + ;	To enter date
Ctrl +:	To enter time
Ctrl + '	To show formula
Ctrl +]	To select an active cell
Alt	To drive menu bar
Alt + Tab	To open the next program
Alt + =	To autosum

CHAPTER FIFTEEN

EXCEL TIPS AND TRICKS

HOW TO USE IDEAS

If you are looking for suggestions on how best to display your Excel data, use Ideas as an inspiration. To do this:

- Click anywhere on the table

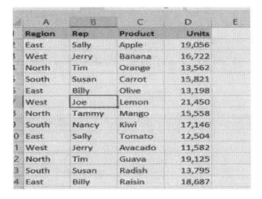

- Go to the Home tab and choose Ideas

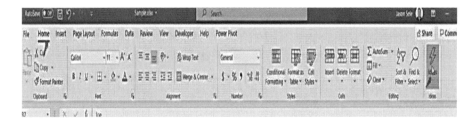

- The ideas will pop up any graph suitable to display your data, then click on insert.

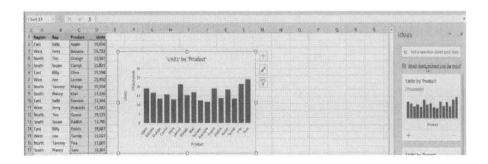

HOW TO REMOVE BLANKS FROM A WORKSHEET

If you want to remove a bunch of empty cells in a set of data,

- Highlight the whole list of data

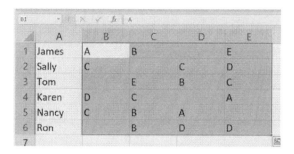

- From the Home tab, go to Find and Select

- Click on Go to special

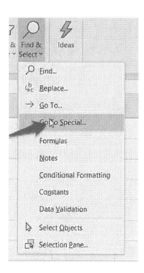

- Then click on Blank and press Ok

- Here in the next page, the blank cell will be highlighted

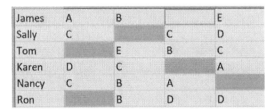

James	A	B		E
Sally	C		C	D
Tom		E	B	C
Karen	D	C		A
Nancy	C	B	A	
Ron		B	D	D

- To delete, right-click on any of the empty cells and select Delete

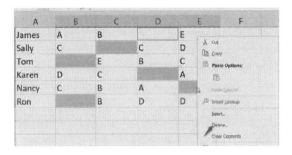

- In the Delete option, select Shift cell left and the blanks cell will be deleted.

HOW TO REMOVE DUPLICATE DATA FROM EXCEL WORKBOOK

If you have a list of data in Excel and you want to remove the duplicates, do the following:

- Hight light the data

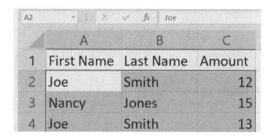

- From the Data tab, select Remove duplicate

- Click on the options that come up depending on the one you want and click on Ok

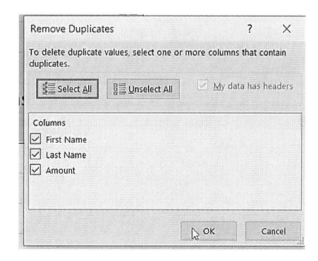

- Here in the worksheet, the change is effected

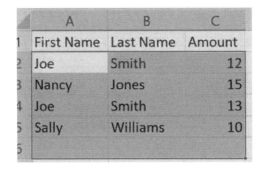

TRANSPOSING ON YOUR WORKSHEET

Transposing allows you to switch the rows and columns on your table and to get this done,

- Highlight the table, right-click, and select copy

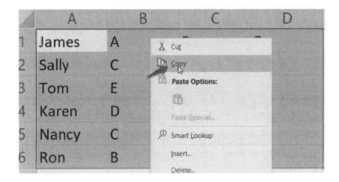

- Select the new location, right-click on it and select Paste Special

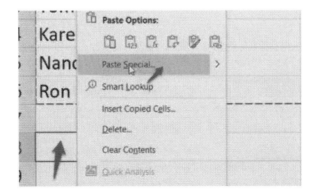

- Select the Transpose and click on Ok

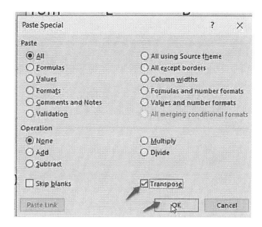

- Here in this, the changes will be effected

James	Sally	Tom	Karen	Nancy	Ron
A	C	E	D	C	B
B	C	B	C	B	D
E	D	C	A	A	D

HOW TO ADD TEXT TO COLUMNS

you can copy texts into your column from a different source by applying the following instructions:

- Copy the data into an Excel worksheet

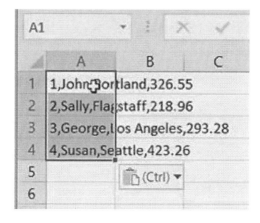

- Go to Data and select Text to column

- Go to the pop-up window and select Comma, check for the preview at the lower part of the pop-up window, and click on Finish

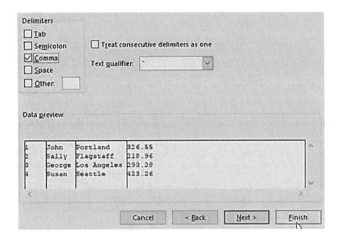

HOW TO INSERT SCREENSHOT TO YOUR EXCEL WORKBOOK

To insert images from other application to Excel worksheet,

- Go to the Insert tab and click on Screenshot

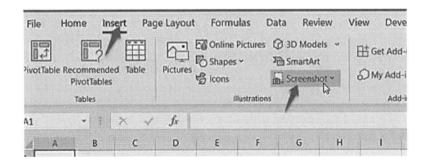

- From the Screenshot tab, select the image available

- Here, the selected image will be displayed on the Excel worksheet

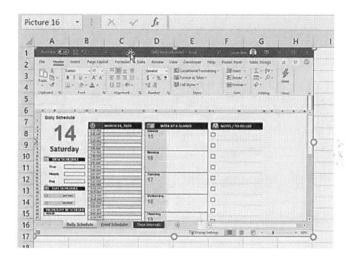

HOW TO INSERT MULTIPLES ROWS

Rather than inserting rows one by one in your worksheet, you can insert three to four rows at once and this helps to save time. To add multiple rows:

- Select as many rows as you want and right-click

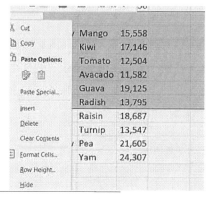

Click on insert and new rows will be added

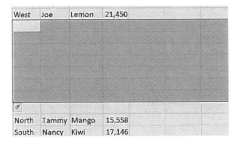

NOTE: The steps above can be applied when adding multiple columns in a worksheet.

HOW TO CREATE PEOPLE GRAPH

Peoples' graph is a kind of graph that is created with a simple two-column table. To do this:

- Go to the Insert tab and click on Transform col data into a cool picture which will bring up a default people graph

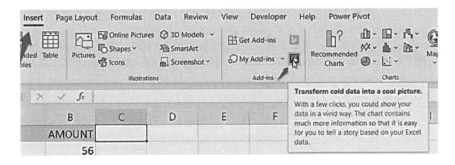

- When the default graph appears, move to select your data

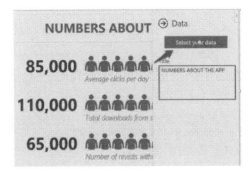

- Go to the simple two-column table to highlight your data and click on Create

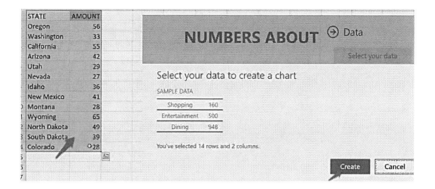

- The changes are seen here in this page

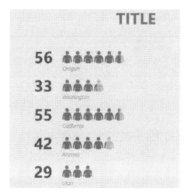

HOW TO HIGHLIGHT TEXT AND NUMBERS

To highlight only numbers in a worksheet;

- Select the whole data in the table

Sr No	Product	Cost	Country
1	Product 1	$247.00	USA
2	Product 2	$168.00	France
3	Product 3	Canada	UK
4	Product 4	$129.00	$156.00
5	Product 5	$133.00	India
6	Product 6	USA	$227.00
7	Product 7	$156.00	France
8	Product 8	India	$575.00

- Press F5 and a window will pop up and then click on Special

- Select Constants, tick on Numbers and click on Ok

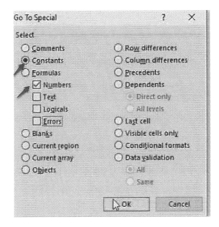

- Here on this page, the numbers will be highlighted

Sr No	Product	Cost	Country
1	Product 1	$247.00	USA
2	Product 2	$168.00	France
3	Product 3	Canada	UK
4	Product 4	$129.00	$156.00
5	Product 5	$133.00	India
6	Product 6	USA	$227.00
7	Product 7	$156.00	France
8	Product 8	India	$578.00

Then go to the fill color to apply to the highlighted numbers

Sr No	Product	Cost	Country
1	Product 1	$247.00	USA
2	Product 2	$168.00	France
3	Product 3	Canada	UK
4	Product 4	$129.00	$156.00
5	Product 5	$133.00	India
6	Product 6	USA	$227.00
7	Product 7	$156.00	France
8	Product 8	India	$578.00

To highlight only texts,

- Select the whole data in the table

Sr No	Product	Cost	Country
1	Product 1	$247.00	USA
2	Product 2	$168.00	France
3	Product 3	Canada	UK
4	Product 4	$129.00	$156.00
5	Product 5	$133.00	India
6	Product 6	USA	$227.00
7	Product 7	$156.00	France
8	Product 8	India	$578.00

- Press F5 and a window will pop up and then click on Special

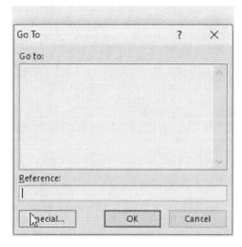

- Select Constants, tick on Texts and click on Ok

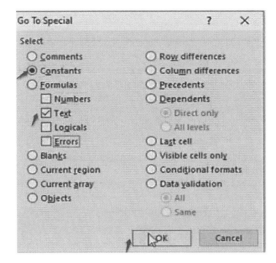

- Here on this page, the texts will be highlighted

Sr No	Product	Cost	Country
1	Product 1	$247.00	USA
2	Product 2	$168.00	France
3	Product 3	Canada	UK
4	Product 4	$129.00	$156.00
5	Product 5	$133.00	India
6	Product 6	USA	$227.00
7	Product 7	$156.00	France
8	Product 8	India	$578.00

- Go to the fill colour to apply to the highlighted numbers

Sr No	Product	Cost	Country
1	Product 1	$247.00	USA
2	Product 2	$168.00	France
3	Product 3	Canada	UK
4	Product 4	$129.00	$156.00
5	Product 5	$133.00	India
6	Product 6	A	$227.00
7	Product 7	$156.00	France
8	Product 8	India	$578.00

HOW TO HIGHLIGHT CELLS THAT HAVE FORMULAS

To select or highlight the cells that have formulas;

- On the table that contains all the cells, press Ctrl + G
- Right here, a window will pop and click on Special

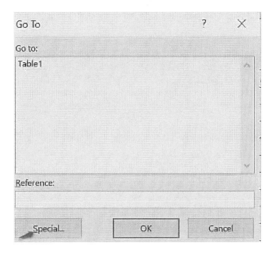

- In the next window that pops up, select Formula and press Ok

- Here in this page, the cell with formulas with be highlighted

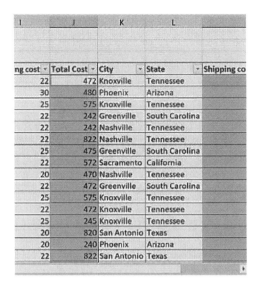

ng cost	Total Cost	City	State	Shipping co
22	472	Knoxville	Tennessee	
30	480	Phoenix	Arizona	
25	575	Knoxville	Tennessee	
22	242	Greenville	South Carolina	
22	242	Nashville	Tennessee	
22	822	Nashville	Tennessee	
25	475	Greenville	South Carolina	
22	572	Sacramento	California	
20	470	Nashville	Tennessee	
22	472	Greenville	South Carolina	
25	575	Knoxville	Tennessee	
22	472	Knoxville	Tennessee	
25	245	Knoxville	Tennessee	
20	820	San Antonio	Texas	
20	240	Phoenix	Arizona	
22	822	San Antonio	Texas	

HOW TO GET DATA FROM THE INTERNET

You can get live data into your Excel worksheet and to get this done, all you need to do is,

- Open your internet browser and go to the website you need to get the data

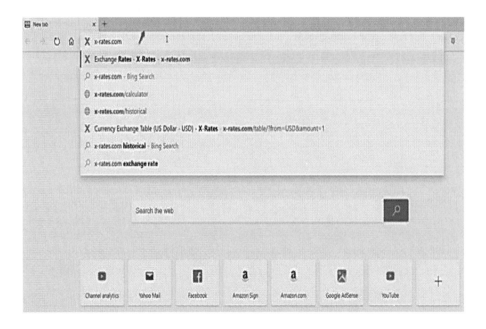

- Copy the URL link from the website

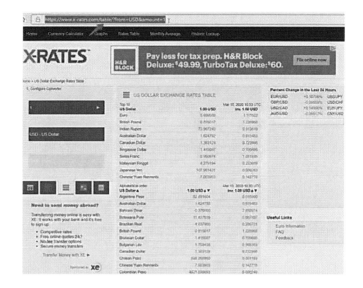

- Go back to Excel, go to Data and select from Web

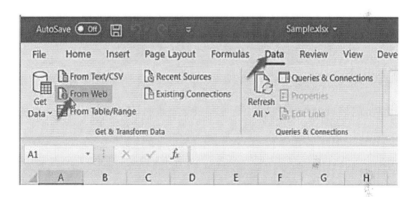

- Paste the copied URL and select Ok

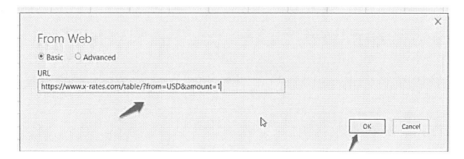

- A window pops up showing you the list of data on the web page, select the data you want and then click on Load

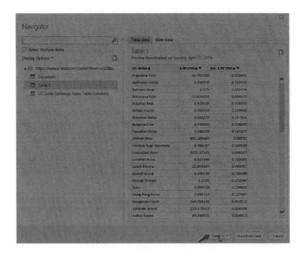

- Finally, on this page, the data is displayed on the Excel Worksheet.

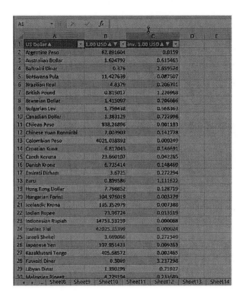

RENAMING A SHEET WITH A DOUBLE CLICK

There are various ways to rename sheets in Excel and the easiest of them all is by double-clicking on the sheet, and then rename it

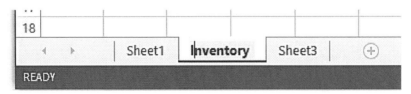

CHANGING THE CASE OF A TEXT

Certain functions are used to change the case of a text. For Example, the UPPER function capitalizes all the characters, the LOWER function changes the text to lower case while the PROPER function capitalizes the first character of a text.

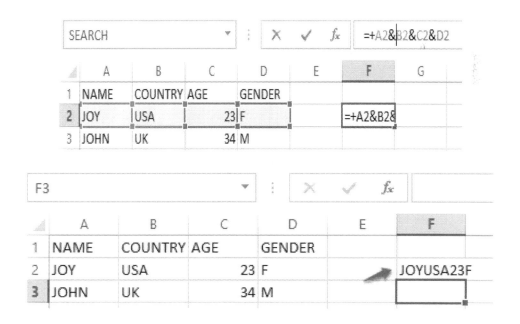

FORMING A TEXT WITH &

With the sign & you can join the texts in different columns into a single cell. Let's join cell A2, B2, C2, and D4 to form JOYUSA23F in cell F2

HOW TO MAKE EXCEL SHOW LEADING ZERO

When a value starts with zero, Excel will automatically delete the zero. To avoid this problem, add a single quote mark before the zero as shown in the table below.

| E3 | | | | ▼ | ⋮ | ✕ | ✓ | f_x | ❘ '040404 |

◢	A	B	C	D	E	F
1	NAME	COUNTRY	AGE	GENDER		
2	JOY	USA	23	F	3223	
3	JOHN	UK	34	M	040404	

EXTENDING FORMULA DOWN

You can extend the formula from a cell by dragging the + cross at the lower bottom corner of the cell and move to the other cells

| C1 | | ▼ | | f_x | =(A1*3+8)/5 |

◢	A	B	C	D	E
1	65		40.6		
2	57				
3	19				
4	2				
5	10				
6	29				
7	17				
8	21				

CHANGING HOW ENTER WORKS

When you click on **Enter** by default, it moves you down to a cell. You can change the method of how Enter works in another direction. To do this,

- Go to **File** and move to **Options**
- Click on the **Advanced** tab and go to **Edit Options**

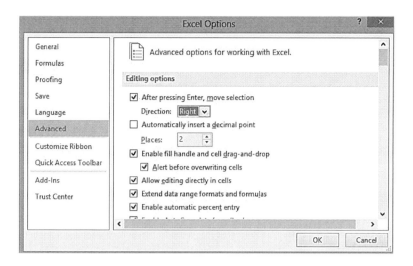

QUICK SELECT FORMULAS

This feature can help save time when trying to input formulas into the cells. As you begin to type the formula, you can scroll down to choose out of the suggested formulas and use the Enter to select the formula automatically.

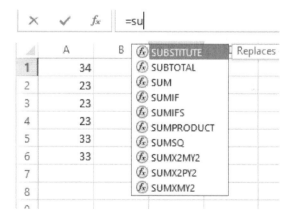

DISABLING THE EXCEL START SCREEN

Probably you hate it when you open your Excel program, only to be welcomed with Excel Start Screen. To disable the Start Screen,

- Go to **File** and move to **Options**
- Go to **General** and move **to Start-up options** to disable the Excel Start Screen

- Then click on Ok

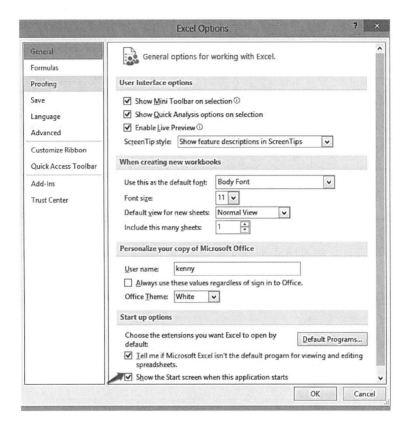

ACTIVATING CURRENT DATE AND TIME

You can insert the current date and time by using the NOW function by using the date and time from the system.

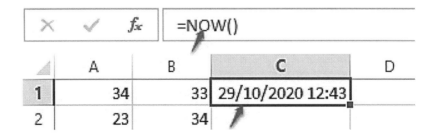

CUSTOMIZING THE STATUS BAR

When you right-click on the status bar, there are a lot of features available you can add.

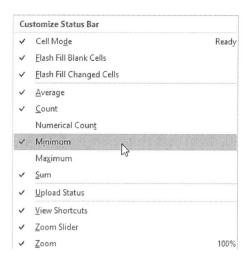

DELETING ERRORS CELLS

To get rid of cells with error values;

- From the **Home tab,** go to **Editing and** click on **Find & Replace**
- Go to **Go To Special and in** the **Go To Special** dialog box, select F**ormula** and then tick **Errors**

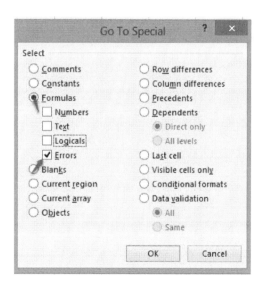

STRIKING THROUGH TEXTS IN EXCEL

To strike through texts in Excel, all you need to do is first select the cell and then press **Ctrl + 5**

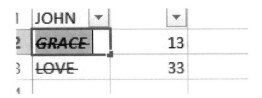

	JOHN	▼		▼
2	~~GRACE~~			13
3	~~LOVE~~			33
4				

HOW TO CLEAR FORMATTING

You can clear any formatting from a cell or a range of cells. To do this;

- From the **Home tab,** go to **Editing**
- Select **Clear** and click on **Clear Format**

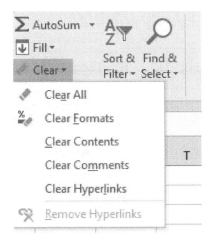

SHARING DATA ONLINE ON EXCEL

You can share excel data or documents online. By implication, you can collaborate with another person to work alongside with you on the Excel worksheet. Not only that, you don't have to go around with your computer, you can choose to save your data to OneCloud and make reference to it anytime, anywhere.

To share Excel file online;

- From the File menu back view, go to Share.
- Then choose any of the options that pop up (**Invite People, Email, and Save to OneDrive**).

NOTE: To save your data or files on **OneCloud**, you must have Microsoft Account on your computer.

EXCEL 2021

BOOK 2

VBA AND MACROS

INTRODUCTION

It has been realized so far to an extent that individuals have a long list of requests and expectations that ordinary Excel cannot meet up with. With this in mind, Excel has been able to go out of lines, to proffer solutions to these limitations, and that is why they have been able to come up with the macro language Visual Basic For Application (VBA). The VBA is a programming language developed by Microsoft, that allows macros to create custom user-generated functions and increase the speed of manual tasks by creating automated processes.

The VBA helps you as an individual to achieve remarkable efficiencies in the day-to-day activities that require the use of Excel. With the use of VBA, you can achieve a lot of things that seem unimaginable and unbelievable.

The VBA contains over 500 functions of which most of them are used in the day-to-day activities of Excel. Not only that, Excel allows you to create your functions, especially when you cannot find any built-in functions that suit your purpose. These functions can be a Sub Procedure or a Function Procedure.

Just like a popular saying that states "Rome was not built in a day". This saying applies to the learning of the Excel VBA. Of a truth, it won't be easy, it will take your time and energy, in fact, there will be days of wanting to give up but with the help of this book, the challenges and constraints will be reduced to what you can handle and at the end of it all, you will be glad to have taken this book to explore the world of VBA.

However, learning the VBA exposes you to a lot of benefits but I will just mention two of these benefits that will catch your attention:

- Learning the VBA will give you an interesting and exciting life; you don't want to imagine yourself having to repeat a task over and over again. With VBA, you get to automate tasks, thus, giving more time to engage in all other exciting projects in Excel.
- Leaning VBA will put more money into your account, Yes! I can see the smile on your face. Do you also know that almost every organization uses Excel? Yes, they do. You having vast knowledge

of Excel, makes you a hot cake that is sought after by every organization.

To use this book, you must have Excel 2016 or later versions on your PC. Not only that, you must have a basic knowledge of Excel to aid your learning process.

With all these in mind, see you in the next section.

CHAPTER SIXTEEN

INTRODUCTION TO EXCEL MACROS

WHAT ARE MACROS IN EXCEL?

Macros are a piece of code created in Excel that is used to automate many tasks such as formatting workbooks, plugging in formulas, formatting cells, highlighting rows, cleaning up data, creating tables, or organizing data. The Macros use the Visual Basic For Application in Excel to create custom user-generated functions and speed up manual tasks by creating automated processes. The Excel macro is a record and playback tool that records Excel steps while the macro will play it back as many times as they automate repetitive tasks.

WHY USE EXCEL MACROS?

- **Speed:** One of the reasons you need to use the macros is that it speeds up your work. Excel on its own is used in so many work processes and with the use of macros, you get to execute your task with speed and efficiency.
- **Mistakes:** Mistakes are bound to occur when you repeatedly apply formulas, sorting and moving data around manually. To avoid errors, you can record a macro and it will act the same way every time you run it.
- **Workbook Tasks:** While using the macros in Excel, you can automate workbook tasks such as listing the sheets, creating a table of contents, hiding specific sheets, opening and closing workbooks, and lots more.
- **Pivot Table Tasks:** The Pivot Tables are one of the tools that make Excel amazing and this can be time-consuming to create, format, update and maintain. Therefore, with macros, you can automate almost every property and action with pivot tables.
- **Process Automation**: At the same time, one can also automate more complex processes with macros & VBA. This consist of creating systems to create, modify, or update several Excel files. For example, many systems like this can be created for forecasting and budgeting processes.

UNDERSTANDING WHICH FILE TYPES ALLOW MACROS

Excel 2019 is compatible with four file types and of all these file types, Macros cannot be stored in the .xlsx file type, and this file type is the default file type. You have to use the **Save As** settings for all your macro workbooks, or you can change the default file type used by Excel 2019.

The available files types are as listed below:

- **Excel Workbook (.xlsx):** Here, files are stored as a series of XML objects which are then zipped into a file. This file type allows for other applications to create and edit Excel workbooks. Unfortunately, this file type cannot store macros files with a .xlsx extension
- **Excel Macro-Enabled Workbook (.xlsm):** This file type is similar to the default .xlsx format, except that it accepts macros files.
- **Excel Binary Workbook (.xlsb):** This file format is designed to handle a larger 1-million- row grid sizes introduced in Excel 2007. The binary file format stores the legacy versions of Excel. One major shortcoming of this file format is that it is prone to get corrupt and just a few lost bits can damage the whole of the file. This file format can also be stored in this format.
- **Excel 97- 2003 Workbook (.xls):** This file format produces files that can be read by any user using the legacy versions of Excel. When macros are saved in this format, one loses access to any cells outside A1:IV65536. Also, anyone, who opens this file in Excel 2003 will also lose access to anything that uses the features introduced in Excel 2007 or later versions.

To avoid having to choose a macro-enabled workbook in the **Save As** dialog box, you can customize the copy of your Excel to always save new file in the .xlsm format using the steps below:

- Go to the **File Menu** and select **Options**
- In the Options dialog box, click on Save from the left navigation pane
- Go to the **Save Files In This Format** drop-down and then select **Excel Macro-enabled Workbook** and then click on **Ok**

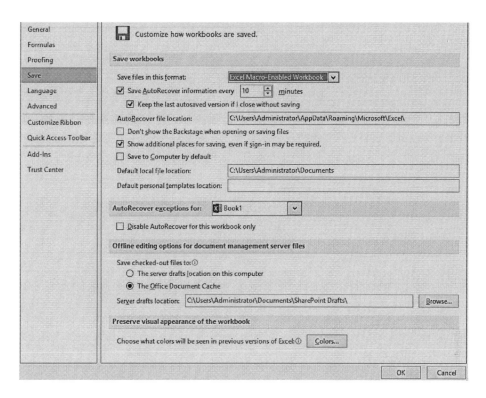

THE DEVELOPER TAB

Before we begin to go deeper into macros and VBA, let's have an overview of the basic tools to use the macros and VBA.

The Developer tab is a built-in tab n Excel that is designed to provide features needed to use the VBA and also perform macro operations. The Developer tab allows quick access to some advanced features and functions that are available in Excel.

You can do the following operations with the Developer tab

- Write macros
- Run macros that have been previously recorded
- Use XML commands
- Use ActiveX controls
- Use form controls in Microsoft Excel
- Create applications to use with Microsoft Office programs
- Work with the ShapeSheet in Microsoft Visio
- Create new shapes and stencils in Microsoft Visio

By default, the Developer tab is hidden, but the good news is that it can be easily unhidden

HOW TO ENABLE THE DEVELOPER TAB

There are two ways of enabling the Developer tab among the ribbons on the Excel workbook screen

The First Step

- Click on the **File Tab** and scroll down to **Option**

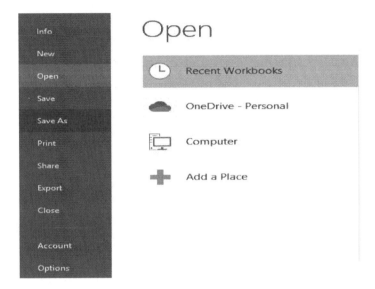

- From the **Option,** click on the **Customize Ribbon** from the left navigation panel   and go to **Main Tabs**

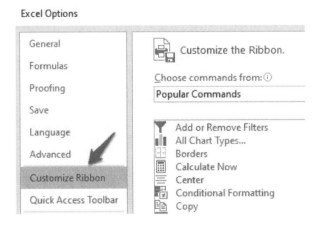

- Click on the **Developer** check box and then hit the **OK** button

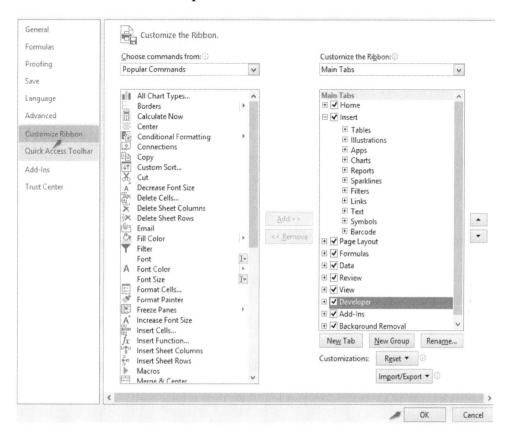

In another way round;

- Right-click on any tab at the top of the Excel window
- Then click on **Customize the Ribbon**

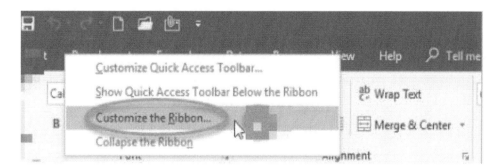

- Then click on the **Developer** check box and then hit the **OK** button

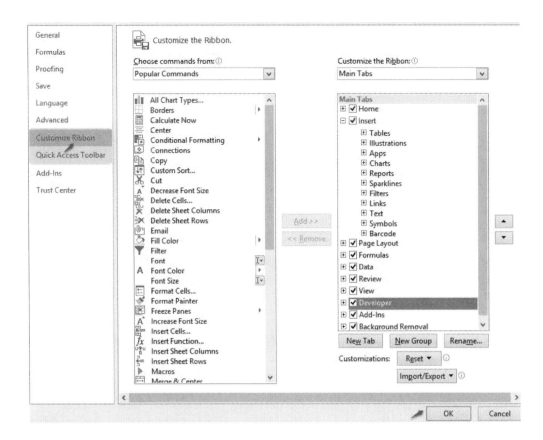

OPTIONS IN THE DEVELOPER TAB

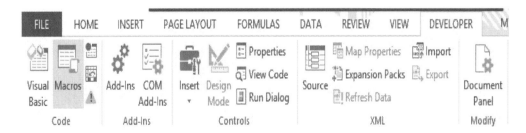

When the Developer tab is turned on, the following options are displayed

- **Visual Basic**: This option launches the VB editor and you can also launch this by using the keyboard shortcut **Alt + F11**
- **Macros:** This option displays the Macro dialog, where one can run or edit a macro from the list of macros. You can also get the keyboard shortcut for this by pressing Alt + F8. Here in this option, you can also record new macros.
- **Record Macro**: This is where the recording of macro takes place

- **Use Relative Reference:** This snaps between using the relative or absolute recording. With the relative recording, Excel records that you move down three cells while with the absolute recording, Excel records that you select cell A4
- **Macro Security:** This is the option that allows you to have access to the Trust Center where you can choose to allow or disallow macros to run on the computer.
- **Add-Ins:** This is an additional program in the Developer tab that contains icons for using regular adds-ins and COM add-ins. Some of the Excel add-ins are built within the application such as Analysis Toolpak and Solver and while others are developed by solution providers to perform a specific function
- **The Controls Group:** This contains the Insert menu where one can access a variety of programming controls that can be placed on the worksheet.
- **XML:** This contains features such as opening the XML Source task pane to manage XML maps, importing and exporting XML documents that are created from other applications or databases. This also manages any expansion packs that may be attached to a worksheet that is being worked on.
- **The Modify Group**: This is where you indicate whether the Document Panel is always displayed for new documents.

RECORDING A MACRO

Here, let's discuss how to create or record a macro. Keep this in mind, recording a macro helps to save the stress of having to execute a task over and over again. Therefore, to record a macro, follow the procedures below:

- Select any cell in the workbook
- Select the **Developer** and click on **Record Macro**

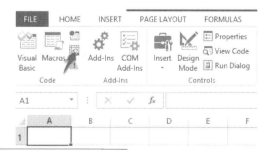

- In the **Macro** dialog box, enter the name of the macro
- Click on the **Shortcut key box** and enter **Shift + N** as the shortcut key (here, you can use any alphabet as your shortcut key).
- Ensure that the Store Macro in settings is **This Workbook** and click on **OK.** When this is done, the Record Macro dialog box closes and the Excel's macro recorder is activated. At this point, Excel keeps track of everything you do and converts them to VBA code.

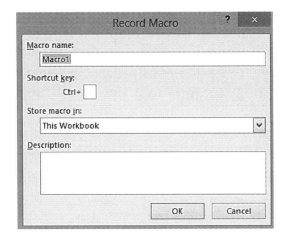

Now let's perform the actions you want to record

- Select an active cell and type your name
- Move the cell pointer to the cell below and enter the formula =**NOW**(); This formula displays the current date and time
- Select the **Formula cell** and press **Ctrl + C** to copy the cell to the **Clipboard**
- Go to **Home**, select **Clipboard** and select **Paste**
- With the date selected, press the **Shift + up arrow** to select the cell and the one above it that contains your name
- Go to **Font group** and formatting to **Bold** and make the font size to 16 point
- Go to the **Developer** and click on **Stop Recording**

TESTING THE RECORDED MACRO

Now let's test the macro recorded to see if it works properly. To test the macro recorded, select an empty cell and press **Ctrl + Shift + N**

As illustrated in the picture below, Excel executes the macro by displaying your name, current date, and time in large and bold letters

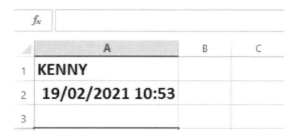

You can also allow Excel to execute the macro by following the procedures below

- Select the **Developer tab** and click on **Macros**
- From the **Macro dialog box**, select the name of the macro and then click on the **Run** button

EXAMINING THE MACRO

After you must have recorded and tested a macro and you are curious to know how the macro looks like, or even wondering where it is stored in the Excel.

To get to the root of this curiosity, all you need to do is follow the steps below to view how the macro look like

- Go to the **Developer tab** and click on the **Visual Basic**

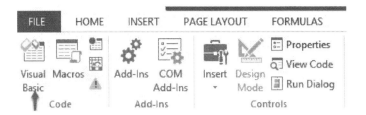

- From the **Visual Basic** window, click on **View** and then select **Project Explorer** to display the project called VBA project (Book1, 2,3, etc) depending on the name used in saving the recorded macro
- From the VBAProject, select the module that corresponds to the name of the recorded macro
- Double click the Module and the VBA code in the modules will be displayed as shown in the image below

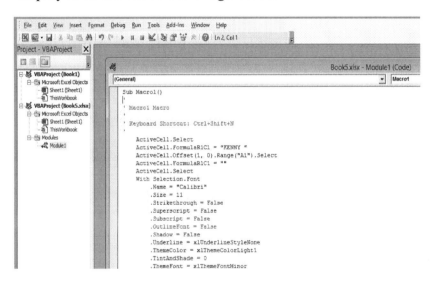

SAVING WORKBOOKS THAT CONTAIN MACROS

In case your workbook has one or more macro, the workbook must be saved as a "macro-enabled" file type. In other words, the file must be saved with an XLSM (macro enabled) extension instead of the usual XLSX extension.

For instance, when you save a workbook containing macro in an extension (XLSX) that does not support macro, Excel displays a warning message telling you to change the file format of the workbook to a macro-enabled file by clicking No and Yes to continue saving as a macro-free workbook.

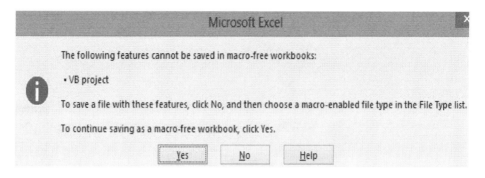

MACRO SECURITY

Before you enable macros, it is essential to understand how dangerous they can be. When a malicious macro is running, it can cause damage or completely wipe off files from your hard disks, disrupt your data, or even corrupt the Microsoft Office installed on your computer.

To prevent these dangers, all you need to do is to enable safe macros.

HOW TO ENABLE MACROS FOR INDIVIDUAL WORKBOOKS?

There are two ways to enable macros for a certain file, either from the workbook or through the backstage view and they are explained as follow

ENABLE THE MACROS VIA SECURITY WARNING BAR OR MESSAGE BAR

When a file that contains a macro is opened, a yellow message bar is displayed with a shield icon and the **Enable Content** button. To enable macro

- Go to the **Message Bar** and click on **Enable Content**

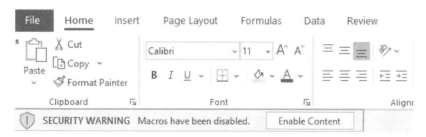

When the macro is enabled, the file becomes a trusted document

ENABLE THE MACRO IN THE BACKSTAGE VIEW

The macros can also be enabled through the backstage view and to get this done, follow the steps below

- From the **File tab**, click on the **Info** in the left navigation pane
- In the **Security Warning** area, click on **Enable Content** and then select **Enable All Content**

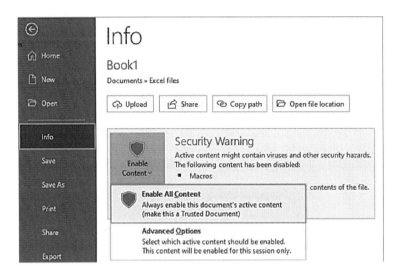

Just like the first step illustrated above, the workbook also becomes a trusted document.

TRUSTED DOCUMENTS IN EXEL

Activating macros either through the message bar or Backstage view, automatically makes the file a trusted document. Some Excel files cannot be made trusted documents; these are files that are opened from an unsafe location e.g. Temp Folder, or when the system administrator only has set its security policy in your organization to disable all macros without notifications. Once a workbook becomes a trusted document, it can no longer be un-trusted again, and the option left is to clear the Trusted Documents list. To do this

- From the **File tab**, select **Options**
- On the left side, select the **Trust Center**, and then click on **Trust Center Settings**

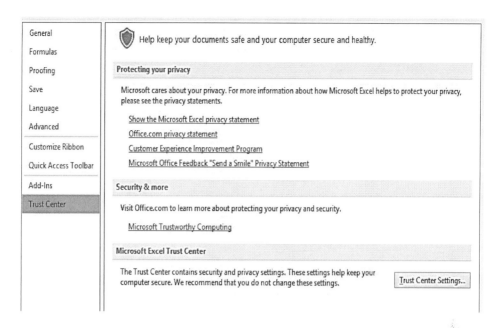

- From the **Trust Center** dialog box, select **Trusted Documents** on the left
- Select **Clear** and then click on **Ok**

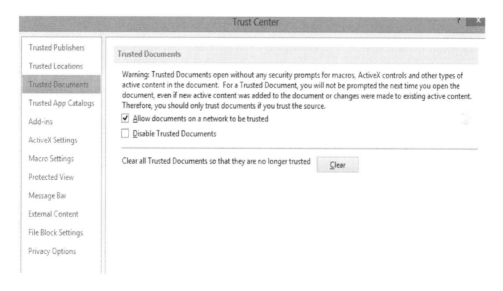

THE TRUST CENTER

The Trust Center is the place in Excel where you configure all the macro security settings. Apart from using the message bar or the Backstage view, you can also enable the macros from the Trust Center

- From the **File tab**, select **Options**
- On the left side, select the **Trust Center**, and then click on **Trust Center Settings**
- From the **Trust Center** dialog box, select **Trusted Documents** on the left and then click on **Enable all macros**
- Then click on **Ok**

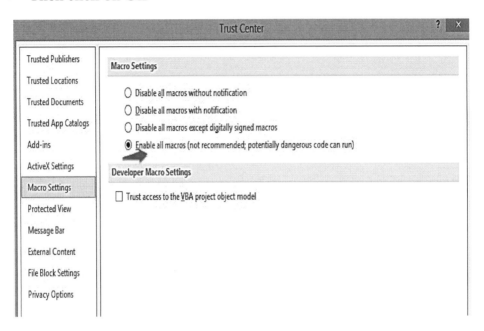

THE MACRO SETTINGS

The macro settings can be found in the Trust Center. In an organization, the system administrator may change the default settings to prevent anyone from changing settings.

To locate the macro settings, follow the procedures below

- From the **File tab**, select **Options**
- On the left side, select the **Trust Center**, and then click on **Trust Center Settings**
- From the **Trust Center** dialog box, select **Macro Settings** on the left
- Select the option you want and then click on **Ok**

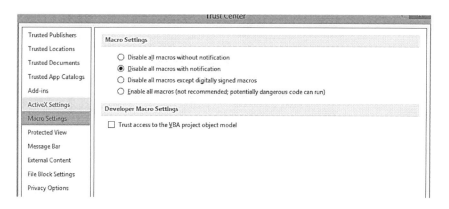

Under the Macro Settings, there are four options available and they are explained below

- **Disable all macros without notification:** When this option is chosen, macros and security alerts are disabled.
- **Disable all macros with notification:** When this option is chosen, macros are disabled and security alerts appear when any macro is present. Macros can be enabled on a case-by-case basis.
- **Disable all macros except digitally signed macros:** Here, macros are disabled but security alerts appear when there are more macros present. If the macro is digitally signed by a trusted publisher, the macro runs if the publisher is trusted. In case you do not trust the publisher, you will be notified to enable the signed macro and trust the publisher.
- **Enable all macros (not recommended, susceptible to macro viruses):** All the macros run when this option is selected. This makes your computer exposed to potentially malicious code.

There is also an additional security option under Developer Macro Settings with a check box.

- **Trust access to the VBA project object model:** This performs the following functions
  - It allows or disallow programmatic access to the Visual Basic for Application (VBA) object from an automation client
  - This security option is for code written to automate an Office program and manipulate the VBA environment and object manipulate the VBA environment and object model

- o It is a per-user and per-application setting, and denies access by default, hindering unauthorized programs from building harmful self-replicating code
- o For automation clients to access the VBA object model, the user running the code must grant access. To enable access, click on the Check box

SETTING UP TRUSTED LOCATION

Rather than manipulating the global macro settings, you can decide to save your macro workbooks in a folder marked to be the trusted location. Any Excel file that is stored in a trusted location or folder is macros enabled and opens without a security warning. When files are stored in a trusted location, macros can still run in certain workbooks even if all other Excel macros are disabled.

To set up a trusted location, follow the steps below:

- From the **File tab**, select **Options**
- On the left side, select the **Trust Center**, and then click on **Trust Center Settings**
- From the **Trust Center** dialog box, select the **Trusted Location** on the left-hand side
- To set up a trusted location, click on **Add new location**

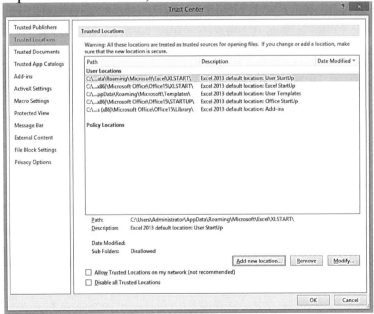

In the Trusted Locations dialog box, do the following:

- Click on the **Browse** button to navigate to the folder you wish to make a trusted location
- Click on **the Subfolder of this location are also trusted** box if you wish to make any folder of the selected folder to be trusted too
- Type a short notice in the **Description field** or you can leave it empty.
- Then click on **OK**

UNDERSTANDING TRUSTED PUBLISHER

WHAT IS A TRUSTED PUBLISHER?

A publisher is a developer who has written or created a macro, ActiveX control, add-in, or extension for use by you and other people. Trusted publishers are reputable developers who have valid credentials and a digital signature issued to them, by a reputable certificate authority.

Trusted publishers have the following criteria

- Their code is signed by their digital signature
- Their digital signature is valid
- Their digital signature is current (not expired)

- The certificate associated with the digital signature was issued by a reputable certificate authority (CA).
- The developer is known to be a trusted publisher.

ADDING TRUSTED PUBLISHER

There are two ways to add a trusted publisher; adding a trusted publisher when the security warning appears and adding a trusted publisher via the Trust Center

ADDING A TRUSTED PUBLISHER WHEN SECURITY WARNING APPEARS

To add a publisher to the list of Trusted Publishers after the security warning has appeared, follow the steps below;

- From the **File tab**, click on the **Info** in the left navigation pane
- In the **Security Warning** area, click on Enable **Content** and then select **Advanced Options**
- **In Microsoft Office Security Options,** then click on **Trust all documents from this publisher**

ADDING A TRUSTED PUBLISHER VIA TRUST CENTER

You can add a publisher to a list of trusted publishers in Trust Center, follow the steps below

- From the **File tab**, select **Options**
- On the left side, select the **Trust Center**, and then click on **Trust Center Settings**
- From the **Trust Center** dialog box, select the **Trusted Publisher on** the left-hand side
- In the list, select the publisher's certificate, and then click on **Ok**

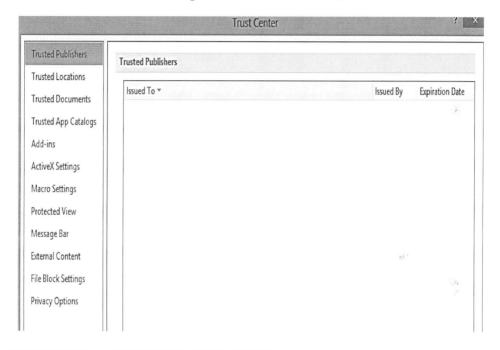

REMOVING A TRUSTED PUBLISHER

In case you feel the need to remove a publisher from the list of trusted publishers, all you need to do is follow the procedures below

- Click on the **File** tab and select **Options**
- On the left side, select the **Trust Center**, and then click on **Trust Center Settings**
- From the **Trust Center** dialog box, select the **Trusted Publisher on** the left-hand side

- In the Trusted Publishers lists, click on any publisher to remove, and then click on **Remove**

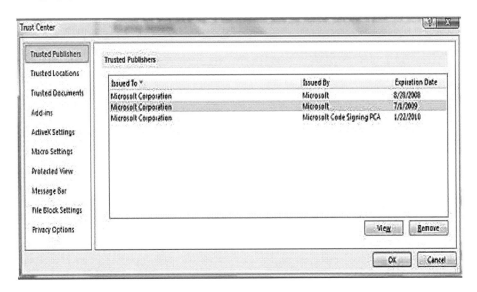

NOTE: In case you do not see the **Remove button** in the Trusted Publishers, then the Office Program is not operating with the administrator rights.

CHAPTER SEVENTEEN

HOW VBA WORKS WITH EXCEL

VBA stands for Visual Basic for Application, a programming language developed by Microsoft, that allows macros to create custom user-generated functions and speed up manual tasks by creating automated processes. The VBA can be used for analyzing scientific data, budgeting, and forecasting, creating invoices and other forms, developing charts from data, etc. In the course of using the VBA, some shortcomings are likely to occur.

- There is a need to know how to write a program and unfortunately, not everyone can write a program
- There are times when the VBA program will not always work correctly. With the help of technical support, solutions can be proffered to this problem
- Due to the continual upgrade on Excel, VBA has become a moving target. Although, Microsoft has tried its best to ensure compatibility among versions, yet, some VBA codes do not work correctly with older or future versions of Excel.

WORKING WITH THE VISUAL BASIC EDITOR

The Visual Basic Editor is a separate application or tool in Excel that allows you to write and edit VBA codes, procedures, and modules.

OPENING THE VB EDITORS

There are three main ways to open the Visual Basic Editor in Excel

- Using a keyboard Shortcut
- Using the Developer Tab
- Using the Worksheet Tabs

USING THE KEYBOARD SHORTCUT

The easiest and fastest way to open the Visual Basic Editor is to use the keyboard shortcut is **ALT + F11.** When you use this shortcut key, a separate window will be opened for the **Visual Basic** editor

USING THE DEVELOPER TAB

You can also open the Visual Basic Editor through the Developer Tab by following the steps below

- Open the **Developer tab**
- From the **Code group**, click on **Visual Basic** and the Visual Basic Editor will be opened

USING THE WORKSHEET TAB

To open the Visual Basic Editor from the worksheet tab, all you need to do is to right-click on any of the worksheet tabs and select **View Code** among the other options listed

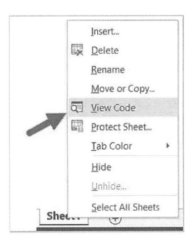

UNDERSTANDING THE VBE COMPONENTS

Opening a VB Editor for the first time can be so confusing and for this purpose, we will be discussing the major six components of the VB Editor.

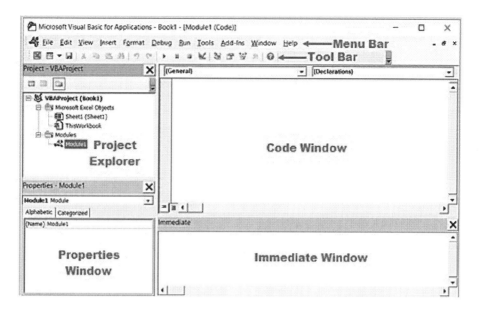

- **Menu Bar:** The VBE menu bar contains a considerate number of drop-down menus that contain commands, and they are used to interact and execute different operations on the VB Editor. Each of the menu commands has shortcut keys associated with them. You can also right-click on any VBE to get the shortcut menu of common commands.

- **Toolbar:** The toolbar which is directly under the menu bar, contains on-screen buttons, menu, icons, and other related elements that can be used while working with the VBE. The toolbar bar can be customized by removing or adding options to it by clicking on the small downward pointing arrow at the end of the toolbar. The toolbar can be moved above the menu bar by clicking on the three grey dots which are located at the beginning of the toolbar and dragging it above the menu bar.

- **Project Explorer:** The Project Explorer is a part of the VB Editor where every workbook that is currently open and this can be add-ins and hidden workbooks. Each Excel workbook or add-in that is currently open appears in the Project Explorer as a separate project. There is a plus icon to the left of objects that is used to collapse or expand the list of objects. The following objects can be found in the Project Explorer
  - All open Workbooks
  - All open Add-ins

To open the Project Explorer, press the keyboard shortcut Ctrl + R, and to close the Project Explorer, just click on the close icon at the top right of the Project Explorer window.

- **Properties Window:** The properties window shows the properties of the object that is being selected in the Project Explorer and permits you to edit these properties. To open the Properties window, use the keyboard shortcut or go to the View tab and click on the Properties window.
- **Code Window:** This is the part of the Visual Basic Editor where you write and edit VBA codes. To open the code window of an object, double-click on it in the Project Explorer area. When a macro is recorded, the code goes into the code window of a module.
- **Immediate Window:** The Immediate Window helps to check errors and debug VBA code. The Immediate Window, by default, is hidden. To unhide the Immediate Window, go to the View menu and click on Immediate Window or use the keyboard shortcut Ctrl + G. To close the Immediate Window, click the Close button in the title bar.

WORKING WITH THE PROJECT WINDOW

ADDING VBA CODE IN MODULE

While recording, a macro automatically creates a module and inserts the code in it. There are, however, some shortcomings when using a macro recorder. For instance, the macro recorder cannot use loops and If Then Else condition.

A module can be used to hold the following types of VBA codes:
- **Declarations**: Declaring variables allows you to indicate the type of data a variable can hold.
- **Subroutines (Procedures)**: This is the code that possesses the steps you need the VBA to perform.
- **Function Procedures:** This is the code that returns a single value and use it to create custom functions

By default, a mode is not part of the workbook but it must be inserted first before using it.

ADDING A MODULE IN THE VB EDITOR

The VBA module is the place where the codes are typed. The codes typed in the module are run to execute a task and perform other tasks. A collection of modules is known as the VBA project.

To add a new module in the VB Editor, all you need to do is;

- Right-click on any object of the workbook on the VB Editor and select **Insert**
- Then select **Module**

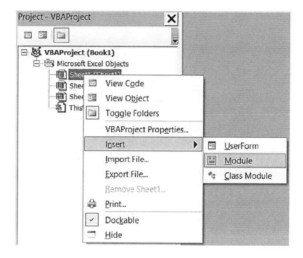

- When the steps above are carried out, the Module is added as shown in the image below.

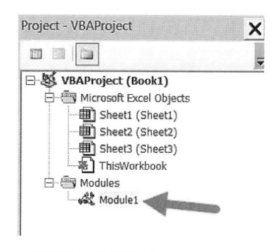

Once the module is created, double-click on the module object in the Project Explorer to open the code window for it.

REMOVING A VBA MODULE

At times, there may be the need to remove a module from the VB Editor, which may be because you no longer need the code again or because it is empty. To remove a module from the VB Editor

- Right-click on the module you wish to remove
- Click on **Remove Module**

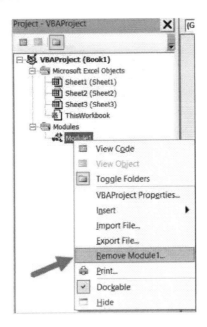

- Click on the **No** button in the **Dialog box** that is displayed

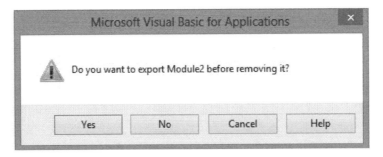

NOTE: *A module can be exported before removing it. when exported, it is saved as a .bas file.*

EXPORTING AND IMPORTING OBJECTS

In the course of working on the VBA project and there arises the need to use an object separately, then you need to learn how to export and import objects in the VBE.

Exporting an object simply means taking a VBA object from a VBA project and saving it in a separate file while importing an object means transferring a VBA object from a separate file to a particular VBA project.

To export an object,

- Click on the object you wish to export
- From the **File menu**, then click on **Export File**

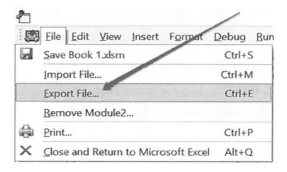

- In the **Export Dialog box**, choose the location to import the file and then click on **Save**

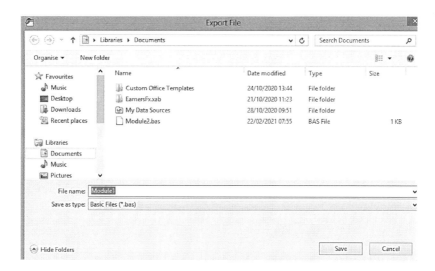

NOTE: *You can also use the Keyboard shortcut key to export files in the VBE. Keep this in mind, the object remains in the project, only a copy of the file is exported.*

To import an object;

- Select the project into which you wish to import the object
- Go to the **File menu** and click on **Import File**

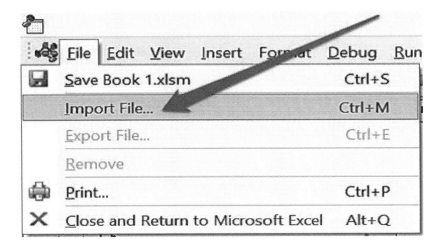

- In the **Import Dialog** box, select the file to be imported and then click on the **Open** button

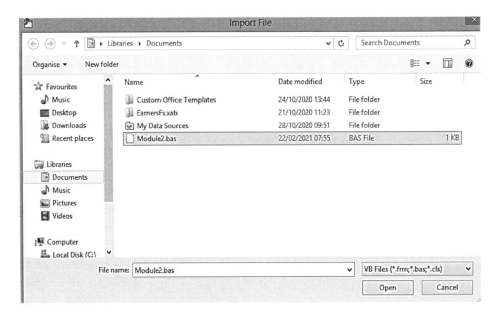

WORKING WITH A CODE WINDOW

MINIMIZING AND MAXIMIZING CODE WINDOWS

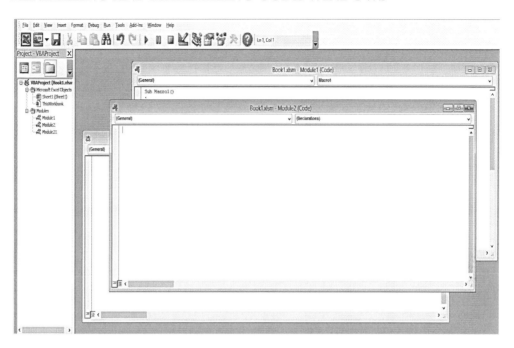

As seen in the image above, the VBE can open as many Code windows as possible at any given time. The Code windows look just like the Excel workbook windows. The Code windows can be minimized, maximized, resized, and hidden.

- To maximize a Code window, all you need to do is click on the Maximize button in the title bar; the maximum button is located next to the X icon in the title bar. To restore a Code window to its original size, click the Restore button.
- To minimize a Code window, click on the minus (-) icon next to the maximize button in the title bar. You can also click on the icon that displays X to close the Code window completely.
- To make two or more Code windows visible on the same page, go to Window, and select the way you want them to be displayed on the page (Horizontally, Vertically, Cascade)
- To switch between two or more Code windows, use the keyboard shortcut Ctrl + F6

GETTING VBA CODE INTO A MODULE

Just like humans can't function without the brain, the VBA module is useless without the VBA code. Before the VBA module can be used for anything meaningful, the VBA code must be inputted in it. To get the VBA code into the VBA modules, the three following ways can be used

- By entering the code directly
- Using the macro recorder
- By copying the code from one module and pasting it to another

ENTERING THE CODE DIRECTLY

Entering the VBA code directly involves typing the code in the VBA module using the keyboard. In this form of getting the code into the module, you can select, copy, cut, and paste the texts as well as doing other things with the texts.

To enter the code directly into the modules

- Open a new worksheet in Excel
- Open the VBE by using the shortcut key Alt+ F11
- Select a new workbook's name from the **Project window**
- Click on **Insert** and then select **Module**
- Then type the following code into the module

```
Sub GuessName ()

        Msg = "Is your name "& Application.UserName & "?"

Ans = MsgBox (Msg, vbYesNo)

        If Ans = vbNo Then MsgBox "Oh, never mind."

        If Ans = vbYes Then MsgBox "I must be psychic!"

End Sub
```

- When the above texts are typed into the module, press F5 and the procedure will be executed. A dialog box will pop us just like the one below

USING THE MACRO RECORDER

One of the ways to input the VBA code in a module is by using the macro recorder. In the previous chapter, the steps needed to record a macro were clearly explained. Here again, we will still go through these steps to record some actions. To do this, follow the steps below

- Select any cell in the workbook
- Select the **Developer** and click on **Record Macro**

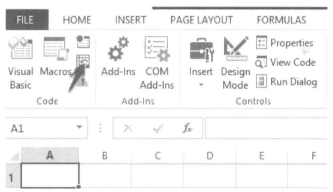

- In the **Macro** dialog box, enter the name of the macro
- Click on the **Shortcut key box** and enter **Shift + N** as the shortcut key (here, you can use any alphabet as your shortcut key)
- Ensure that the Store Macro in settings is **This Workbook** and click on **OK.** When this is done, the Record Macro dialog box closes and the Excel's macro recorder is activated. At this point, Excel keeps track of everything you do and converts them to VBA code.

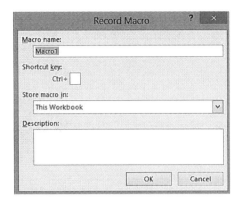

Now let's perform the actions you want to record

- Click on the **New Sheet** icon at the right of the last sheet tab to insert a new worksheet
- Select the whole of **Column I** and press **Ctrl + Shift + Right Arrow**. When this is done, right-click on any of the columns and click on **Hide** from the shortcut menu and all the selected columns will be hidden.
- Select the whole of **Row 9** and press **Ctrl + Shift + Down Arrow**. When this is done, right-click on any of the columns and click on **Hide** from the shortcut menu and all the selected columns will be hidden.
- Select **C1**
- Go to the **Developer** and click on **Stop Recording** and the actions recorded are stopped and recorded

If you have followed the steps above, press Alt + F11 to activate the VBE and then locate the workbook's name in the Project window. Then double click on the module to view the Code window. When you do these, the following codes are generated

Sub AMES ()

'

' AMES Macro

'

' Keyboard Shortcut: Ctrl+Shift+J

'

Sheets.Add After: =ActiveSheet

Columns ("I: I"). Select

Range (Selection, Selection.End(xlToRight)). Select

Selection.EntireColumn. Hidden = True

Rows ("9:9"). Select

Range (Selection, Selection.End(xlDown)). Select

Selection.EntireRow. Hidden = True

Range("C1"). Select

End Sub

To test run the macro recorded, open any worksheet and use the shortcut key you assigned while creating the macro (**Ctrl+Shift+J**) or you can follow the steps below

- Select the **Developer tab** and click on **Macros**
- From the **Macro dialog box**, select the name of the macro and then click on the **Run** button

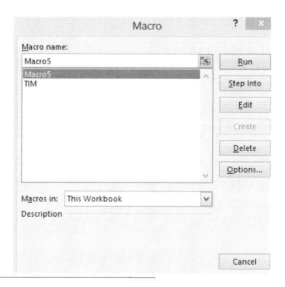

When the macro is tested, your worksheet contains 8 visible rows and 8 visible columns as shown in the image below

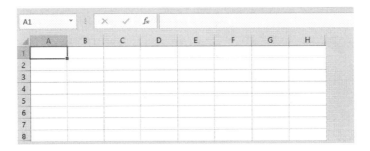

COPYING THE VBA CODE

The last method of getting codes into the module is by copying from another module. This will save the stress of having to re-enter the codes over again. You can open the module and use the shortcut keys Ctrl + C to copy and Ctrl + V to paste.

CUSTOMIZING THE VB EDITOR

Customizing your VB Editor is very important. You get to change the VB appearance to what suits your purposes and also to your comfortability. To customize your VB, the first thing to do is to open the Options dialog. To open the Option dialogue

- Ensure that the VB is open
- Then from **Tools**, click on **Option** and the **Options dialog** will be displayed as shown below

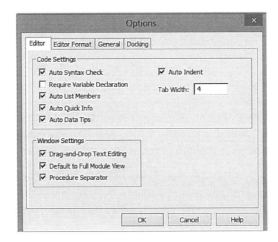

As shown in the image above, the Options dialog box has four tabs that are used for customizing in the VB Editor

- Editor Tab
- Editor Format Tab
- General Tab
- Docking Tab

Let's quickly check these tabs out and how important they are in customizing the VB Editor

EDITOR TAB

The Editor tab is the place where you can change the settings for Code windows and Project windows. Briefly, let's discuss the options available in this tab.

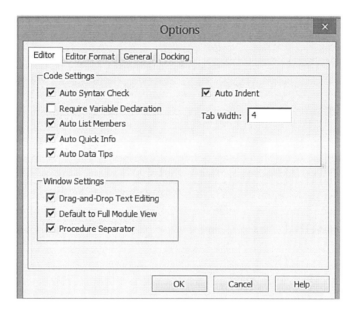

Auto Syntax Check

This is one of the options in the Editor tab that helps check for syntax errors while entering the VBA code. When the Auto Syntax Check is enabled, a dialog box is displayed when a syntax error is made. When the Auto Syntax Check is disabled and a syntax error is detected, there is a color change usually red in the code, to note the error.

Require Variable Declaration

This option when enabled inserts the statement **Option Explicit** at the beginning of each new VBA module you insert. When this setting is changed, it only affects new modules and not existing modules. Enabling the Required Variable Declaration reduces the risk of errors occurring in the wrong spellings of variable names. Not only that, this option when enabled, saves time when debugging and also allows for a better understanding of the Visual Basic for Applications (VBA)

Auto List Members

When typing a VBA code, this option displays a list of logical options to complete the code being typed. This feature is also called IntelliSense and helps to quickly select the property and method from the list to save time. Besides, this feature discourages spellings errors

Auto Quick Info Options

This option, when enabled helps to display information about functions, their arguments, properties, and methods as they are being typed.

Auto Data Tips

When the Auto Data Tips option is enabled, the VBE shows the value of the variable on which the cursor is placed when the codes are being debugged.

Auto Indent Setting

While typing, the VBA codes can become disorganized and not readable, but with the indentation, the chances of the codes being readable increase. So, when the Auto Indent Setting is enabled, the indentation of each line of the VBA code is the same as the previous line's indentation.

You can also set the indentation width of your codes by inputting the value in the Table Width box, and by default, 4 is the number of characters to be indented

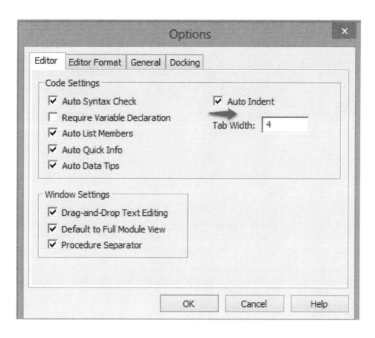

Drag and Drop Text Editing

The Drag and Drop Text Editing when enabled, allows you to copy and move texts by dragging and dropping the texts to the desired location with your mouse.

Default to Full Module View

When the Default to Full Module View is enabled, the VBA procedures are displayed on a single scrollable list, and if it is not enabled, the VBA procedures can only be displayed one at a time.

Procedure Separator

When the Procedure Separated option is enabled, a line in form of a divider is placed between two procedures.

EDITOR FORMAT TAB

The Editor Format tab is where you customize the way the VBA codes will look in the VBA windows. The Editor Format regulates the way the Visual Basic Editor using the option available in it. Now, let's discuss the options available in the Editor Format tab.

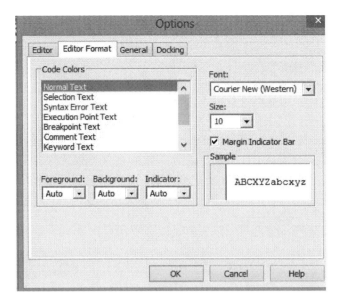

Code Colors Options

The Color Colors option allows you to set the text color and background color that can be displayed for the VBA codes

Font Option

The Font option allows you to select the font type in which the VBA code in the Programming Window will be displayed. The default font for the VB Editor is the Courier new.

Size Settings

The Size Setting option allows you to specify the font size to be used in the Code Window.

Margin Indicator Bar Option

This is a grey bar that is displayed on the left side of the Programming Window of the VBA. When this is turned off, the graphical indicator will not be seen when debugging the VBA codes

THE GENERAL TAB

In the image below, there are several options available in the General tab of which we will quickly explain

---

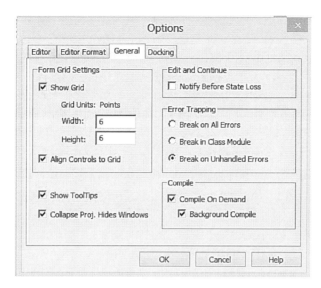

Form Grid Settings

This option in the General tab allows you to control the way the VBA handles UserForms

Show ToolTips

This option is what helps the VBA to display information that helps understand a particular toolbar button. When this option is enabled, ToolTips are displayed automatically when you click on a particular button.

Collapse Proj. Hides Windows

When this option is enabled on any project, it hides any window that is related to that project. And when this is disabled, the windows hidden are restored to their normal position

Edit and Continue & Notify Before State Loss

When this option is enabled, the VBE pops up with notification provided the following conditions are met

- When you are running VBA code
- When an operation you are carrying out requires that the variables in the module be reset.

Error Trapping

This option is concerned with how errors are trapped and handled in the course of running the VBA code. There are three option available

- **Break All Errors:** When you activate this feature, a break mode is entered when there is an error in the VBA code. This can come in handy when debugging.
- **Break-in Class Module:** When this is enabled, the break mode is entered when an error occurred in the VBA code within a class module
- **Break on Unhandled Errors:** When this option is enabled, the break mode will not be entered as long as there is an error handler that traps the error. If there is no adequate error handler, the break mode will be entered.

Compile

The Compile setting gives you access to control and coordinate the movement at which the VBA code is compiled. The Compile setting has two options and they are as follow

Compile On Demand: When this option is enabled, Procedure 1 is the only procedure that is compiled at the beginning of the process. The Compile On Demand means that the VB Editor compiles the VBA code as is needed.

Background Compile: This is option is only accessible when the Compile On-Demand is enabled. The Background Compile means that the idle time is used for purpose of compiling a program in the background.

DOCKING TAB

The Docking tab is a part of the VB Editor that is used to set or determine the behavior of the different windows of the Visual Basic Editor. The Docking tab allows you to fix the position of a window so that it doesn't float around and also allows you to view all the different windows at the same time.

CHAPTER EIGHTEEN

INTRODUCING THE EXCEL OBJECT MODEL

WHAT IS EXCEL OBJECT MODEL?

All applications such as Excel, Access, Word, and PowerPoint that use the VBA have their object models. The Excel object model is a large hierarchy of all the objects used in the VBA. All objects and their properties and method in Excel VBA can be viewed or seen in the Object Browser located in the VBE code window. To locate the Object Browser

- Go to the **VB Editor** and click on **View**
- Then click on **Object Browser** or press **F2**

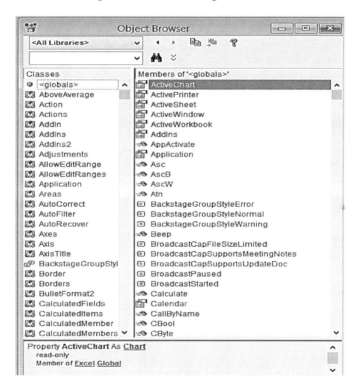

THE EXCEL OBJECT MODEL HIERARCHY

While learning about the Excel object model, the first step to take is to get to know the basic structure of the object model hierarchy. The Excel object model and its hierarchy are listed below:

- Application
- Workbook
- Worksheet
- Range

The Application Object: This is the host application in which the entire Excel application is represented. The Application object reveals explicit information about the running application. The Application contains the following VBA objects

- Add-ins
- Windows
- Workbooks
- Worksheet functions

The Workbook Object: This is the next in the Excel Model hierarchy that represents a single workbook within the Excel application. Some of the objects that can be found within the Workbook objects are as follows:

- Charts containing Chart objects
- Names containing Name objects
- VBA project containing open projects.
- Windows containing Window objects in the specified Excel workbook

The Worksheet Object: Next to the Workbook Object is the Worksheet Object, and this represents a single worksheet within the workbook. The Worksheet object can contain the following VBA objects

- ChartObjects containing ChartObjects objects
- Comment, which represents a cell comment
- Hyperlink, which represents a hyperlink
- Name, which indicates a defined name for a particular cell range
- PageSetup, which is used to store printing information
- PivotTable, which contains PivotTable objects.

The Range Object: This is the last in the Excel Model hierarchy that represents cells, rows, columns, selections of cells with contiguous blocks of cells, or 3-D ranges.

REFERENCING AND ACCESSING OBJECTS IN EXCEL

Most times when working with the VBA, you will need to use a particular object from the collection. For this reason, here, I will be teaching you how to reference an object in a collection or even a collection of objects.

There are two ways to reference objects and they will be explained below

- *Using The VBA Object Name*
- *Using The Index Number*

Using The VBA Object Name

In this method, the syntax that is used to reference an object is **Collection_name("Object_name)**. To use the VBA object name while referencing an object, follow the steps below

- The name of the specified collection (collection_name) comes first
- After inputting the collection_name, let the parentheses follow ()
- Inside the parenthesis, input the name of the individual VBA object with a quotation around it ("Object_name")
  Worksheet("Sheet1")

Or

Sheets("Sheet1")

Using The Index Number

To use this method of referencing objects in a collection of objects, use the syntax **Collection_name("Index_name").** To use the index number to reference an object, follow the steps below

- The name of the specified collection (collection_name) comes first

- After inputting the collection_name, let the parentheses follow ()
- Inside the parenthesis, input the number of the individual VBA object with a quotation around it (1)

Worksheet(1)

Or

Sheets(1)

NAVIGATING THROUGH THE HIERARCHY

To work with the Application object, all you need to do is type application. All objects in Excel's model object are under the Application object and you can locate all these objects by navigating down the hierarchy and connecting each object with the (.) operator.

To locate the Workbook object named Book2.xlsx, start with the Application object and move down to the Workbook collection object.

Application.Workbooks ("Book1.xlsx")

To move to another specific worksheet, add a dot operator and locate the Worksheets collection object

Application.Workbooks ("Book1.xlsx").Worksheet(2)

To get the value from cell A2 on the second Worksheet of the Workbook named Book2.xlsx, you will need to move one level to the Range object by adding a dot (.) separator to the Range object

Application.Workbooks ("Book1.xlsx").Worksheet(2).Range("A2").Value

SIMPLIFYING OBJECT REFERENCES

DIVING INTO OBJECT PROPERTIES AND METHODS

Knowing how to reference objects is important, yet, it is very important to know how to

- Read or modify an object's properties
- Indicate a method of action to be used with an object.

With all these in place, you can accomplish something meaningful with VBA objects

OBJECT PROPERTIES

Every VBA object in Excel has properties. Properties are the attributes that describe the object. These attributes can be size, color, screen location, width, height, etc. The object's properties define how it looks, behaves, and even whether it is visible. With the object's properties, VBA can do the following

- Check the current setting of a property
- Change the property's settings

For instance, a cell Range object has just a single property called Value. The Value property saves the value that is contained in the cell. The characteristics of an object can be changed when you change the value of its properties. The VBA code can be written to display the Value property or better still, you can set the Value property to a specific value.

To establish the value of a property, follow the reference of the object with a period, the property name, an equal sign, and the new property value. For example, the procedure below changes the caption of a Visual Basic form by establishing the Caption property

```
Sub ChangeName(newTitle)

    myForm.Caption = newTitle

End Sub
```

OBJECT METHODS

Methods are the actions that can be performed by an object. A method can change the properties of an object.

The example below uses the ClearContents to delete the content of 12 cells on a Range object in the active sheet.

```
Sub ClearRange()
```

```
       Range("A2:A13").ClearContents

End Sub
```

Again, to select a range, you need to use the Select method, to copy a range from another worksheet to another, you also need to use the Copy method. The example below copies data from Range A2 to B6.

```
Sub sbExampleRangeMethods()

        Range("A2").Select

        Selection. Copy

        Range("B6).Select

        AciveSheet.Paste

End Sub
```

OBJECT EVENTS

An event is an action that is recognized or acknowledged by an object and such events may include clicking the mouse, pressing a key on the keyboard, o activating different worksheets in a workbook. An event can also happen as a result of a user action or program code.

USING THE VBA'S HELP SYSTEM

The VBA Help system is a tool in Excel that helps define every object, property, and method available. This also helps to know more about the VBA.

To use the VBA Help system in Excel 2013 and 2016, you must be connected to the internet while in Excel 2007 and 2010, the VBA Help system is stored in the local drive and can provide sensitive information even without the need to connect to the internet.

To access the VBA Help system;

- Go to the VB Editor and click on **Help**

- Select **Microsoft Visual Basic for Application Help** and you will be directed to the internet
- You can also use **Alt + H twice** to open the VBA Help system.

USING THE OBJECT BROWSER

As explained earlier in this chapter, the Object Browser is a tool in the VB Editor used for viewing all objects and their properties. To locate the Object Browser

- Go to the **VB Editor** and click on **View**
- Then click on **Object Browser** or press **F2**

The first drop-down list at the top contains all the lists of the objects available in the libraries; in the All-Libraries menu, you can go through Excel's objects by selecting Excel from the drop-down list. The second drop-down list is where you input any object you wish to search for

USING THE AUTO LIST MEMBER

This is a tool in the VBA that gives a list of properties and methods as you type. This tool saves you the stress of having to repeat a word that has been typed already. When you type c in the list, the list is constricted to any object that begins with c. At this point, all you need to do is highlight the object you need and the press Tab

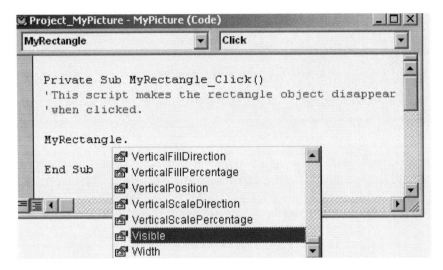

CHAPTER NINETEEN

UNDERSTANDING EXCEL VBA PROCEDURES

WHAT IS A PROCEDURE?

A procedure is the main building block of an Excel VBA program. The procedure is the block of a statement which is enclosed by a particular declaration statement and End declaration. The VBA procedures are written and stored in the module and viewed in the VB Editor.

TYPES OF PROCEDURE

There are two most common types of VBA procedures and they are as follow

- Sub procedures
- Function procedures

THE SUB PROCEDURES

The Sub procedures are VBA statements written to perform or command actions such as creating the chart, analyzing data, copying, and pasting data, coloring cells, etc. in Excel.

THE FUNCTION PROCEDURES

The function procedures are also VBA statements created to make the Excel perform or execute any type of calculation that will be used many times in your computer code.

THE DIFFERENCE BETWEEN THE SUB AND THE FUNCTION PROCEDURES

The Sub and the Function procedures have some differences and they are listed below

HOW TO WRITE A SUB PROCEDURE IN EXCEL

SUB PROCEDURES	FUNCTION PROCEDURES
A Sub procedure executes a task and does not return a value	A function procedure returns a value of the task executed.
A Sub procedure can be recalled from anywhere in the program and multiple types	Functions are called by a variable.
A Sub procedure cannot be directly used in a spreadsheet as formulas	Functions are directly used in formulas
In the Sub procedure, the value must be inserted by the users into the desired cell to get the result of the sub	The function procedures can be used to perform a task over and over again and return a value
The VBA sub can be executed by the Excel user	The VBA function cannot be executed by the Excel user

To write a Sub procedure, the following rules must be followed

- The Sub procedure must begin with declaration statement **Sub** and end with declaration statement **End**
- The subroutine must not contain any space
- The Sub procedure should not be started with a number or special character. Rather, a letter or underscore should be used
- Period (.) and spaces () are not allowed.
- The first character must be a letter
- The maximum number of characters a name can contain is 225

The example below shows a Sub procedure

```
Sub ShowMessage()

    MsgBox "Who are you?!"

End Sub
```

HOW TO WRITE A FUNCTION PROCEDURE IN EXCEL

To write or customize a Function procedure, follow the steps below

- Open the **VB Editor** and choose a particular workbook in the Project
- From the **Menu**, go to the **Modules** to insert a standard VBA module
- Right in the **Module,** enter the word Function and followed by the function name. In case the function uses an argument, input the list of arguments in the parentheses
- Put in the VBA code that will execute the task intended. Here, the program stores the value of the result in a variable, using the same name as the function.
- Finally, close the function with the **End** Function

Here is an example of the Function procedure

```
Function CubeRoot(number)

    CubeRoot = number ^ (1 / 5)

End Function
```

NAMING THE SUBS AND FUNCTION PROCEDURES

Just like giving names to humans, the Subs and Function procedures must be given a name. To name a Sub or Function procedure, the following rules must be obeyed.

- Use letters, numbers, and punctuation characters, but the first character must be a letter.
- Spaces and period are not allowed in the name

333

- Whether it is a lowercase or uppercase character, the VBA does not care.
- Characters such as $, %, &, +, ^, @, etc. cannot be used to name a procedure
- While writing the Function procedure in the formula, do not use a name that looks like a cell address (A2 or B23)

EXECUTING THE SUB PROCEDURES

You may not have an in-depth knowledge of what it takes to develop a Sub procedure but here, I will be taking you on how to execute a Sub procedure. Executing a Sub procedure simply means that you want to run or call a Sub procedure. However, there are several ways of executing the Sub procedure and a few of them are mentioned below

- **From The Macro Dialog Box:** One of the most common ways to execute the Sub procedure is the Macro dialog box which can be located in the Developer tab
- By using the Ctrl + Shift + Key shortcut designated to the Sub procedure
- Clicking on a button or a shape on a worksheet that has been assigned to the Sub procedure
- The Sub procedure can be executed from another procedure
- The Sub procedure can be executed from a button that has been added to the Quick Access toolbar
- The Sub procedure can also be executed from a custom item added to the Ribbon
- When an event occurs, a Sub procedure can also be executed.
- The Sub procedure can also be executed from the Immediate window in the VBE by typing the name of the procedure and pressing **Enter**

Before we begin to execute a Sub procedure using a different method, let's enter a Sub procedure in the module

- Open a new workbook and open the **VBE Editor** from the **Developer tab**
- In the **Project window,** select the worksheet
- Click on **Insert** to insert the module

334

- Then begin to enter the following Sub procedures in the module

```
Sub ShowCubeRoot()

    Num = InputBox("Enter a positive number")

    MsgBox Num ^ (1/5) & " is the cube root."

End Sub
```

- The procedure requires a number from the user

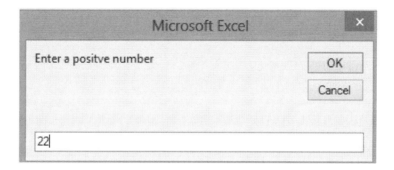

- Here, the procedure then gives the cube root of the number in the message box as shown in the image below

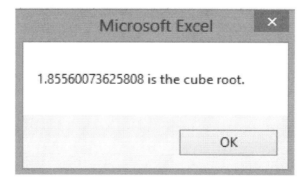

Here, let's take look at how to execute the procedure above using different methods.

EXECUTING THE SUB PROCEDURE DIRECTLY

One of the quickest and easiest ways to execute a procedure is directly executing the procedures from the modules. To do this, follow the steps below

- Open the **VB Editor** and select the module holding the procedure
- Navigate the mouse cursor to anywhere in the procedure's code
- Go to **Run** and select **Run Sub/UserForm** or you can use the shortcut key **F5**
- React to the input box and then click on **Ok**

NOTE: *The **Run/UserForm** command cannot execute a Sub procedure that contains arguments. If the Sub procedure contains one or more arguments, it can only be executed when it is called from another procedure. By so doing, the arguments are supplied.*

EXECUTING THE PROCEDURE FROM THE MACRO DIALOG BOX

Another way to also execute the Sub procedures is from Excel and this can be achieved using the Macro dialog box. Follow the steps below to execute this action

- Open the Excel worksheet and go to **the Developer**
- Select the **Macro** and click on **Run**

NOTE:

- *The Macro dialog box doesn't display the Sub procedures that use arguments. The reason is that the arguments cannot be indicated in the Macro dialog box.*
- *You can also execute the Sub procedure through the Macro by using the shortcut key assigned to it*

EXECUTING THE SUB PROCEDURE FROM A BUTTON OR SHAPE

Another interesting way to execute the Sub procedure is by assigning the macro to a button or shape. Follow the steps below to assign macro to a button

- Open the worksheet
- From the **Developer tab**, go to **Insert** and select **Button tool** in the **Form Controls group**

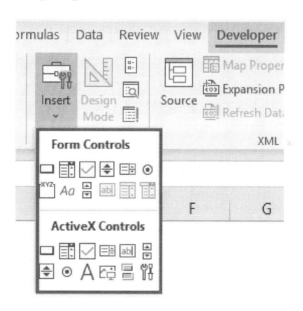

- Click on the worksheet you wish to create the button on
- Here, Excel displays the Assign Macro dialog box and then select the macro you wish to assign to the button or shape
- Finally, click on **OK**. After these are done, the button appears on the worksheet to execute the procedure

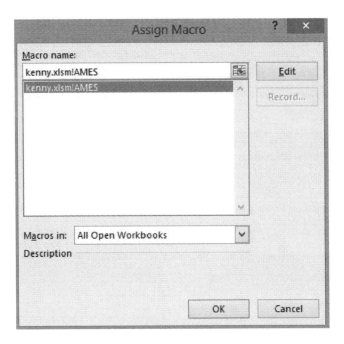

Not only can you assign macro to a button, but you can also assign macro to any shape or object. Now let's assign a rectangular shape to the macro using the steps below

- Go to the **Insert tab** and click on **Illustration**
- Select **Shapes** and click on the rectangle to insert it on the worksheet
- Right-click on the rectangle and then choose the macro from the Assign Macro dialog box
- Then click on Ok. After these are done, the rectangle appears on the worksheet to execute the procedure

NOTE: *The Assign Macro dialog box allows you to record a macro and also create a New button, and with this New button, Excel allows you to insert Sub procedure with the name you want.*

EXECUTING FUNCTION PROCEDURES

The Function procedures can be executed in two ways

- By calling the function from another Sub or Function procedure
- By using the function in a worksheet

CALLING THE FUNCTION FROM A SUB PROCEDURE

The Excel Function procedure cannot be called directly and that is why it must be called from other procedures. Now let's use the CubeRoot function as an example. Keep these in mind, there are two stages involved in this method; the first stage displays an input box to contain the CubeRoot of the number and the second stage uses the MsgBox function to reveal to the user the result after it has been processed by the CubeRoot function

Now let's write the following procedures in the VBA module and press F5 to execute

Function CubeRoot(number)

CubeRoot = number ^ (1 / 3)

End Function

Sub CallerSub()

Ans = CubeRoot(125)

MsgBox Ans

End Sub

When the CallerSub procedure is executed, Excel displays a message box that contains the value of the Ans variable to be 5 as shown in the image below

CALLING A FUNCTION FROM A WORKSHEET FORMULA

Calling a function from a worksheet formula is easier than you think. If you are used to working with Excel formulas, you won't find this difficult.

For instance, to find the Cube root of the data in cell A2 in the table below, all you need to do is enter the formula in an active cell

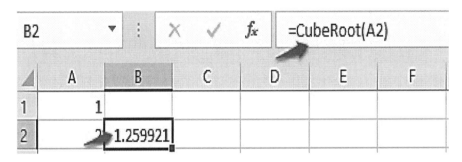

To get the Cuberoot, enter =**Cuberoot(A2)** as shown in the image below to get your answer to be

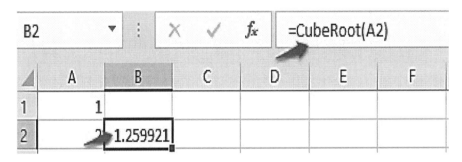

You can also use the Insert Function to also find the Cuberroot of Cell A2. To do this, follow the steps below

- From the **Formula tab,** click on **Insert Function** and the Insert Function dialog box will be displayed
- Click on the drop-down menu under **Or Select a Category** and then click on **User Defined**
- Scroll down to Cuberoot and click on **Ok**

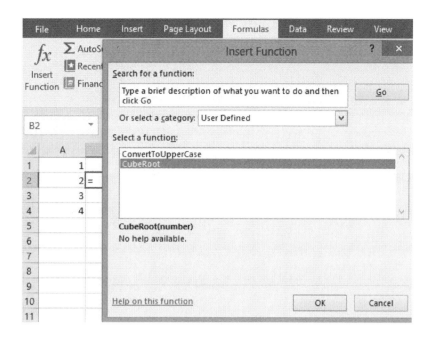

- In the **Function Argument** dialog box, enter the argument A2 and then click on **Ok**

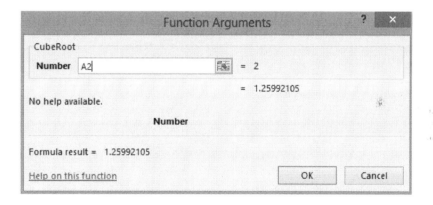

- As expected, the answer will be 1.259921 as shown in the image below

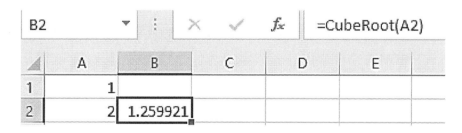

CHAPTER TWENTY

USING THE EXCEL MACRO RECORDER

WHAT IS AN EXCEL MACRO RECORDER?

The Macro Recorder is an essential tool in the Excel VBA that helps record every task performed on Excel. When the task is recorded once, it can be executed several times with a click of a button. The Macro Recorder records all the steps in the Visual Basic for Application (VBA) code. The Macro Recorder registers every move you take and even if you click on a button you don't intend to, the Macro Recorder will also record it. when this occurs, you can record again or edit the VBA code in the module.

The Macro Recorder is located on the Developer tab as discussed earlier in chapter 1

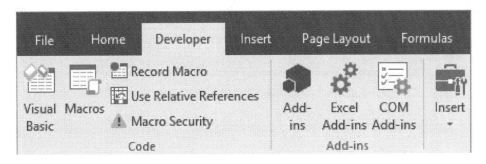

BASICS OF USING THE MACRO RECORDER

When using the Macro Recorder, some basic steps must be taken into consideration of which have been explained in chapter 1 of this book. However, I will be referring to them again and they are as follows:

- Have a clue of what task you intend to do with the Macro recorder
- Get things set up properly to determine how efficient the macro will work
- Choose to make the cell reference in the macro to be absolute or relative
- Click on the **Record Macro button** on the **Developer tab**
- Input the name, shortcut key, macro location, and description
- Click on **Ok**

- Then carry out the tasks you wish to perform and when you are done, then click on the **Stop Recording button** on **the Developer tab**
- **Finally, test the macro to see if it works correctly.**

The Macro Recorder can only work with the Sub procedures and cannot work with Function procedures.

LIMITATION TO THE USE OF THE MACRO RECORDER

In as much as the Macro Recorder is simple and straightforward, there are certain tasks the Macro Recorder cannot generate codes for and they are listed below

- Allocating values to variables
- Identifying data types
- Put on view pop up messages
- Put on view custom dialog boxes
- Performing any type of repetitive looping
- Performing any type of conditional actions using the If-Then statement

RECORDING IN THE ABSOLUTE OR RELATIVE MODE

The Excel macros can be recorded in the absolute reference or relative reference. Recording the macro in the absolute reference places the recorded steps in the cells where it has been recorded, whether it is an active cell or not. And by default, the macro uses the absolute reference for recording. On the other hand, macro recorded in the relative reference can perform the task recorded at different parts on the worksheet.

RECORDING IN THE ABSOLUTE MODE

Now let's take a look at how to record a macro in the absolute mode. To get this done, follow the steps below

- From the **Developer tab**, go to **Use Relative Reference** that is no highlighted
- Go to **Record Macro** and type **Absolute** as the name of the macro

- Then click on Ok to start the recording

- Click on cell **C1** and type **FEB** in the cell
- Move to cell D1 and type MAR
- Move to cell E1 and type APRIL
- Go back to cell C1 to activate again and stop the macro recorder
- Press Alt +F11 to open the VB Edior
- Open the Module 1 module and the code below will be generated

```
Sub Absolute()

'

' Absolute Macro

'

    Range("C1").Select

    ActiveCell.FormulaR1C1 = "FEB"

    Range("D1").Select

    ActiveCell.FormulaR1C1 = "MAR"
```

```
Range("E1").Select

ActiveCell.FormulaR1C1 = "APRIL"

Range("C1").Select

End Sub
```

When this task is executed, the macro selects cell C1 and input the three-month name (FEB, MAR, and APRIL) in the range C1:E1 respectively as shown in the image below

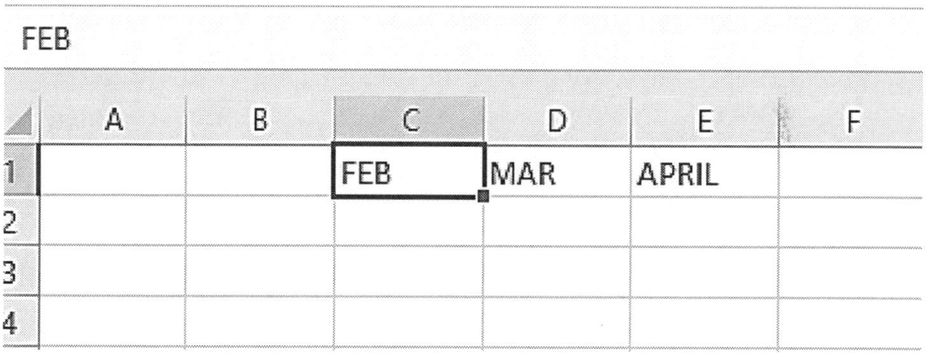

FEB

	A	B	C	D	E	F
1			FEB	MAR	APRIL	
2						
3						
4						

RECORDING IN RELATIVE MODE

At times, you may need your recorded macro to work with cell locations in a reference mode. For example, you may want the macro to start entering the day names in the current active cell. In this scenario, the relative reference should be used.

To use the relative mode, follow the steps below

- Open the cell C1
- From the **Developer tab**, go **Record Macro** and type **Relative** as the name of the macro
- Click on **Ok** to start the recording

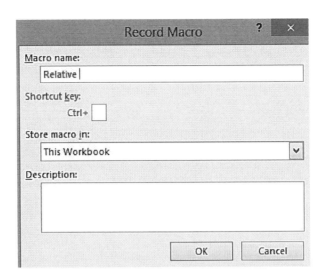

- Then click on the **Use Relative Reference** button to change the recording mode to relative (This changes the color from the rest of the ribbons)
- Click on cell **C1** and type **FEB** in the cell
- Move to cell D1 and type MAR
- Move to cell E1 and type APRIL
- Go back to cell C1 to activate again and stop the macro recorder
- Press Alt +F11 to open the VB Editor
- Open the Module 1 module and the code below will be generated

```
Sub Relative()

'

' Relative Macro

'

    ActiveCell.Select

    ActiveCell.FormulaR1C1 = "FEB"

    ActiveCell.Offset(0, 1).Range("A1").Select

    ActiveCell.FormulaR1C1 = "MAR"

    ActiveCell.Offset(0, 1).Range("A1").Select
```

```
    ActiveCell.FormulaR1C1 = "APRIL"

    ActiveCell.Offset(0, -2).Range("A1").Select

End Sub
```

If you look at the example above, you realize that there is a slight difference between the relative mode and the absolute mode. For the relative mode, the beginning of the cell must be activated before recording can take place.

RECORDING OPTIONS

In the Macro Recorder dialog box, there are some options needed to record your actions to create a VBA. Briefly, we will talk about them and how they are used.

MACRO NAME

This is where you enter the name of the Sub procedure you are recording. Excel uses Macro1, Macro 2, etc to record each macro by default. However, you can decide to change the name to whatever name you desire

SHORTCUT KEY

The Shortcut key gives you an easy and fast option to execute your macro by pressing a shortcut combination e.g Ctrl + Shift + W. you can also change the shortcut key to anyone you desire

STORE MACRO IN

This option specifies where Excel will store the macro that is being recorded. By default, Excel saves the macro in a module in the active workbook.

DESCRIPTION

This is where you type brief information of what you expect the macro recorded to do. This option is optional

CHAPTER TWENTY-ONE

ESSENTIAL VBA LANGUAGE ELEMENTS

USING COMMENTS IN THE VBA CODE

A comment is a descriptive text found within a code to describe what you are doing and why you are doing it. by default, comments are displayed in **green** color, and not only that, they cannot be executed by Excel VBA. To add a comment in Excel's VBA code,

- Open the VB Editor
- Precede the code in the VBA with an apostrophe

```
' Keyboard Shortcut: Ctrl+Shift+J
'
    Application.Left = 541.75
    Application.Top = 112.75
    Application.Width = 668.25
    Application.Height = 454.5
    Application.Left = 199
    Application.Top = 110.5
    Sheets.Add After:=ActiveSheet
    Columns("I:I").Select
    Range(Selection, Selection.End(xlToRight)).Select
    Selection.EntireColumn.Hidden = True
    Rows("9:9").Select
    Range("C9").Activate
    Range(Selection, Selection.End(xlDown)).Select
    Selection.EntireRow.Hidden = True
    ActiveWindow.SmallScroll Down:=-3
    Range("C1").Select
End Sub
```

However, there is an exception to the application of apostrophe indicating a comment; the VBA will not understand an apostrophe inside a set of quotation marks as a comment indicator. As earlier said, any text with a comment cannot be executed by the VBA and due to this, you don't need to delete any statement you don't want the VBA to execute. All you just need to do is add an apostrophe to the statement and the VBA will not execute it.

With the following tips, you can make the best use of comments

- Give short and clear information about each Sub and Function you wish to write by using the comment
- Keep track of any change made on the procedure by using comments

- As you begin to develop code, use the comments.
- Ensure to use the comments to give concise information on any solution proffer to curb bugs in Excel

USING VBA VARIABLES, CONSTANTS, AND DATA TYPES

WHAT ARE VBA VARAIBLES?

Variable are specific values that are stored in the computer's memory and are used to execute the VBA code. One of the advantages of using the variables instead of a constant is that you can change the value of the variable when the code is being used. However, the variables must be named and for this reason, you will have to declare the data type of your variable. Declaring the data type implies that you are telling the program, the type of data you wish your variable to store. You can also use the equal sign operator to assign values to your variables

While using naming the variables in VBA, some of these rules should be enforced

- You can use alphabets, numbers, and punctuation, but the first character must be an alphabet.
- Special characters such as #, $,%, &,! etc cannot be used to name a variable
- The VBA does not distinguish between uppercase and lowercase in the naming of variables
- You cannot use space or period when naming a variable. Rather, you use an underscore character e.g My_Watch
- You cannot use mathematical operators in naming a variable
- There are some reserved words that the VBA does not permit while naming the variable. These are words such as Next, Sub, Dim, End, For, etc.
- VBA does not allow you to create a variable with names that correspond with Excel's object model such as Workbook and Range
- The name of the variable should not exceed 255 characters in length.

WHAT ARE THE DATA TYPE OF VARIABLES?

To allow for the efficient and effective use of the variables, it is very important to learn how to specify the data type of the variable. The data types of variables are mainly categorized in two and they are explained below

- **Numerical Data Types**: The numerical data types are used when you intend to store numbers only and examples of these are currency, long, integer, date, time, etc
- **Non-Numerical Data Types:** The non-numerical data type save characters or values that do not contain numbers. Examples are String, Boolean. Object, variant.

The following data types both (numerical and non-numerical) are briefly explained in the table below:

Numerical Data Types

Data Type	Byte Used	Ranges of Values
Byte	1 byte	0 to 255
Integer	2 bytes	-32, 768 to 32,767
Long	4 bytes	-2,147,483,648 to 2,147,483,648
Single	4 bytes	-3.40 to $-1.40E-45$ for negative values; $1.40E-45$ to 3.40 for positive values
Double	8 bytes	$-1.79E308$ to $-4.94E-324$ for negative value $4.94E-324$ to 1.79 for

		positive values
Currency	8 bytes	-922,337,203,685,477.5808 to 922,337,203,685,477.5807
Decimal	12 bytes	+/- 79,228,162,514,264,337,593,950,335 if no decimal is used. 7.9281625142643375935543950555 (28 decimal places)

Data Type	Byte Used	Ranges of Values
String (Fixed length)	Length of string	1 to 65,400 characters
String (Variable Length)	Length + 10 bytes	0 to 2 billion characters
Boolean	2 bytes	True or False
Date	8 bytes	January 1, 100 to December 31, 9999
Object	4 bytes	Any embedded object

Varaint (numeric)	16 bytes	Any value as large as Double
Variant (text)	Length + 22 bytes	Same as variable length string

DECLARING VARIABLES

Here in this section, we will discuss how to declare a variable to a particular data type. If you don't declare a variable to a particular data type, VBA will automatically set the variable to a variant, which is the default data type.

To declare a variable to any data type, follow the steps below

- Use the keyword Dim in the starting
- Indicate the name for the variable
- Use the keyword As after the name
- Indicate the Data Type for the variable for the value you wish to assign to it

E.g

Sub Macro ()

Dim Num As Interger

Num = 99

MsgBox " Guru & Num

End Sub

USING THE OPTION EXPLICIT

Using the Option Explicit implies that you have to declare all your variables. Instead of declaring your variables one by one, you use the Option Explicit to declare them all at once when it is enabled in the setting.

To add the Option Explicit, do the following

- From the **VB Editor**, go to **Tools**
- Click on **Options** and go to the **Editor tab**
- From the **Editor tab,** click on **Check Required Variable Declaration**

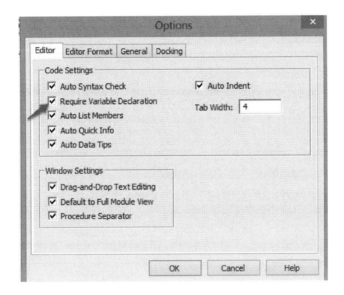

WHY DO YOU NEED TO DECLARE YOUR VARIABLES

It is very good to declare your variables in the and some of the reasons are stated below

- **Memory And Calculation Speed:** When you do not declare your variables, by default, it is a variant and this takes more memory than any other data type. Therefore, declaring your variable helps your macro to run faster and also efficiently use the memory.
- **Prevention of Typo Bugs:** Declaring the variables help to prevent you from introducing bugs into your code by accidentally typing a variable name incorrectly

- **Highlighting Unexpected Data Values**: If you declare a variable to have a specific data type, and you attempt to assign the wrong type of data to it, this will generate an error in your program which, if not handled within your code, can cause your program to crash

CONSTANTS IN VBA

A constant is similar to a variable but stores a value that cannot be changed. One of the advantages of using the constant is that it makes it easy to write and understand code, and also allows you to control all fixed values from one place. To declare constant in VBA, use the keyword **Const.** declaring a constant is shown in the VBA code

```
Sub DeclaringAConstant()

Const NumberofDays = 1

MsgBox NumberofDays

End Sub
```

When the following codes are executed in the VB Editor, the result is as shown in the image below

There are, however, two different kinds of constants in the VBA and they are

Intrinsic Constant: These are constants that are built into the VBA language. An example of this is the built-in constant vbOKcancel which are used in a message box

User-Defined Constants: These are the type of constant you create by assigning value to it. To create a user-defined constant, follow the procedure below

- Start with the keyword "Const"
- Indicate a name for the variable
- After the name, use the keyword "As"
- Specify the Data Type for the variable depending on the value you wish to assign to it
- Equals to "=" sign
- The value you wish to assign to in the end

USING ASSIGNMENTS STATEMENTS

Assignments statements are VBA instructions that are used for mathematical evaluation and also for assigning the result to a variable or an object. The assignment statement allows the value of the expression on the right side of the equal sign to be stored in the variable indicated on the left side of the equal sign. The following codes are an example of the assignment statements

```
x = 3
```

```
x = x + 3
```

```
x = (y * 4) / (z * 2)
```

```
HouseCost = 395000
```

```
FileOpen = True
```

```
Range("TheYear").Value = 2021
```

THE EQUAL SIGN

The equal sign in the assignment statement is very important and it uses the equal sign as an operator. When the assignment statement is executed, it increases the value of z by 1. In a nutshell, if z is 14, then while executing to it, z is increased to 15

SMOOTH OPERATORS

Operators are very important while using the VBA. There are several operators apart from the equal sign. These operators are applicable in worksheet formulas

The operators are listed below

Arithmetic Operators

OPERATORS	OPERATOR SYMBOLS
Addition	+
Multiplication	*
Division	/
Subtraction	-
Exponentiation	^
String concatenation	&
Integer division	\

Logical Operators

OPERATORS	FUNCTIONS
Not	Carry out logical negation on an expression
And	Carry out logical conjunction on two expression
Or	Carry out logical disjunction on two expressions
Xor	Carry out logical exclusion on two expression
Eqv	To carry out logical equivalence on two expressions
Imp	To carry out logical implication on two expression

WORKING WITH ARRAYS

Arrays are types of variables that are used to store lists of data of the same type. To refer to a particular variable in the array, you need to use the array name and the index number in parenthesis. When you learn the VBA array, you get to benefit from the points listed below

- It allows you to group data that are related and also make the manipulation of data easier

- It makes the process of getting information from data easier

- It makes coding more readable and easier to maintain

- It allows you to increase the pace or speed of your VBA application

DECLARING ARRAYS

Declaring the array is just the same way as declaring the variables and the reason is that, the array is the same as the variable.

- Use the keyword Dim or Public statement in the starting
- Indicate or specify the numbers of elements in the array i.e, specify the index number, the keyword, and the last index number inside a parenthesis

The example below shows how to declare an array of 100 integers

Dim MyArray (1 to 20) As Integer

ONE DIMENSIONAL ARRAY

This is an array that has all the elements are contained in a single row or column. A good example is listing of some numbers. In the example below, let's declare a array by listing out some numbers using the codes below

```
Sub StaticArray_Ex()

 Dim x(1 To 5) As Integer

 x(1) = 10

 x(2) = 40

 x(3) = 50

 x(4) = 60

 x(5) = 80

 Range("A1").Value = x(1)

 Range("A2").Value = x(2)
```

```
Range("A3").Value = x(3)

Range("A4").Value = x(4)

Range("A5").Value = x(5)

End Sub
```

The result of the codes above are shown in the image below

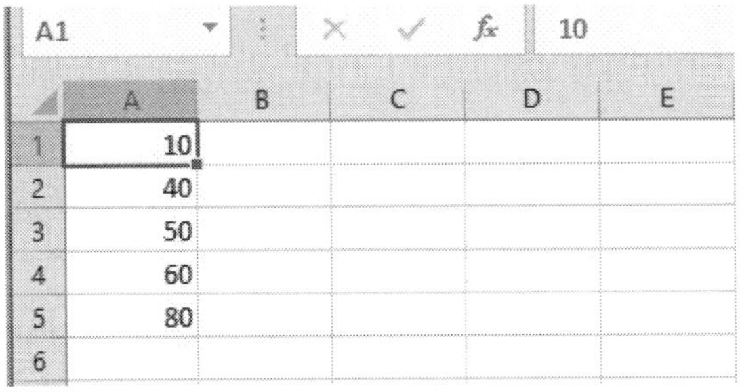

MULTIDIMENSIONAL ARRAYS

Multi-dimensional arrays are arrays that contain more than one dimension, they usually contain two or three dimensions.

The following example declares the multidimension array

```
Sub Populate2D()

'declare the 2D array

   Dim intA(2, 3) As Integer

'declare variables

   Dim rw As Integer

   Dim col As Integer

'populate the array

   intA(0, 0) = 45

   intA(0, 1) = 55
```

```
  intA(0, 2) = 23
  intA(0, 3) = 64
  intA(1, 0) = 65
  intA(1, 1) = 70
  intA(1, 2) = 75
  intA(1, 3) = 67
  intA(2, 0) = 85
  intA(2, 1) = 90
  intA(2, 2) = 78
  intA(2, 3) = 100
'loop through the array and populate Excel
  For rw = 0 To 2
    For col = 0 To 2
      Cells(rw + 1, col + 1).Value = intA(rw, col)
    Next col
  Next rw
End Sub
```

C5

	A	B	C	D	E	F
1	45	55	23	60		
2	65	70	75	80		
3	85	90	78	100		
4						
5						
6						

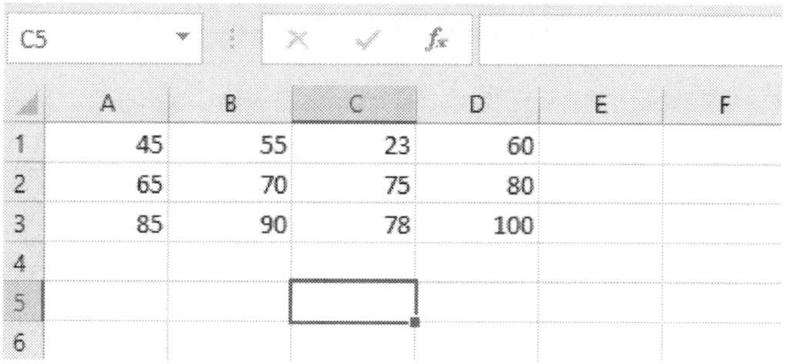

DYNAMIC ARRAYS

The dynamic array is an array that allows the user to resize the array and add more values to the array while the code is running. The dynamic array comes in handy when the user does not know the exact size of the array at design time. Before the dynamic array can be used, you must use the ReDim statement to define the initial numbers of the elements in the array e.g **ReDim arValues(3)**

To create a dynamic array in a VBA, follow the steps below

- Define the subprocedure

- Declare the array with its name

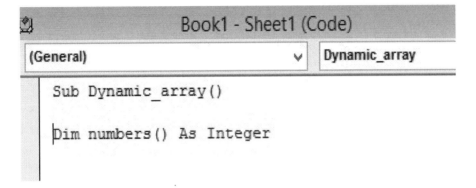

- Use the ReDim statement to specify the initial number of elements the array can hold

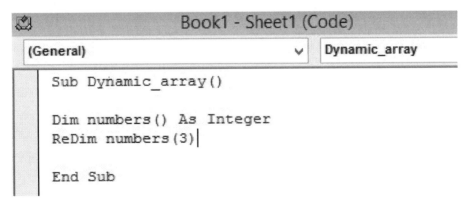

- Input the specified values in the codes

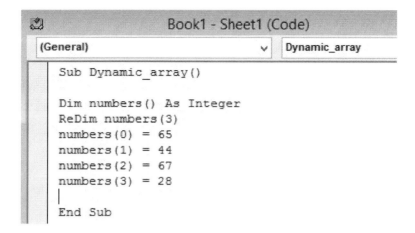

- Assign the values to the ranges in sheet 1

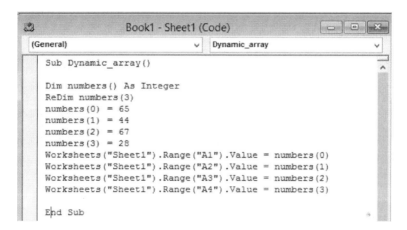

- Finally, run the code by using the Run button or keyboard shortcut F5, and the result be displayed as shown in the image below

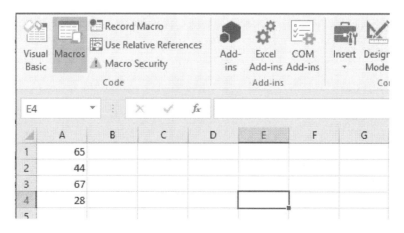

CHAPTER TWENTY-TWO

WORKING WITH RANGE OBJECT

In chapter three of this book, we briefly discuss the range object as the last in the Excel Model hierarchy that represents cells, rows, columns, selections of cells with contiguous blocks of cells, or 3-D ranges contained in the Worksheet.

To work well with the Range objects, you must have a clear understanding of how to work with the three main parts of a reference to Excel's VBA Range object and they are briefly explained below

- **Object Qualifier**: The object qualifier is used for referencing the object i.e., it helps to indicate the worksheet or workbook being referred
- **Property: This is what stores information about the object in the worksheet or workbook**
- **Method:** This is the action that will be executed by the object. The Range object can execute actions such as copied, pasted, selected, cleared, sorted, etc.

By referring to a cell or range of cells in Excel, you can perform the tasks stated below

- Reading the value from the range
- Entering a value into the range
- Changing the format of the range objects

When referring to a Range object, the address must be surrounded by a double quote e.g.

("A2, D5")

In case the Range carries a name, all you need to do is enclose the name with double quotes too e.g.

Range ("GroceryList")

You can also refer to a range that is outside the active cell. All that is needed to do is qualifying the range reference with the name of the worksheet from the active workbook e.g

Worksheets ("Sheet 3"). Range (A5, B7)

To refer to a range in a different workbook, you can use an expression such as this

Workbooks ("Payroll.xlsx").Worksheets ("Sheet"). Range ("A2, D5")

To refer to an entire row in a Range object, use the format of the expression below

Range ("4:4)

To refer also to a column, use the expression below

Range ("F: F)

REFERRING TO EXCEL RANGE OBJECT

In this section, we will be talking about some of the ways to refer to a range in Excel. Below are some of the various ways to refer to a range object

THE CELLS PROPERTY

The Cell property is all the cells of the specified range objects, which can be a worksheet or a range of cells.

The Cells property uses two arguments, which involve a row number and a column number. You can also refer to the column using letters. The sample below shows the syntax that is used to refer to cell C2 on Sheet 3

Worksheets ("Sheet3"). Cells (2, 3)

You can as well use the Cells property to refer to a multiple-cell range. The example below shows the syntax to be used

Range (Cells(1, 2), Cells (5, 7)

THE OFFSET PROPERTY

Another way to refer to a range object in Excel is the Offset property. The Offset property is used with the Range property to specify a new location and the new location is based on cells that are specified.   Just like the Cells property, the Offset property uses two arguments; the first argument is the number of rows to offset and the second argument is the number of columns to offset.

The following is the syntax for the Offset property

`Range. Offset (Rowoffset, Columnoffset)`

The syntax below refers to a cell one row below cell A1 and two columns to the right of cell A1

`Range ("A1). Offset(1, 2)`

The Offset property also uses negative arguments. A negative row offset refers to a row above the range while a negative column offset refers to a column to the left of the range. The syntax is shown below

`Range ("C2"). Offset ( -1, -2)`

THE RANGE OBJECT PROPERTIES

The Range object has a lot of properties and here in this section, I will be explaining some of the commonly used properties in Range

THE VALUE PROPERTY

The Value property is the property used in the range object to assign a value to a specific range. This is a read-write property that allows you to either read or change a value in the range objects.

Use the following codes to assign value to the Range object using the value property

`Sub Value()`

`Range("A1:C4").Value = "Exel Champs"`

366

End Sub

The result of the VBA code is shown in the picture below

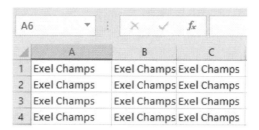

Use the codes below to display the value represented in cell A1

Sub Value()

MsgBox Worksheets("Sheet1").Range("A1").Value

End Sub

The result of the VBA codes is shown below

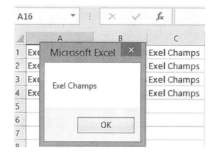

THE TEXT PROPERTY

The Text property is a read-only string that returns a string that represents the text that is displayed in a cell. The Text property returns Null if the range includes more than one cell. The statement below displays a message box that contains the text in cell A1

Sub Text()

MsgBox Worksheets("Sheet1").Range("A1").Text

End Sub

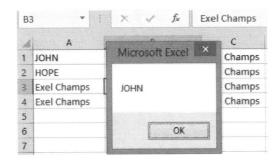

THE COUNT PROPERTY

The Count property is a read-only property that counts or returns the number of cells within a range including the nonblank cells. To count the number of cells within a cell range, use the following VBA codes or statement

Sub Count()

MsgBox Worksheets("Sheet1").Range("A1:C4").Count

End Sub

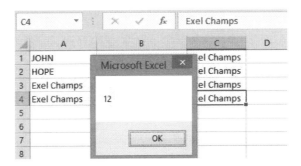

THE COLUMN AND ROW PROPERTIES

The Column property is a read-only property that returns the column number of a cell within a cell range. To return the column number of cell C4 within the cell range, use the following VBA codes or statement

Sub Colunm()

MsgBox Worksheets("Sheet1").Range("C3").Column

End Sub

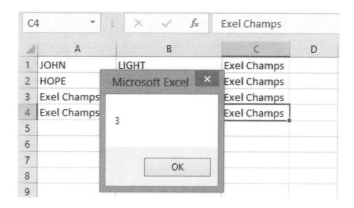

The Row property is also a read-only property that returns the row number of a cell within a cell range. To return the row number of cell B2 within the cell range, use the following statement

Sub Colunm()

MsgBox Worksheets("Sheet1").Range("B2").Row

End Sub

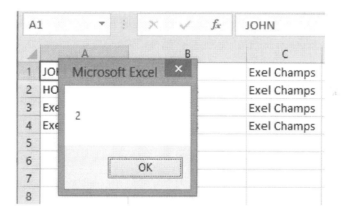

THE ADDRESS PROPERTY

The Address property is also a read-only property that displays the cell address of a Range object as absolute reference. The absolute reference uses a dollar sign before the column letter and before the row number. To get the address property of the Range object, use the following statement and the message box will be displayed indicating the address of the range object

```
Sub Address()

MsgBox Range(Cells(1,1), Cells(5,5) .Address

End Sub
```

THE HASFORMULA PROPERTY

This is a read-only property that returns when a single cell in the range has a formula and returns false when a cell does not have a formula. When the range has more than one cell, the HasFormula property returns TRUE provided all the cells are TRUE but returns FALSE when all the cell do not contain a formula. This property returns Null if there is a combination of formulas and non-formula in the range.

```
Sub HasFormula()

Dim FormulaTest As Variant

FormlaTest = Range("A1:C5").HasFormula

End Sub
```

THE FONT PROPERTY

The Font property returns a font object within the Range object in Excel. The Font property allows you to access a lot of other properties such as color property, bold property, application property, italic property, themeColor property, fontStyle properties, etc.

With the following statements, the Font property uses the bold and color properties

```vba
Sub Font()

Range("A1:C4").Font.Color = vbRed

End Sub
```

```vba
Sub Bold()

Range("A1").Font.Bold = True

End Sub
```

The result of the statements above are shown in the image below

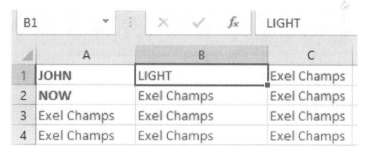

THE INTERIOR PROPERTY

This is another property that returns the interior of a specified object. This type of property works the same as the Font.

The statement below changes the Color property of the Interior object in the Range object

```vba
Sub SetColor()

Worksheets("Sheet1").Range("A1").Interior.ColorIndex = 8 ' Cyan

End Sub
```

The result is shown in the image below

	A	B	C	D
1	JOHN	LIGHT	Exel Champs	
2	NOW	Exel Champs	Exel Champs	
3	Exel Champs	Exel Champs	Exel Champs	
4	Exel Champs	Exel Champs	Exel Champs	
5				

THE FORMULA PROPERTY

This is a read and writes property that returns a formula in a cell. With this property, you can either view or insert a formula in a cell. While using the Formula property, keep these points in mind

- The value of the formula must start and end in a quotation mark
- The formula string must start with an equal sign after the first quotation mark

Let's use the following statement to input a SUM formula into cell A5

Sub Formula_Property()

Worksheets("Sheet1").Range("A5").Formula = "=SUM(A1:A4)"

End Sub

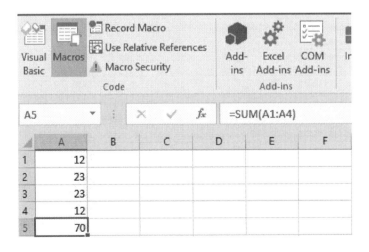

THE NUMBER FORMAT PROPERTY

The NumberFormat property is a read and write property that sets or returns the number format for a particular object in VBA. Let's use the following statement to change the number format of cell A4 to percentage with one decimal place

Sub NumberFormat()

Worksheets("Sheet1").Range("A4").NumberFormat = "0.0%"

End Sub

A4			⊗ ✓ fx	1200%	
	A	B	C	D	E
1	12				
2	23				
3	23				
4	1200.0%				
5	70				

THE RANGE OBJECT METHODS

As earlier said in this chapter, a method is an action that will be executed by the object. The Range object has a lot of methods to execute but for this study, we will be pointing out some of the most commonly used Range object methods

THE SELECT METHOD

The Select method is used to select or highlight a range of cells. The following statement will be used to highlight a range of cell on the Excel worksheet

Sub SelectCell()

Worksheets("Sheet1").Range("A1:B5").Select

End Sub

The result of the statement is shown below

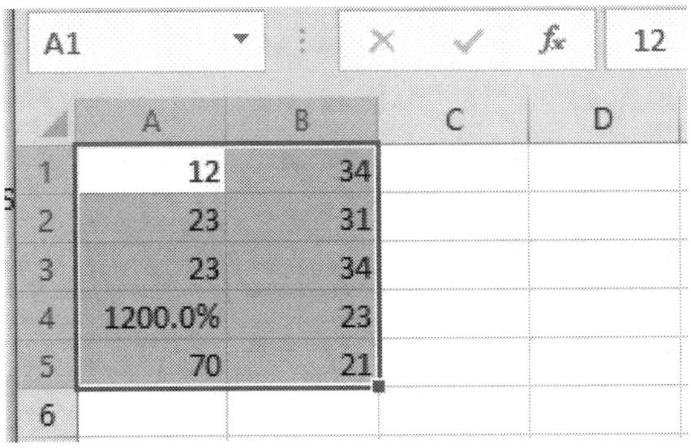

THE COPY AND PASTE METHODS

The Copy and Paste method allow you to copy a range of cells and then paste it into the worksheet. Let's use the statements below to copy the range A1:B5 and then paste it to cell D1 in the same worksheet

Sub SelectCell()

Worksheets("Sheet1").Range("A1:B5").Copy Range("D1")

End Sub

The result of the VBA statement is displayed in the image below

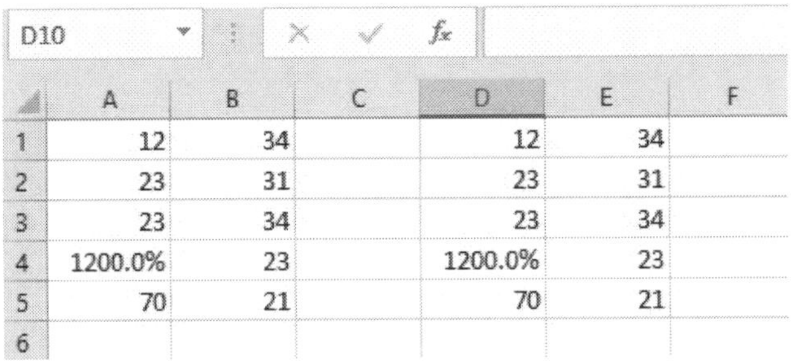

THE CLEAR METHOD

The Clear method is used to delete all the contents within a range including the cell formatting. To clear a range of cells, use the VBA statement below

Sub ClearContent()

Worksheets("Sheet1").Range("A1").Clear

End Sub

The result of the VBA statement is displayed in the image below

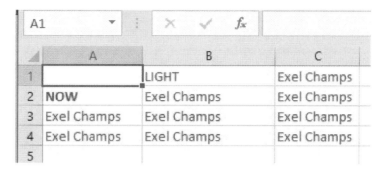

THE DELETE METHOD

The Delete method is used for deleting a range and move the remaining cells to fill up the range that was deleted. The following statement can be used to delete range cell A1:B1

Sub DeleteContent()

Worksheets("Sheet1").Range("A1:B1").Delete

End Sub

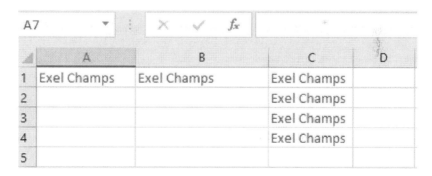

CHAPTER TWENTY-THREE

THE VBA AND WORKSHEET FUNCTIONS

WHAT IS A FUNCTION?

A function is a built-in formula in Excel that is specifically created for carrying out mathematical, statistical, and logical operations. A function is also a group of reusable codes and can be called anywhere in your program. Here in VBA, there are three ways you get to derive your function

- VBA built-in function
- Worksheet function provided by Excel
- Custom function; this can be created or written by you or someone else

Now let's take these functions by one and see how we can make the best use of the functions in VBA

USING THE BUILT-IN FUNCTIONS IN VBA

The VBA has so many built-in functions and these functions are entered in Excel's programming environment called Visual Basic for Application (VBA). Briefly, we will be going through some of the examples of the built-in function in the VBA and they are as follow

DISPLAYING THE SYSTEM DATE OR TIME

Here, we will be using the VBA's Date function to display the current system date in a message box. To get this done, use the statement below

```
Sub ShowDate()

Dim ShowDate As Date

ShowDate = Date

MsgBox (ShowDate)

End Sub
```

In case you want to get system time and date at the same time, use the statement below

Sub ShowDate()

MsgBox (NOW)

End Sub

FINDING A STRING LENGTH

To find the length of a string, the VBA uses the LEN function which returns the length of the text string. To find the length of the string in cell A4, use the following procedures or statement

Sub LENGTH()

Dim L As String

L = Range("A4")

L = Len("A4")

Range("B1").Value = L

End Sub

The table below shows the result of the statement used in the VB Editor

	A	B	C	D
1	passiion	4		
2	diety			
3	hatred			
4	love			
5				

IDENTIFYING THE TYPE OF A SELECTED OBJECT

To identify the type of selected object on the worksheet, the VBA uses the TypeName function. The TypeName function can identify the selection of the objects in the worksheet to be a range, rectangle, ChatArea, etc. To identify the type of selected object in the worksheet, use the following procedure

Sub ShowSelectionType()

Dim SelType As String

SelType = TypeName(Selection)

MsgBox SelType

End Sub

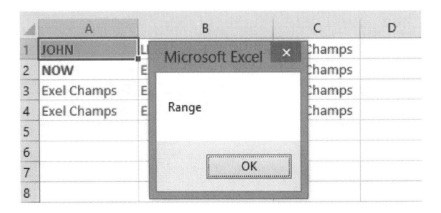

THE VBA FUNCTION THAT DOES MORE THAN JUST RETURN A VALUE

There are some VBA functions that not only can they return a value, they also have some other benefits that come in handy when dealing with the VBA. Below are these functions

- **MsgBox:** This function displays a dialog box that contains a message and a button. Also, the function brings a code that displays the button the users are to click on
- **InputBox:** This function pops up a dialog box that requires the user to put in a piece of information. Whatever is inputted into the dialog box by the user is returned
- **Shell:** This function is used to execute another program. It returns the task ID of the other program.

COMMONLY USED BUILT-IN FUNCTIONS IN VBA

Like I said at the beginning of this chapter that VBA has a lot of built-in functions. So, we will be mentioning some of the most common built-in functions and they are as follows

VBA MESSAGE FUNCTIONS

Functions	Uses
InputBox	This shows a dialog box instructing the user to input
MsgBox	This shows a modal message box

VBA TEXT FUNCTIONS

Function	Uses
Format	This function applies a format to an expression and returns the result as a string
InStr	This returns the position of a substring
InStrrev	This function returns the position of a substring within a string searching from right to the left
Left	This returns a substring from the start of a provided string
Len	This returns the length of a provided string
LCase	This converts a supplied string to lower case
Ltrim	This removes leading spaces from a supplied string
Mid	This returns a substring from the middle of the supplied string
Replace	This function replaces a substring within a supplied text string

Right	This returns a substring from the end of a provided string
RTim	This removes trailing spaces from a given string
Space	This creates a string that consists of a specified number of spaces
StrComp	This compares two string and returns an integer showing the result of the comparison
StrConv	This converts a string into a specified format
String	This creates a string consisting of several repeated characters
StrReverse	This reverses a supplied string
Trim	This helps to remove leading and trailing spaces from a supplied string
UCase	This converts a supplied string to upper case letters

VBA INFORMATION FUNCTIONS

Functions	Uses
IsArray	This tests whether a supplied variable is an array or not
IsDate	This is checks if a supplied expression is a date
IsEmpty	This checks if the supplied variant is empty
IsError	This tests if a supplied expression has an error or not
IsMissing	This checks if an optional argument to a procedure is missing
IsNull	This tests if the expression supplied is Null
IsNumeric	This tests if the expression given is numerical
IsObject	This tests if a supplied variable represents an object value

VBA ERROR HANDLING FUNCTIONS

FUNCTION	USES
CVErr	This function produces an Error data type for a supplied error code
Error	This returns the error message that is corresponding to the error code supplied

VBA PROGRAM FLOW FUNCTIONS

FUNCTIONS	USES
Choose	This selects a value from a list of arguments
IIf	This function assesses an expression and returns one of the two values,
Switch	This evaluates a list of Boolean expression and returns a value associated with the first true expression

VBA CONVERSION FUNCTION

FUNCTTION	USES
Asc	This returns an integer representing the code for a supplied character
CBool	This converts an expression to Boolean data type
CCur	This converts an expression to a Currency data type
CByte	This converts an expression to a Byte data type
CDate	This changes an expression or statement to a Date data type
CDbl	This converts an expression or statement to a Date data type
CDec	This converts an expression to a Decimal data type
Chr	This returns the character corresponding to a supplied character code
Cint	This converts an expression to an Integer data type

CIng	This changes a statement to a Long data type
CSng	This changes a statement to a single data type
CStr	This converts an expression to a Variant data type
CVar	This converts an expression to a Variant data type
FormatCurrency	This function applies a currency format to an expression and returns the result as a string
FormatDate Time	
	This function applies a number format to an expression and returns the result as a string
FormatNumber	This applies a number format to an expression and returns the result as a string
FormatPercent	This applies percentage format to an expression or number and returns the value as a string

Hex	This converts a number value to hexadecimal notation and returns the result as a string
Oct	This converts a number value to octal notation and returns the result as a string
Str	This converts a numeric value to a string

VBA DATE AND TIME FUNCTION

FUNCTIONS	USES
Date	This returns the current date
DateAdd	This adds a time interval to a date or time
DateDiff	This returns the number of an interval between two dates or times
DatePart	This returns a part of supplied date or time; this can be a month, year, or day
DateSerial	This returns a date from a supplied year, month, and day number

DateValue	This returns a date from a string representing a date or time
Day	This returns the day number from 1 to 31 from the date supplied
Hour	This returns the hour component of a supplied time
Minute	This returns the minute component of a supplied time
Month	This returns the month number starting from 1 to 12 from the date given
MonthName	This function returns the month name starting from 1 to 12 for the month given
Now	This function returns the current date and time.
Second	This function returns the second component of the time supplied.
Time	This returns the current time
Timer	This is a function that calculates the number of seconds that have gone since midnight

TimeSerial	This returns a Time from a supplied hour, minute, and second
Timevalue	This returns a time from a string representing time and date
Weekday	This returns the weekday name for a supplied integer ranging from 1 to 7
Year	This returns the year of the given date

VBA MATH AND TRIG FUNCTION

FUNCTIONS	USES
Abs	This returns the absolute value of a number
Atn	This calculates the arctangent of the number supplied
Cos	This function calculates the cosine of a supplied angle
Exp	This function calculates the value of e^x for a supplied value of x.

Fix	This function shortens a number to an integer rounding negative numbers to zero
Int	This function returns the integer portion of a number i.e rounding negative numbers away from zero
Log	This function calculates the natural logarithm of the number given
Rnd	This function returns a random number between 0 and 1
Round	This rounds a number to a specified number of decimal places
Sgn	This function returns an integer that represents the arithmetic sign of a number
Sin	This calculates the sine of a supplied angle
Tan	This function calculates the tangent of a supplied angle
Sqr	This calculates the square root of a number

VBA FINANCIAL FUNCTIONS

FUNCTIONS	USES
DDB	This function returns or calculates the depreciation of an asset over a given period using the Double Declining Balance Method
FV	This function returns the future value of a loan or investment
IPmt	This function calculates the interest part of a payment, during a specific time for a loan or investment
IRR	This function estimates the internal rate of return fie series of periodic cash flow
MIRR	This calculates the modified internal rate of return for a series of periodic cash flows
NPer	This returns the number of periods for a loan or investment
NPV	This calculates the net present value of an investment

PPmt	This calculates the principal part of payment over a given period
Pmt	This calculates the constant periodic payments for a loan or investment
PV	This calculates the present value of a loan or investment
Rate	This calculates the interest rate per period for a loan or investment
SLN	This returns the straight-line depreciation of an asset for a single period
SYD	This returns the sum-of-year digit depreciation over a given period in the lifespan of an asset

VBA ARRAY FUNCTIONS

FUNCTIONS	USES
Array	This function creates an array that contains a supplied set of values

Filter	This returns a subset of a supplied string array that is based on the criteria provided
Join	This function joins two or more substrings into a single string
LBound	This returns the lowest subscript for a dimension of an array
Split	This function separates text string into several substrings
UBound	This returns the highest subscripts for a dimension of an array.

VBA FILE MANAGEMENT FUNCTIONS

FUNCTIONS	USES
CurDir	This function returns the current path as s string
Dir	This function return s the first file or directory name that matches a specific pattern and attributes
FileAttr	This function returns the mode of a file that is opened using the Open statement

FileDate Time	This function returns the last modified date and time of a given file, directory, or folder
FileLen	This function returns the length of a supplied file, directory, or folder
GetAttr	This function returns an integer that represents the attributes or features of a supplied file, directory, or folder

USING THE WORKSHEET FUNCTION IN VBA

You may not always find the function you need in the VBA built-in functions and fortunately, you can use the functions available in the Excel worksheet in the VBA procedures to execute any operations. The functions in the Excel worksheet can only be accessed in the Worksheet Function object, which is contained in the Application object. Below is a perfect example of how to use Excel's SUM function in a VBA statement

Total = Application.worksheetFunction.Sum (Range ("A1:A4))

THE WORKSHEET FUNCTION EXAMPLES

Here in this section, let's quickly go through how to use the worksheet functions in the VBA procedures. Below are the examples

FINDING THE MAXIMUM VALUE IN A RANGE

The VBA codes below is an example of how the Excel's Max worksheet function is used in the VBA procedure to find the maximum value from range A1:A4 and returned in cell B1

```vba
Sub ShowMax()

Dim maxvalue As Long

maxvalue = Application.WorksheetFunction.Max(Range("A1:A4").Value)

Range("B1").Value = maxvalue

End Sub
```

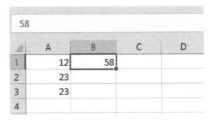

FINDING THE SUM VALUE IN A RANGE

The VBA codes below is an example of how the Excel's Average worksheet function is used in the VBA procedure to find the sum value from range A1:A3 and returned in cell B1

```vba
Sub ShowSum()

Dim averagevalue As Long

sumvalue = Application.WorksheetFunction.SUM(Range("A1:A3").Value)

Range("B1").Value = sumvalue

End Sub
```

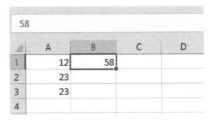

FINDING THE PRODUCT VALUE IN A RANGE

The VBA codes below is an example of how the Excel's worksheet function is used in the VBA procedure to find the sum value from range A1:A3 and returned in cell B1

```
Sub ShowProduct()

Dim productvalue As Long

productvalue = Application.WorksheetFunction.Product(Range("A1:A3").Value)

Range("B1").Value = productvalue

End Sub
```

	A	B	C	D	E
	6348				
1	12	6348			
2	23				
3	23				
4					
5					

INPUTTING THE WORKSHEET FUNCTIONS IN THE VBA MODULES

First and foremost, if you wish to enter the worksheet functions in the VBA codes, you will need to enable Auto List Members Option in the Visual Basic Editor. The Auto List Member option gives a drop-down of all the Worksheet functions that can be used. In the VB editor, input Application. Worksheefunction preceded by a period, and a list of all Excel function will be displayed to pick anyone to use

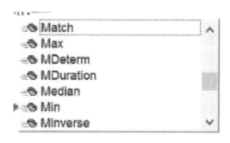

USING CUSTOM FUNCTIONS

The Custom function is the third category of the functions that can be used in the VBA procedures. The Custom function is also referred to as the User-Defined Function (UDF). With the Custom function, you can create any macro that is accessed and used within the worksheet. In a nutshell, you can create any function with the custom function and by implication, you are not restricted to the functions provided by Excel only.

To create a custom function, you must determine what information the function must return and what information should be provided to make the function produce the desired result.

The custom function starts with **Function** and end with **End Function**

Here is an example of what custom function looks like;

```
Function NumXs(rng As Range) As Integer
Dim iCnt As Integer
Dim c As Range
Dim sTemp As String
Dim J As Integer
iCnt = 0
For Each c In rng.Cells
  sTemp = c.Value
  For J = 1 To Len(sTemp)
    If Mid(sTemp,J,1)= "X" Then iCnt = iCnt + 1
  Next J
Next c
NumXs = iCnt
End Function
```

In the next chapter of this book, I will be discussing how to create functions using the custom functions.

CHAPTER TWENTY-FOUR

THE USER DEFINED FUNCTION (UDF) IN EXCEL VBA

The User-defined function or custom function is a function that is created and provided by the user of a program to do any kind of operations on the VBA. The custom function allows you to execute operations that cannot be executed using the Excel worksheet functions and the built-in VBA functions.

The following rules must be followed when using the user-defined function

- A custom function must start with a Function and end with an End Function
- The name of the function cannot have spaces in it
- The function name must not carry the existing function.
- You can also use an underscore if you wish to separate words e.g Get_Value

WHY SHOULD USE THE USER DEFINED FUNCTION

There are so many benefits to the use of user-defined functions and some of them are explained below

- The User-defined function is created when there are no existing built-in functions that will execute the task
- The User-defined function can be used to replace the Sub procedures. The sub procedures do not return a value and they are not dynamic, therefore, there is a need to create a custom function
- The User-defined function is used to create an advanced array of formulas and matrix functions
- With the custom function, you can simplify formulas that may be too long

LIMITATIONS OF USER DEFINED FUNCTIONS

Whatever has advantages, also have disadvantages and however, the user-defined function is not an exception and they are as follow

- The user-defined functions cannot be recorded like the Excel macro
- The user-defined functions cannot alter or change the structure or format of a worksheet or cell
- The user-defined functions find it difficult to track errors
- When you add the user defined functions to your workbook, the macro flag is triggered
- The user-defined functions cannot place a value apart from the cell containing the formula
- Calling the function or macro from the user-defined functions are liable to encounter the limitations of user-defined functions
- The user-defined functions in VBA are very much slower than the functions compiled in C++ OR FORTRAN

WRITING FUNCTIONS

To write a function in Excel VBA, follow the following procedures

- Start by writing function in the VBA modules; this helps to tell the VBA that the code is not a subroutine but a function
- What follows next is the name of the function that will be used in the worksheet. e.g COUNTIF.
- What comes next is adding of comment; any codes written in green is a comment and it is introduced by adding an apostrophe to the start of the codes
- The next line of the code declares the variable to any data type. The variable is where the value of the data is being analyzed into the formula
- Then in the Function procedure, type in the formula codes and then close it with the End Function

ARGUMENTS IN A USER DEFINED FUNCTION IN VBA

A FUNCTION WITH NO ARGUMENT

There are so many functions that do not use arguments of which some of them are NOW, RAND, TODAY, etc.

The codes below will give you the name of the file without using any arguments, as the result it needs to display requires no arguments

```
Function myPath() As String

Dim myLocation As String

Dim myName As String

myLocation = ActiveWorkbook.FullName

myName = ActiveWorkbook.Name

If myLocation = myName Then

myPath = "File is not saved yet."

Else

myPath = myLocation

End If

End Function
```

The function above will return the name and location of the file as shown in the image below

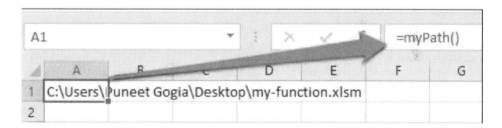

While using the Excel built-in functions, ensure to include a set of empty parentheses, to avoid Excel interpreting the function as a named range

A FUNCTION WITH ONE ARGUMENT

There are also a lot of functions that require just one argument, and one of them is the function of extracting an address or URL from a hyperlink.

The codes below return the address of the hyperlink with just an argument

```
Function giveMeURL(rng As Range) As String

On Error Resume Next

giveMeURL = rng.Hyperlinks(1).Address

End Function
```

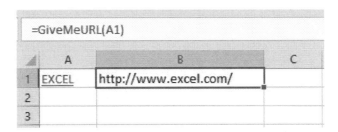

A FUNCTION WITH MULIPIE ARGUMENTS

The VBA custom functions can also take multiple arguments just like the worksheet functions

The code below will remove a letter from a text string and keep the remaining part

```
Function removeFirstC(rng As String, cnt As Long) As String

removeFirstC = Right(rng, Len(rng) - cnt)

End Function
```

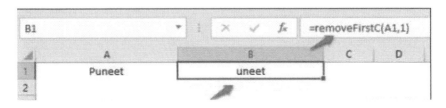

Here in the function above, two arguments are involved to execute its operations

- **Rng**: This is the argument that specifies the cell to remove the first character of the text.
- **Cnt**: This is the argument that indicates the count of the characters to remove

CHAPTER TWENTY-FIVE

ERROR HANDLING TECHNIQUES

No matter how intelligent you are on the VBA, you will be faced with errors at one point or the other. Therefore, it is pertinent to learn how to write specific codes on how to handle errors when they occur and handle them as they come

Error handling is the process of anticipating, detecting, and proffering solutions to an error that occurs while the VBA application is running. This process occurs when the codes are being written before the occurrence of any error.

To have a better understanding of error handling, we must first have a deep understanding of the different types of error handling

TYPES OF ERROR

There are four types of error in Excel VBA

- Syntax errors
- Compilation errors
- Runtime errors
- Logical errors

The Syntax Error: The syntax error occurs when the VBA finds abnormalities with the syntax in the code. The error can be misspelling, missing, or incorrect punctuations. The VBA Editor recognizes syntax errors with red highlighting and when this is run, the VB Editor displays a message box notifying you of the syntax errors after entering a line code

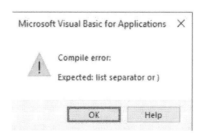

To turn on or off the Syntax error dialog

- Go to **Tools** and click on **Options**
- Then go to **Editor** and click on **Auto Syntax Check** to either enable or disable

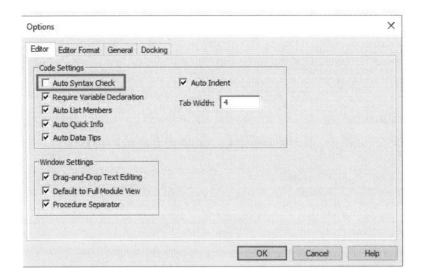

Compilation Errors: The compilation error occurs when something required for the code to run is missing. The following are good examples of compilation error

- **If** statement without corresponding **End If** statement
- **For** without **Next**
- **Select** without **End Select**
- Calling a Sub or Function that does not exist
- Calling a Sub or Function with the wrong parameter
- Giving a Sub or Function the same name as a module
- Variables not declared (Option Explicit must be present at the top of the module)

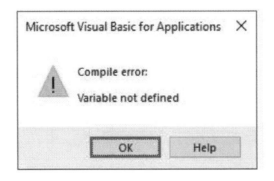

Runtime Errors: The runtime error occurs when an impossible mathematical statements or terms are present in a statement. This error occurs when the code is running. When the Runtime error occurs, the code will stop and show the error dialog box

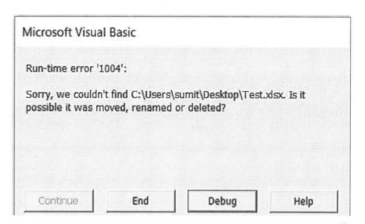

The following are other examples of runtime errors

- A database not being available
- The user entering invalid data
- A cell containing text instead of a number

The Logical Error: The logic error occurs when there is a mistake in the logic that drives the script in the VBA and causes you not to get the expected result. The logical error is the most difficult error to rectify, and this will error will make the code stop working but will lead to a wrong answer. The logical error can occur

- When one uses the wrong variable in the code
- When runs into an endless loop

THE ON ERROR STATEMENT IN VBA

THE VBA On Error statement is a statement that is used for error handling. This statement tells the VBA what actions to take when faced with errors. There are four different methods to use this statement

- On Error GoTo 0
- On Error Resume Next

- On Error GoTo (Label)
- On Error GoTo -1

ON ERROR GOTO 0

The On Error GoTo 0 is the default settings in VBA. This statement resets the code on the line that causes an error and show a message that indicates the error

ON ERROR RESUME NEXT

The On Error Resume next ignores errors encountered in the VBA and continues to run the code. One of the limitations of this error handling method is that you may not be able to see the errors corrected or that are needed to be corrected.

ON ERROR GOTO (LABEL)

The On Error Goto (Label) is another method of error handling that tells the VBA what to do when your code encounters an error. This sends an error that occurs to a specific label so that the code will be executed.

ON ERROR GOTO -1

Unlike the other three error handling methods, the On Error Goto -1 is used to clear the current error that occurs in a code rather than setting a particular behavior.

THE ERR OBJECT

The Err Object is used to get the details of any error that occurs in a code. The Err Object has the following properties

- **Description:** This gives a short description of the error that occurs. This pops up each time an error occurs in the modules E.g Type Mismatch
- **Number:** This is the ID number that represents the error that occurs in the modules. E.g Type Mismatch is 29
- **Source**: This is the project name where the error occurs
- **HelpContext:** This is the help context id for the error in the help file

- **HelpFile:** This is the string that indicates the folder location and the file name of the help file

ERR OBJECTS METHODS

While the Err properties are concerned about showing useful information about errors, the Err Object methods are concerned about carrying out actions that help you with error handling, and of which we have the following

- Clear: This is used to clear property settings of the Err object. In other words, it clears the description and number.
- Raise: This allows you to create errors.

CHAPTER TWENTY-SIX

SIMPLE DIALOG BOXES

The Simple dialog box is an excellent alternative to a userform that is used to obtain information, clarify commands and display messages. The Simple dialog boxes are built into the VBA and help to save time because there is no need to code and also build a userform. The VBA allows access to show different kinds of dialog boxes, which can be used in replacement of a UserForm. The Simple dialog boxes are as follow

- The MsgBox function
- The InputBox function
- The GetOpenFilename method
- The GetSaveAsFilename method
- The FileDialog method

THE MsgBox FUNCTION

The MsgBox is one of the dialog boxes in Excel is used for displaying information and get some basic inputs. Each time the MsgBox is displayed, the codes in the VBA are stopped, and to continue the running process, you will need to click on any button in the MsgBox.

The MsgBox function can be used in two ways

- To show or display a message to the user
- To get a response or feedback from the user

THE ANATOMY OF A MsgBox IN EXCEL

The MsgBox in Excel has the following parts and they are as follow

- Title
- Prompt
- Button
- Close Icon

Title: This displays or shows what the message box is all about and if nothing is specified in the title, it displays the application name which is Microsoft Excel

Prompt: This is the text or message that is displayed in the message box

Buttons: These involve six different buttons setup and the default button is Ok and can be customized to button such as Yes/No, Yes/No/Cancel. Retry/Ignore, etc.

Close Icon: This is where you close the message box by clicking on the close icon

SYNTAX OF THE VBA MSGBOX FUNCTION

Just like the other VBA functions, the MsgBox function also has a syntax function that allows it to execute its operation

MSGBOX(PROMPT [, BUTTONS] [, TITLE] [, HELPFILE, CONTEXT])

- **Prompt:** This is a required argument that displays the message that is seen in the MsgBox. The prompt can use up to 1024 characters and can also be used in displaying the values of variables
- **Buttons:** This argument determines what buttons and icons are to be displayed in the MsgBox. E.g using the vbOKOnly will only display the OK button and using the vbOKCancel will display OK and Cancel buttons
- **Title:** This argument indicates what caption to be used in the message dialog box and it is displayed in the title bar of the Msgbox. In case this was not specified, the name of the application will be displayed.
- **Helpfile:** This is where you specify the help file that should be accessed when you click on the Help button. The help button only appears when you use the button code for it. while using the help file, it is needed to specify the context argument.
- **Context:** This is the numeric expression used by the Help context to assign a number to the appropriate Help topic

THE EXCEL VBA MsgBox BUTTONS CONSTANTS

Here in this section, we will be discussing the different types of button and they can be used in the VBA MsgBox

MsgBox BUTTON (vbOKOnly)

This is the MsgBox button that shows only the Ok button and this is the default MsgBox button. The example below is an image of the vbOKOnly

To get the vbOKOnly button. all you need to do is use the vbOKOnly constant

```
Sub DefaultMsgBox()

MsgBox "This is a sample box"

End Sub
```

The result of the code is seen in the image below

MsgBox BUTTONS (OK & Cancel)

This MsgBox button displays the OK and the Cancel buttons. To show this in the MsgBox, use the vbOKcancel constant as shown below

```
Sub MsgBoxOKCancel()

MsgBox "Do you wish to stop?", vbOKCancel

End Sub
```

The result of the code is seen in the image below

MsgBox BUTTONS (Abort, Retry, and Ignore)

This MsgBox button shows the Abort, Retry, and Ignore buttons. To show this in the MsgBox, use the vbAbortRetryIgnore constant as shown below

```
Sub MsgBoxAbortRetryIgnore()

MsgBox "What do you wish to do?", vbAbortRetryIgnore

End Sub
```

The result of the code is seen in the image below

MsgBox BUTTONS (Yes and No)

This MsgBox button shows the Yes and No buttons. To show this in the MsgBox, use the vbYesNo constant as shown below

```
Sub MsgBoxYesNo()

MsgBox "Should we stop?", vbYesNo

End Sub
```

The result of the code is seen in the image below

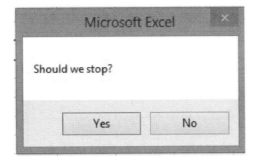

MsgBox BUTTONS (Yes, No, and Cancel)

This MsgBox button shows the Yes, No, and Cancel buttons. To show this in the MsgBox, use the vbYesNoCancel constant as shown below

```
Sub MsgBoxYesNoCancel()

MsgBox "Should we stop?", vbYesNoCancel

End Sub
```

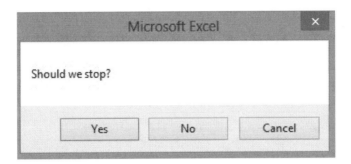

MsgBox BUTTONS (Retry and Cancel)

This MsgBox button shows the Retry and Cancel buttons. To show this in the MsgBox, use the vbRetryCancel constant as shown below

```
Sub MsgBoxRetryCancel()

MsgBox "What do you want to do now?", vbRetryCancel

End Sub
```

MsgBox BUTTONS (Help)

This MsgBox button shows the Help button. For the Help button to work, it must be used with the help and context arguments in the MsgBox functions. **To show this in the MsgBox, you can use the** vbMsgBoxHelpButton constant as written below

Sub MsgBoxRetryHelp()

MsgBox "What do you want to do next?", vbMsgBoxHelpButton

End Sub

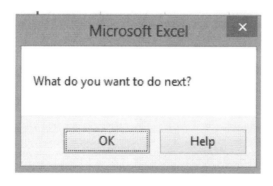

The vbMsgBoxHelpButton constant can be used with other button constants and this can be seen in the instance below

Sub MsgBoxRetryHelp()

MsgBox "What do you want to do next?", vbRetryCancel + vbMsgBoxHelpButton

End Sub

EXCEL VBA MsgBox ICON CONSTANTS

Apart from the Msg buttons, some icons can be customized and displayed in the MsgBox dialog. It can be the red critical icon or the blue information icon. Now let's have a look at these icons

MsgBox ICONS (Critical)

In the MsgBox, the vbCritical icon displays a critical message icon. To display the critical message icon in the MsgBox, use the vbCritical constant as shown below

```
Sub MsgBoxCriticalIcon()

MsgBox "This is a sample box", vbCritical

End Sub
```

You can as well add the Yes and No buttons to the vbCritical icon by using the following code

```
Sub MsgBoxCriticalIcon()
```

MsgBox "This is a sample box", vbYesNo + vbCritical

End Sub

MsgBox ICONS (Question)

In the MsgBox, the vbQuestion icon displays a question message icon. To display the question icon message in the MsgBox, use the vbquestion constant as shown below

Sub MsgBoxQuestionIcon()

MsgBox "This is a sample box", vbYesNo + vbQuestion

End Sub

MsgBox ICONS (Exclamation)

In the MsgBox, the vbExclamation icon displays a warning message icon. To display the exclamation icon message, use the vbExclamation constant as shown below

Sub MsgBoxExclamationIcon()

MsgBox "This is a sample box", vbYesNo + vbExclamation

End Sub

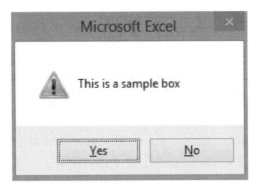

MsgBox ICONS (Information)

In the MsgBox, the vbInformation icon displays an information message icon. To display the information icon message, use the vbInformation constant as shown below

Sub MsgBoxInformationIcon()

MsgBox "This is a sample box", vbYesNo + vbInformation

End Sub

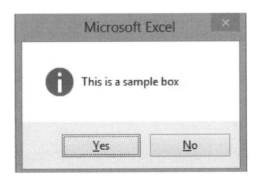

THE InputBox FUNCTION

The InputBox function is a specially designed dialog box that allows the user to enter a piece of information. This information can be displayed in form of value, text string, or a range address. The InputBox has two buttons which are Ok and Cancel. Also, the InputBox function is a good substitute for creating a Userform when you need to get only one value.

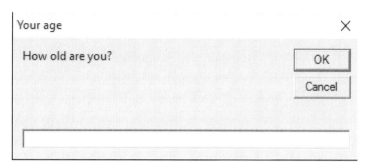

THE InputBox SYNTAX

The InputBox function uses the following arguments to execute its operation in the Excel VBA and they are as follow

The InputBox(PROMPT, [TITLE], [DEFAULT], [XPOS], [YPOS], [HELPFILE, CONTEXT])

- **Prompt(Required Argument):** This is the text displayed as the message in the dialog box and the maximum length of the prompt is up to 1024 characters, depending on the width of the characters used.
- **Title(Optional Argument):** This is the text displayed in the title bar of the dialog box. If the title is omitted, the application name is placed in the title bar.
- **Default (Optional Argument):** This is the text displayed in the text box as the default response if there is no other text provided. In case this is omitted, the text box is displayed empty.
- **Xpos (Optional Argument):** This is the position of the X-axis that represents the prompt distance from the left side of the screen horizontally. If the X pos is omitted, the input box is horizontally centered.

- **Ypos (Optional Argument):** This is the position of the Y-axis that represents the prompt distance from the left side of the screen vertically. If the Y pos is omitted, the input box is vertically centered.
- **Helpfile (Optional Argument):** This is the text that specifies the helpfile to be used in providing context-sensitive Help for the dialog box. When the help file is provided, the context must also be provided.
- **Context (Optional Argument):** This is the number that the Help context number assigned to the right Help topic by the Help author. When the context is provided, the helpfile must also be provided.

AN InputBox EXAMPLE

Let's find the area of a rectangle by getting values from the user at run time with the help of two input boxes I.e one for length and one for width using the statements below

Function findArea()

Dim Length As Double

Dim Width As Double

Length = InputBox("Enter Length ", "Enter a Number")

Width = InputBox("Enter Width", "Enter a Number")

findArea = Length * Width

End Function

- After input the code is inputted in the modules, the First input box (length) is displayed. Enter the value into the input box

- After inputting the first value, the second input box (width) is displayed

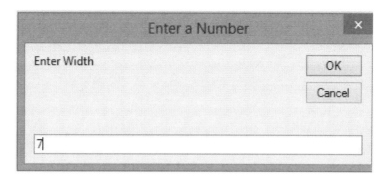

- After entering the second number, click on the OK button. The area is displayed as shown in the following image

THE GetOpenFilename METHOD

The GetOpenFileName is a method used to obtain a valid filename and its full path. This is a process of displaying a dialog box to open files using the built-in method of the Application object. This method does not really open the file specified, rather, it returns a string that contains the path and the file name selected by the user.

THE SYNTAX OF GetOpenFilename METHOD

The GetOpenFilename method uses the following arguments to execute its operations

GetOpenFilename (FILEFILTER, FILTERINDEX, TITLE, BUTTONT EXT, MULTISELECT)

- **File Filter:** This is the string that displays what type of file that should be displayed in the dialog box. For example, Excel file .xlsx.
- **File Index:** This determines the number of file filters to be displayed in the dialog box. If this argument is omitted or greater than the number of filters present, the first file filter is used.
- **Title:** This specifies the text to be displayed in the title bar of the dialog box. If this argument is omitted, the default title is used
- **Button Text:** This is used to customize the texts for the buttons (Macintosh only)
- **MultiSelect**: If TRUE, you can select multiple files to be selected. If FALSE, you can only allow a single file selection.

A GetOpenFilename EXAMPLE

Using the following statement to locate the file name

```
Sub OpenFile()

Dim A As String

A = Application.GetOpenFilename()

MsgBox A

End Sub
```

- After these codes have been compiled in the VB Editor, press the F5 function key and click on the run button and the file you wish to select will be displayed.
- Then click on Open

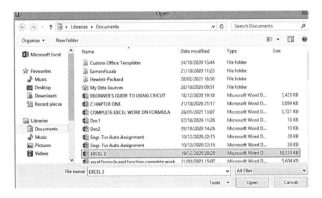

- Here, the path of the file selected will be displayed

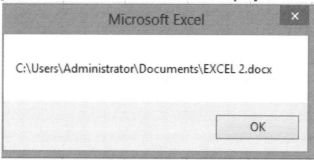

THE GetSaveAsFilename METHOD

The GetSaveAsFilename Method is a method in Excel that helps to display Save As dialog box and gets a file name from the user without having to save or open any file

THE SYNTAX OF GetOpenFilename METHOD

The GetOpenFilename method uses the following arguments to execute its operations

GetSaveAsFilename([initialFilename], [fileFilter], [filterIndex], [title], [buttonText])

- **Initial Filename:** This specifies the filename that is displayed in the File name box. When this argument is omitted, Excel uses the active workbook's name
- **File Filter:** This argument is used to determine or specify the types of files to display in the dialog box e.g Excel file .xlsx. With this argument, you can pick any from different filters to use from
- **File Index:** This argument determines the number of file filters to be displayed in the dialog box. If this argument is omitted or greater than the number of filters present, the first file filter is used.
- **Title:** This specifies the text to be displayed in the title bar of the dialog box. If this argument is omitted, the default title is used
- **Button Text:** This is used to customize the texts for the buttons (Macintosh only)

A GetOpenFilename EXAMPLE

In the example below, a dialog box will be opened asking the user to select a location to save the file. The path of the file will be displayed in cell A2. To do this, use the following code

```
Sub Example1()

Dim varResult As Variant

varResult = Application.GetSaveAsFilename

If varResult <> False Then

Cells(2, 1) = varResult

End If

End Sub
```

- After these codes have been compiled in the VB Editor, press the F5 function key and click on the run button and the file you wish to save will be displayed.
- Then click on **Save**

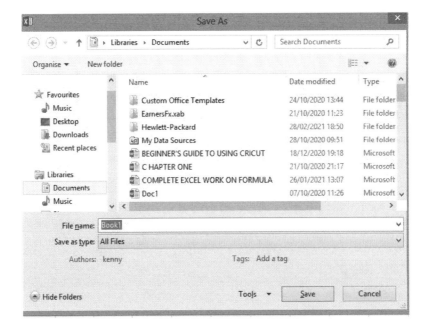

- Here in cell A2, the path of the file will be displayed

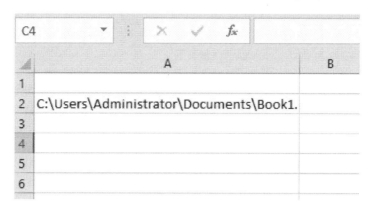

CHAPTER TWENTY-SEVEN

USERFORM BASICS

WHAT IS USERFORMS

The UserForm is a custom-built dialog box that allows the entry of data more controllable and easier to use by the users. It allows you to create a new Excel custom Window with select Form or Active X controls such as Buttons, ListBox, CheckBox, and all other controls.

WHY SHOULD YOU USE THE USERFORMS

The following are the reasons why you should use the Userforms

- The users should be able to make decisions while using the User forms that can't be captured by the limited controls available in Message or Input boxes
- The macro requires the user to make several different data entries
- The user input required is too specialized or complex for Message or Input boxes
- To restrict the choices user can make or the data they can input by establishing sophisticated or complex data validation and controlling rules
- To ensure that user can easily move a data entry without confusion

HOW TO CREATE AN EXCEL USER FORM

In case you have used the built-in UserForms and they do not meet your needs, then you can create your own UserForms and to create yours and to do this, follow the procedure below

- Open the **Visual Basic Editor** from the **Developer tab** or use **Alt + F11**
- Go to **Insert** and click on **UserForm** and the **Userform** will be displayed on the VB Editor
- You can customize the UserForm or its control

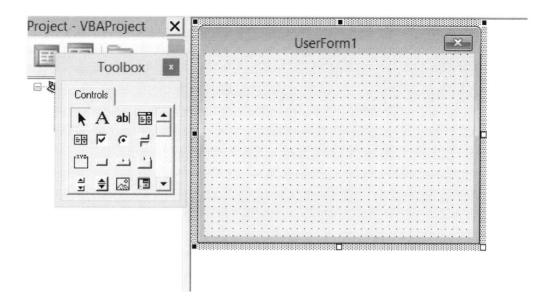

- Assign a VBA code to the Userform and then load the Userform

HOW TO INSERT A NEW USER FORM INTO THE EXCEL WORKSHEET

To insert a UserForm object into a worksheet, all you need to do is follow the steps below

- Open the **Visual Basic Editor** from the **Developer tab** or use **Alt + F11**
- Go to the **Project Explorer** and select the worksheet you wish to insert the UserForm
- Then go to **Insert and** click on **UserForm** and the UserForm will be displayed on the VB editor

ADDING CONTROLS TO A USER FORM

Provided that the UserForm has been activated, the Toolbox is displayed as shown in the image above on how to create a UserForm. The Toolbox contains the controls needed to be added to your UserForm. To add any control to the UserForm

- Select any control you want in the **Toolbox** and drag to the UserForm
- You can move or adjust the sizes to whatever you want

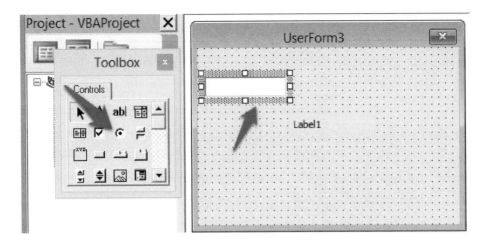

In case you open the Userform and the ToolBox does not come up, click on the **Toolbox button** in the VBE Toolbar, and automatically, the Toolbox will be displayed.

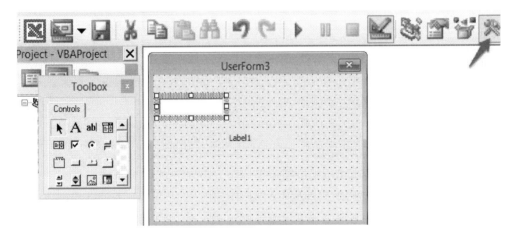

In the table below, I will quickly list all the controls in the Toolbox and their functions, though, all these functions will be explicitly explained on the next page

CONTROLS	FUNCTIONS
Label	To display texts
Textbox	To permit a user to input text

Combobox	To show or display a drop-down list
Listbox	To show a list of items
checkBox	This is used to display on/off or yes/no options
OptionButton	This is used where there are two or more group thus, allowing the user to select any option among several options
ToggleButton	This switches between on or off button
Frame	This is a container that can contain other controls
CommonButton	This is a clickable button
TabStrip	This displays tabs
MultiPage	This is a tabbed container for other objects
ScrollBar	This is a draggable bar
SpinButton	This is a clickable button that is used for changing value

Image	This control helps t
RefEdit	This control allows the user to select a range

CHANGING PROPERTIES FOR A USERFORM CONTROL

The Properties Window is always displayed on the lower-left corner of the VBE. The Properties for controls include the name, width, height, value, and caption. clicking on the **Properties Window** in the VBE Toolbar and automatically, the Properties Window. The Properties Window can be opened by will be displayed or use the **F4 keyboard shortcut.**

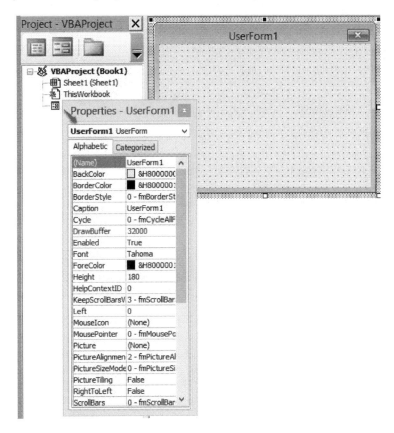

The Properties window contains two parts; the left column contains the name of the properties while the right column shows the current property setting.

NAMING OF NAME USERFORMS

The principles adhere to while naming the Sub procedures are very applicable to the UserForms. Below are the rules to consider while setting the names of your UserForm and UserForm controls

- The maximum name length is 40 characters
- The first character of the name must be a letter
- The characters apart from the first character containing letter can include letters, numbers, and underscores (_)
- The names must not include spaces, periods, mathematical operators, comparison operators, or some punctuation characters

To change the name of the UserForm, follow the procedures below

- Click on the UserForm in the Project window
- Click in the name field of the Properties Window
- Then type in the new name

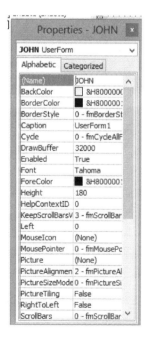

ASSIGNING THE VBA CODE TO THE USER FORM

After finishing the design on the UserForm, there is a need to create and assign macro

That will enable the UserForm to work. To do this, follow the two simple steps

- Navigate to the Code window of the UserForm (you can also use the Keyboard shortcut: F7
- Input the right code into the Code window and the code will be displayed in the worksheet

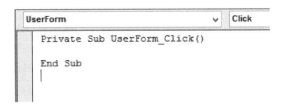

TOGGLING BETWEEN THE CODE AND THE USERFORM WINDOWS

There are two major windows while working with UserForm and you can switch or toggle from these windows i.e, Code and UserForm Windows. To do this

- From **Project Explorer**, right-click on the **UserForm**
- To go to the **Code window**, click on **View Code**
- To go to the **UserForm**, click on the **UserForm window**

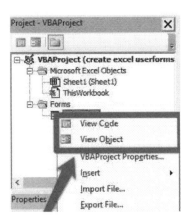

you can also toggle between the Code window and the UserForm window by using the keyboard shortcut

- The F7 and shift + F7 keyboard shortcuts; the F7 is used for displaying the Code window while the Shift + F7 is used for displaying the UserForm window

THE USERFORM EXAMPLES

Briefly, I will be introducing to you in this section, how to add some control tools on the UserForms, and later in the next chapter, we will talk about each control in the Toolbox.

ADDING THE CommandButtons

The CommandButtons are clickable buttons added to the dialog box. To add a CommonButtons, follow the steps below

- From the Toolbox, drag the CommandButton to the dialog box to create a button
- Right-click on the CommandButton and go to the Properties window to change the properties below
  - ***Name to Okbutton***
  - ***Caption to Ok***
  - ***Default to True***
- Add another CommandButton to the dialog box and also change the following properties
  - ***Name to Cancelbutton***
  - ***Caption to Cancel***
  - ***Default to True***
- You can as well as your controls on the dialog box if you wish and it will be displayed as shown in the image below

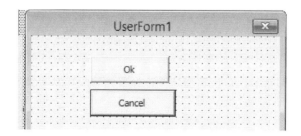

ADDING A TextBox BUTTON

The TextBox allows the user to input text or data to the form. To add the Textbox to your UserForm. Follow the steps below

- From the Toolbox, drag the TEXTButton to the dialog box to create a button
- Double click on the newly selected **TextBox** button to input any text and then click on **Enter**

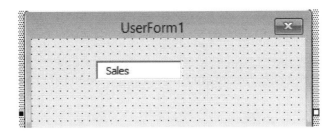

ADDING A LABEL BUTTON

The label button is used to display text in the UserForm. Here we will be adding the label buttons to the text box buttons already added in the UserForm

- From the Toolbox, drag the **Label button** to the dialog box to create a button
- Right-click on the Label button and go to the **Properties window** to change **the Name properties** to **Name**
- Add another **Label button** to the dialog box and also change the **Name Properties** to **Address**

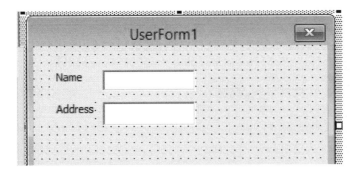

CHAPTER TWENTY-EIGHT

THE USERFORM CONTROLS

With the UserForm Controls, you can make a selection, input text, click on a button, etc. on the UserForms. The VBA uses these controls to determine what operations to be executed. But before we, let's have a comprehensive knowledge of the control properties.

THE CONTROL PROPERTIES

For every control added to the UserForm, some properties help to determine how the controls should execute their operation on the dialog box. To change the control properties, there are two methods to use

- **At Design Time:** This involves manually using the Properties window from the Toolbar or uses the shortcut key F4
- **At Runtime:** This is when the macro is being run and this is possible when writing the VBA code. Codes written here are not permanent.
- Like earlier said, each control has its properties, and now we will be listing some of the common properties that are found in so many controls

PROPERTY	WHAT IT DOES
Accelerator	This is the letter that is underlined in the control's caption. You will need to press this key together with the Alt key to pick this control
AutoSize	This allows the control to resize itself automatically depending on the text in the caption when it is True

Backcolor	This is the background color of the control
Forecolor	This is the color of the font
Font	This is used for making changes to the size, format, and appearance of the control's font excluding the color
Caption	This is the text that appears on the control. For a CommandButton, it appears on the button, for a Frame, it appears at the top and for a Label, it appears within
Name	This is the control's name and by default, the control's name is always dependant on the control type
Value	This is the value the control carries
Visible	The control is hidden if False and vice versa
Width and Height	These are what decides the width and height sizes of the control
ControlSource	This is the property that links the control to a cell on a worksheet

THE USERFORMS DIALOG BOX CONTROL

Here in this section, I will be introducing the controls on the dialog box. In few minutes, let's have in-depth knowledge about the controls in the dialog box

CheckBox CONTROL

The CheckBox is one of the controls in the Toolbox that is used for obtaining binary choices such as yes or no, true or false, on or off, etc. When a checkbox is selected, a checkmark or tick appears on the Windows form

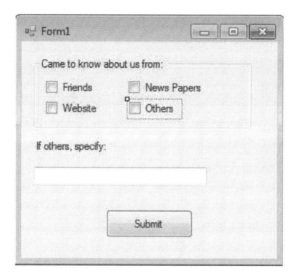

The following are the properties of the ChekBox Control

- **Default:** This is used to get the default size of the checkbox
- **AutoCheck**: This property sets the value showing whether the checked or checkedState value and the appearance changes automatically when the check box is selected.
- **CheckAlign:** This is used to set the horizontal and vertical alignment of the checkmark on the check box

- **Checkstate**: This is used to set or check the state of a check box
- **Text:** This is used to get or set the caption of a check boy
- **ThreeState:** This is used to set or get a set value specifying whether or not a check box should permit three checks rather than two.
- **Style**: This is used to determine whether the control acts like a drop-down list or a ComboBox
- **Checked**: This is used to set a value specifying whether the check box is selected or not.
- **Appearance**: This is used to determine the appearance of the check box control by setting a value
- **FlatStyle**: This is used to set the flat appearance of a checkbox

CommandButton CONTROL

The CommonButton is a common clickable and a push button that is used to issue commands in a form. When you view the Windows dialog and see Ok and cancel, they are from the command buttons

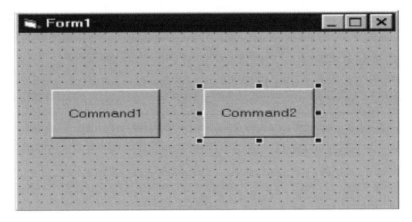

Some of the following are the properties of CommandButton control

- **Caption:** This is the text used to label the command button.
- **Back Color**: This is the color to be used for the command button's background
- **ForeColor**: This is the color used for the command button's foreground, including the color of the text caption
- **Cancel:** When this is True, pressing the Esc button will run the macro attached to the button

- **Default:** When this is True, Pressing the Enter button will run the macro attached to the button
- Effects: This is used to determine the Bold, Italic, Underline, and Strikeout
- **Color Palette**: This is used to display the available colors

ComboBox CONTROL

The ComboBox control is one of the controls in the Toolbox that is used to display a drop-down list of several items. This control is combined with a text box that allows users to input an item and also, choose from a drop-down list

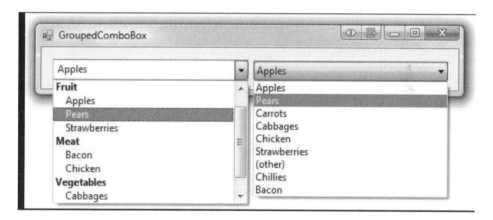

The following are some of the properties in the ComboBox control

- **AllowSelection**: This sets a value specifying if the list allows selection of list items
- **AutoCompleteMode:** This is used to set an option that helps control how automatic completion works for the ComboBox
- **AutoCompleteCustomSource:** This is used to set a custom system collection
- **ListRow:** This specifies the number of items to display when the list drops down
- **ControlSource**: This is the cell that saves the values that are selected in the ComboBox
- **Sorted:** This sets a value specifying if the items in the combo box are sorted

- **Style**: This is used to set the control to either a drop-list or a ComboBox
- **ListStyle:** This displays the appearance of the list items
- **RowSource:** This is the range address that contains the list of items that are displayed in the Combox
- **Value:** This is the text of the item selected by the user and display in the ComboBox
- **DropDownStyle:** This sets a value indicating the style of the ComboBox

Frame CONTROL

The Frame control which is also known as the group box permits the user to group other controls such as the option buttons

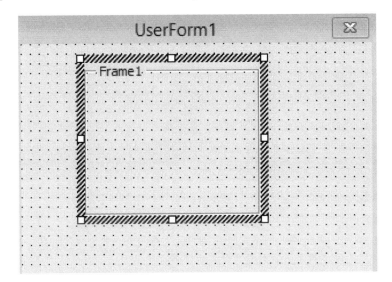

The following are some of the properties used in the Frame control

- **Picture**: This is used to specify the picture at the background of the frame
- **PictureAlignment:** This is used to set the alignment or position of the picture
- **PictureSizemode:** This is used to specify or set the picture size to be used in the control
- **BorderStyle:** This displays the frame's appearance
- **Caption:** This is the text displayed at the top of the frame.

Image CONTROL

As the name implies, Image control helps to add graphics or pictures to the userform. It allows you to display pictures as part of the data in the userform

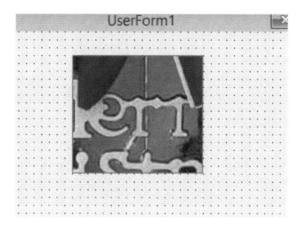

The following are some of the properties of Image control

- **Picture:** This is used to specify the image that is displayed in the userform
- **PictureSizeMode:** This is used to set the size of the picture displayed

Label CONTROL

The Labe control; is used to display some informative texts in the dialog box.

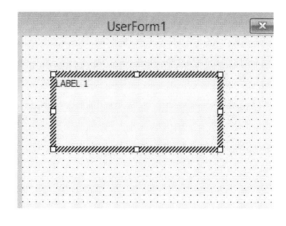

The following are the properties of the Label control

- **Autosize:** This is used to set the value indicating if the control should be resized automatically to show all its content.
- **BorderStyle**: The BorderStyle property sets the border style of the control
- **FlatStyle:** This is used to set the flat style appearance of the Label control
- **Font**: This is used to set the font that is displayed by the control in the dialog box
- **FontHeight:** This is used to set the height of the font of the control.
- **ForeColor:** This is used to set the foreground of the control
- **PreferredHeight:** This is used to set the preferred width of the control
- **TabStop:** This is used to set a value specifying if the user can tab to the Label.
- **Text:** This is used to set the text related to the control
- **TextAlign:** This is used to set the text alignment in the label

ListBox CONTROL

The ListBox control displays a list of items the user can select from. This allows the users to add items at the design time by using the properties window or at the runtime.

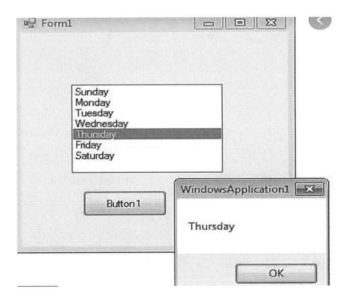

The following are the commonly used properties in the ListBox control

- **AllowSelection**: This is used to get value specifying if the Listbox allows selection of list items
- **BorderStyle:** This property sets the border type to be drawn around the list box.
- **ColumnWidth:** This is used to set the width of columns in the column list box
- **ControlSource:** This stores the value selected in the list box
- **HorizontalExtent**: This defines the horizontal scrolling area of a list box
- **HorizontalScrollBar:** This is used to set a value that defines if a horizontal scrollbar is displayed in the list box
- **ItemHeight:** This is used to define the height of an item in the list box
- **CanSelect:** This is used to obtain a value specifying if the ListBox control can be selected.
- **Visible:** This is used to obtain a value that determines if the ListBox control and its components are displayed on the Windows Form
- **SelectionMode:** This is used to determine the methods in which the items can be selected in the listed property and it has the following values for selection
  - None
  - One
  - MultiSimple
  - MultiExtended
- **TopIndex:** This is used to set the index of the first visible item of a list box
- **MultiColumn**: This permits the columns of an item to be displayed by setting the True value in the list box
- **Value**: This is the text of the item selected in the list box
- **RowSource**: This is the range address containing the list of items revealed in the list box

Multipage CONTROL

A MultiPage control is another example of a container control that is used for creating a dialog box that contains many tabs, thereby, allowing the user to switch in between them. By default, only two tabs are created and other tabs can be added later on

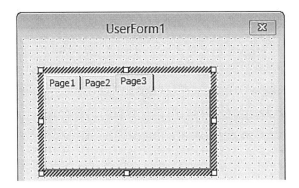

The following are some of the MultiPage control properties

- **Style**: This is used to set the appearance of the control I.e, how the tabs on the dialog box will be displayed
- **Value:** This is used to set which page or tab is to be displayed. For instance, value 0 displays the first page, value 1 displays the second page, etc.

OptionButton CONTROL

The OptionButton control which is also known as the Radio button is a control used to select only one selection from multiple selections within a group. Here in this type of control, clicking on an option turns it on and automatically turns other options in the group off

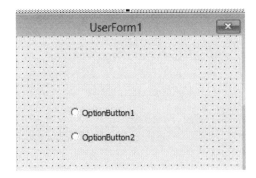

The following are the properties of the OptionButton control

- **Value:** if True, the OptionButton is selected but if False, the OptionButton is not selected
- **ControlSource:** This is the worksheet cell that is associated with the option button. The cell shows True when the control is selected and it shows False when the control is deselected
- **Accelerator:** This is the letter that allows users to select the option using the keyboard. For instance, if the accelerator selects A for an option, pressing Alt + C will select the control.
- **Caption:** This is the text used to tag the option button
- **Back Color:** This is the color used for the option button background.
- **ForeColor:** The is the color to be used for the options button's foreground
- **Color Palette:** This shows the colors available to be used in the option button
- **Alignment:** This is used to place the option to either left or right of the caption within the size of the control.

RefEdit CONTROL

The RefEdit control is a control that allows a user to select a range of cells from the worksheet in Excel. By default, this control cannot be found in the Toolbox. To locate this control, right-click on any control, click on Additional Controls, and then scroll down to select the RefEdit.Ctrl.

ScrollBar CONTROL

The ScrollBar control is a control that allows the user to navigate through a large information in two directions (vertical and horizontal scroll bars) by clicking a button that displays an arrow.

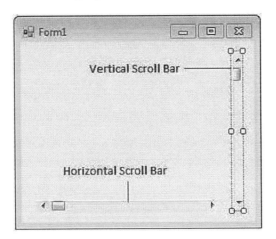

The following are some of the properties ScrollBar control

- **AutoSize:** This is used to set a value that defines if the ScrollBar is automatically resized to fit its content
- **BackColor:** This is used to set the background color of the control
- **ForeColor**: This is used to set the foreground color of the scroll bar control
- **Maximum**: This is used to get the maximum value of the Scroll Bar control and by default, it is 100
- **Minimum**: This is used to get the minimum value of the Scroll Bar control and by default, it is 0
- **LargeChange:** This is used to set the value to be added or subtracted from the Value property when the scroll box is moved a large distance
- **SmallChange:** This is used to set the value to be added or subtracted from the Value property when the scroll box is moved a small distance
- **Value:** This is used to set a numerical value that indicates the current position of the scroll box on the scroll bar control
- **ImeMode:** This sets the Input Method Editor (IME) mode that is supported by this control

SpinButton CONTROL

The SprintButton control is a control that is used to increase or decrease a value by moving the arrows on the control, either up or down. The SpinButton can either be horizontal or vertical

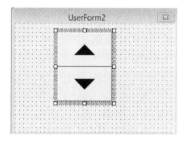

The following are the properties of SpinButton control

- **Value**: This is the value that indicates the current position of the control
- **Min** This is what indicates the lower value of the control
- **Max**: This is what indicates the upper value of the control
- **ControlSource**: This is the worksheet cell that displays the control value
- **SmallChange**: T
- his is the range at which the value of the control is changed by just a click

TextBox CONTROL

The TextBox control is a control that allows the user to enter text into the dialog box. By default, it accepts a single line of text but It can, however, be adjusted to take multiple texts and even add a scroll bar to it.

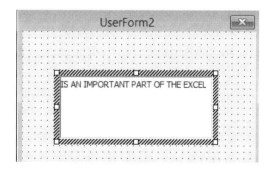

The following are the properties of the TextxBox control

- **AutoCompleteMode:** This is used to set the option that defines how automatic completion works for the TextBox
- **AutoSize:** When set to True, the control adjusts its size automatically, based on the number of texts
- **CompleteSource**: This is the cell containing the text used in the TextBox
- **CharacterCasing**: This is used to specify if a character will lowercase or uppercase as they are been typed in the dialog box
- **Font:** This is used to determine the font of the text displayed by the control
- **FontHeight**: This is used to specify the height of the font displayed in the control
- **ForeColor:** This is used to set the foreground color of the control
- **Textalign:** This is what determines how texts are aligned in the TextBox
- **WordWrap:** This is what determines if the texts will be wrapped up in the dialog box
- ScrollBar: This property specifies the type of scrollbars to be used in the control. It can be horizontal, vertical, both, or none
- **TextLength**: This is used to set the length of the text in the control
- **Text:** This is used to set the current text in the TextBox
- **Lines:** This is used to determine the lines of text in the control
- **Multiline**: This is what specifies that the control is a multiline TextBox control

ToggleButton CONTROL

The ToggleButton control allows the user to toggle or move between two states. The ToggleButton contains two states which are Yes or No. This control can interchange between an enable and disable state when you click on it. With this control, you can carry out tasks such as hide and unhide columns, hide and unhide rows, hid and unhide charts, etc.

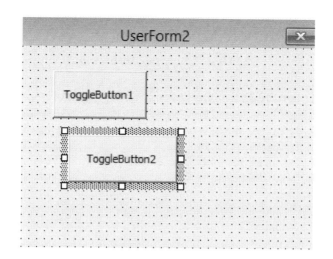

CHAPTER TWENTY-NINE

THE EXCEL ADD-INS

One of the most important features in Excel is the Excel Add-ins. Here in this chapter, we will be discussing what add-in is and most importantly, the functions of the add-ins to the performance of Excel

WHAT IS EXCEL ADD-IN

The Excel Add-in is a program that can be attached to Excel to enhance its functionality. Once an add-in is added to Excel, it provides an outstanding method of improving the way Excel functions. The Excel add-in has a file extension **(.xlam)** and can be opened by default when Excel starts up or load.

WHY SHOULD YOU USE ADD-INS?

While getting yourself acquainted with Excel, a time may come where you will need to start using the add-ins. When such time comes, these are the benefits you get to enjoy

- **Simplify FormuLa**: With the use of Excel-add ins, the user-defined or custom worksheet functions can be written in a way to help make formulas simpler
- **Customizing The Toolbar And Menu Bar:** With the Excel add-ins, the toolbar and menubar can be customized; they can also be removed for new ones to be added.
- **Interaction With Excel Objects**: The Excel add-in allows the user to interact with the Excel objects and also read and write data
- **Easier Access For User:** When you have saved your add-ins to a location, it is displayed in the Add-ins dialog box with a friendly name and clear information of what it does. With this in place, the user can easily access your add-ins
- **Discourages Confusion: With the add-ins, a novice or learner can use your files without getting confused:**
- **Unnecessary Display Of Message When Unloading:** Each time the add-in is to be closed, the dialog box will not display any message to the requesting if the changes made on the files be saved.

CHANGING OR CONVERTING AN EXCEL WORKBOOK TO AN ADD-IN

To convert or change a workbook to an add-in, there are two ways to go about it and they are listed below

- Using the Save As option
- Using the VB Editor

Before we convert the workbook to an add-in, it is advisable to add description information to your add-ins. The reason for this is to ensure that the add-ins are easy to use, especially when the Add-ins dialog box displays the description of the add-in when it is selected.

To add description information to the add-ins

- Open the workbook
- Click on **File** and Excel will display the Document Properties pane at the right side of the window
- Click on **Properties** and from the drop-down menu, select **Advanced Properties**
- Input the name of the add-in in the **Title field**
- Input a short description about the add-in in the **Comment field** and then click on **Ok**

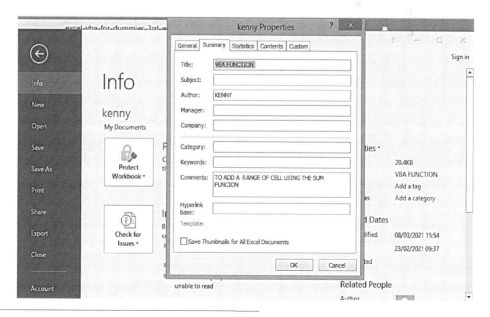

USING THE SAVE AS OPTION TO CONVERT A FILE TO AN ADD-IN

To convert a workbook to Add-in, follow the procedures below

- Open the workbook
- Click on **File** and then select **Save As**
- In the **Save As a field**, navigate through the list and then select **Excel Add-in**
- Then click on **Save**

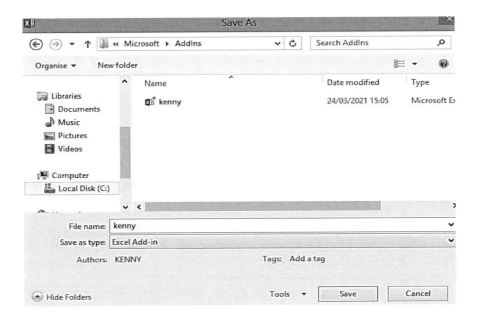

USING THE VB EDITOR TO CONVERT A FILE TO AN ADD-IN

Apart from using the Save As option, you can also VB Editor Editor to convert a file to an add-in. To do this, follow the steps below

- Open the workbook you intend to convert to an add-in
- Open the **VB Editor**
- Go to the **Project Explorer** and click **This Workbook**
- Click on the **Properties window** on the **Toolbar** at the top of the **VB Editor**
- From the **Properties window**, locate the **IsAddin** and change it to True

- Press **Ctrl + G** to display the Immediate window
- In the **Immediate window**, save the file, using the **.xlam** extension

OPENING THE ADD-IN

To open the add-ins, follow the steps below

- Go to the Developer tab and click on the Add-in; here, Excel displays the Add-ins dialog
- Click on the **Browse button**
- **Search and select the add-in created**
- Then click on **Ok** to close the Browse dialog box
- On the next page, the Add-Ins dialog has a checkmark for your new add-in
- Finally, click on **Ok** to close the dialog box

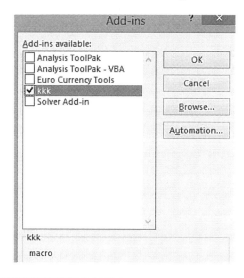

PROTECTING THE VBA CODE

You can protect your VBA code from being viewed by others by adding a password that only you can access. To do this, follow the steps below

- Open the **VB Editor** and select the workbook in the Project window.
- Click on **Tools** on the **Tool Bar** and then select **VBA Project Properties**
- When the VBA Project Properties dialog box appears, click on the **Protection tab**
- Click on the **Lock Project** and enter the desired password twice as displayed in the dialog box
- Then click on **OK**

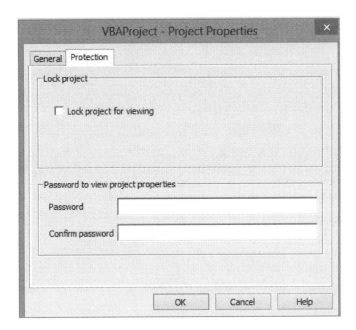

EDITING THE ADD-IN

Just as a workbook can be edited, the add-in also can be edited. To edit your add-in

- Open the XLAM file you wish to edit
- Open the VB Editor and double click on the Project's name in the Project window

- Incase the add-in is protected, input the password and click **Ok**
- Then make the desired changes to the add-in through the codes
- Then save the file from the VBE

CHAPTER THIRTY

EXCEL VBA SHORTCUTS, TIPS AND TRICKS

Here in this chapter, I will be taking you on some tips and tricks, that will make your work on VBA more efficient. Using the VBA tips and tricks doesn't mean you won't make mistakes, but it will minimize the numbers of mistakes to be made.

Below, some of the tips and tricks are listed.

ADD COMMENTS TO YOUR CODE

Adding comments to your code is one of the most important things to do while writing a code. Adding comments to your codes allows anyone to understand what you are doing with the codes. By default, the comment is displayed in green color and does not affect the running of the code.

To add a comment in Excel's VBA code,

- Open the VB Editor
- Precede the code in the VBA with an apostrophe

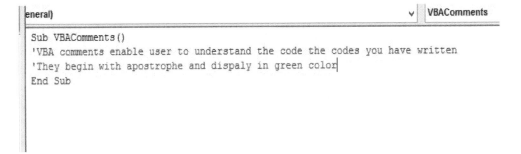

DECLARE ALL VARIABLES

Another thing to take note of is declaring your variables. Declaring your variables to a specific data type allows your code to run faster, and avoids typographical error. For instance, use an integer variable named Count, and declare Dim Count as Integer.

Instead of declaring your variables one after the other, you can use the Option Explicit. To add the Option Explicit to your code, do the following

- From the **VB Editor**, go to **Tools**
- Click on **Options** and go to the **Editor tab**
- From the **Editor tab,** click on **Check Required Variable Declaration**

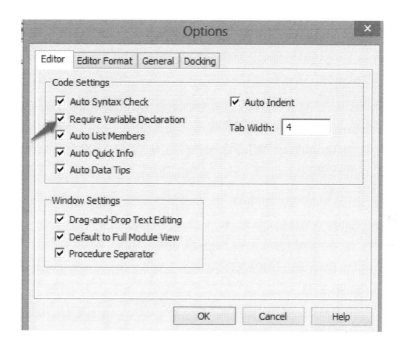

After the steps above must have been taken, the **Option Explicit** is displayed at the top of the module.

NAME VARIABLES AND FUNCTIONS USING CLEAR AND NAMES

When naming the VBA variables and functions, use names that can be clearly understood and interpreted. When this is strictly followed, any user can use the codes without making any mistake or error

BREAK YOUR WORK INTO SMALLER CHUNKS

It is unprofessional to put all your codes in one procedure. The reason is that, when you go back to check the procedures, you may end up making mistakes and at the same time, introducing bugs into the codes. Therefore, to avoid this, it is better to split the codes into smaller chunks, where you designate to each chunk the task to execute. With this tip, you will find the writing of codes to be bug-free.

DISPLAY ONE PROCEDURE AT A TIME

The Code windows in the VBA display all the procedures in the module, one after the other, which can be distracting at times, especially, when trying to write out codes. To ensure that only one procedure is visible, follow the steps below

- Open the **VBE** and select **Tools Options**
- Click on the **Editor Tab** in the **Options dialog box**
- Then remove the checkmark from Default to **Full Module View Check Box**

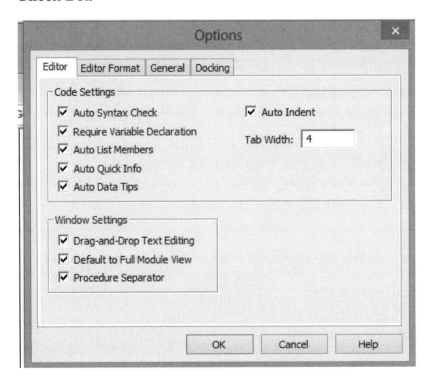

USE THE OPTION EXPLICIT

Using the Option Explicit at the beginning of a VBA code helps to avoid spelling errors in the VBA code. When the Option Explicit detects any variables that are not declared, it returns a Compile Error. Not only, but Option Explicit also highlights the undeclared variable and tells us of the problem.

RE-USE COMMONLY USED FUNCTION TO SAVE TIME

When you develop a habit of keeping your most commonly used VBA routines in a place, this will help reduce the time you will be exhausting in coding or model building. You can even assign a shortcut to make it quick to access for use.

TEST YOUR CODE REGULARLY TO AVOID RUN-TIME ERRORS error.

As a professional, it is pertinent that you test your code from time to time to detect any mistake and error and to be able to handle any run time that may pop up in the VBA codes

ENSURE TO BACKUP YOUR FILES

It can be so disheartening after working for several hours, but only for your system to crash or dies with everything you have spent coding, go down the drain. To avert this calamity, ensure to have a good back up plan

USE IMMEDIATE WINDOW

The Immediate window is used to test and execute VBA statements and also help in debugging codes. Here in this window, you can write any VBA statement and get a quick result. To use the Immediate window

- Go to **VB Editor**, select **View** and then click on **Immediate Window** (You can also use shortcut key **Ctrl + G**

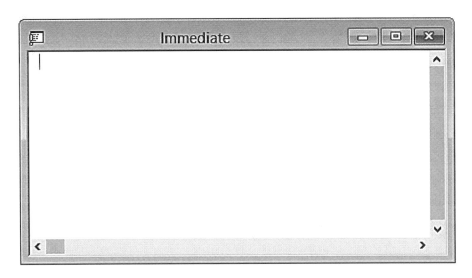

LEARN HOW TO DEVELOP YOUR CODE

It is very good to use the macros for creating codes but most times, there will be some limitations that will require you to create your codes without using the macro. For this reason, it is advisable that as a programmer, you must be able to write your codes.

USE PROPER LINE INDENTATION

As a professional, ensure that the lines in your VBA codes are properly indented so that the code structure will be clearly visible and well understood by anyone that comes across your codes.

AVOID WRONG SPELLINGS

One of the reasons why the VBA codes encounter the errors is because of wrong spellings. Therefore, as a programmer, ensure that codes are well spelled out especially texts in UserForms and message boxes.

USE THE VBA TO VIEW ALL BUILT-IN FUNCTIONS AND CONSTANT

It can be so difficult to remember all the built-in functions and constants in Excel, but with the "VBA., you can see the lists of all the VBA functions and constants. To get this done, all you need to id type VBA. In the module

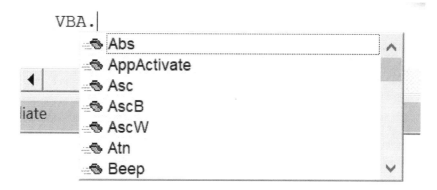

LOWER CASE ALL CODE

Using the lower case to write your code, helps to capitalize all codes that are correctly spelled. In case the codes are not capitalized, check the VBA codes for any spelling errors

USE SHORTCUT KEYS

The VBA shortcut keys are very essential while working with VBA to ease the rigorous stress of writing out codes in the modules. Below are some of the shortcut keys

SHORTCUT KEYS	FUNCTIONS
Tab	To insert a level of indentation to the highlighted block of code
BackSpace	To delete one character to the left of the cursor
Enter	To add or create a new line
Insert	To toggle insert mode on or off

Home	To move the cursor to the start of the current line
End	To move the cursor to the end of the current line
Page Up	To move the viewable area of the module up one page
Page Down	To move the viewable area of the module down one page
Up	To move the cursor up one line
Down	To move the cursor down one line
Left	To move the cursor one character to the left
Right	To move the cursor one character to the right
F1	To open the Visual Editor Help
F2	To open the Visual basic Object browser
F3	To perform the Find Next command

F4	To open the Properties window
F5	To run the current procedure
F6	To move the cursor between split windows
F7	To move to the Code window
F8	To step into code
F9	To toggle code breakpoints on or off
F10	To activate focus on the menu bar
Alt + A	To open the Add-ins menu
Alt + D	To open the Debug menu
Alt + E	To open the Edit menu
Alt + F	To open the File menu
Alt + J	To open the Insert menu
Alt + O	To open the Format menu

Alt + R	To open the Run menu
Alt + Q	To close the Virtual basic Editor
Alt + T	Open the Tools menu
Alt + V	To open the View menu
Alt + W	To open the Window menu
Alt + F4	To close the Visual Basic Editor
Alt + F5	To run the Error Handler
Alt + F6	To switch between last two windows
Alt + F7	To step Error Handler
Alt + F11	To switch between the Visual Basic Editor and
Alt + Tab	To navigate through all open Windows applications
Alt + Space Bar	To open the Visual Basic Editor menu
Alt + Back Space	To undo last command

Ctrl + A	To select all text in the current module
Ctrl + C	To copy the current selection
Ctrl + E	To export the currently selected module
Ctrl + F	To open the Find dialog box
Ctrl + G	To open the immediate window
Ctrl + H	To open the Replace dialog
Ctrl + I	To display Quick Info for the objects selected
Ctrl +J	To show the lists of available properties or methods
Ctrl + K	To send an object back when creating a user form
Ctrl + L	To show the call stack
Ctrl + M	To import a module file
Ctrl + N	To create a new line

Ctrl + P	To open the Print VBAProject dialog box
Ctrl + R	To open the Project window
Ctrl + S	To save the current project
Ctrl + T	To open the Components dialog box
Ctrl + V	To paste the last item copied to the clipboard
Ctrl + W	Equivalent to Debug
Ctrl + x	To cut the current selection
Ctrl + Y	To cut the entire current line
Ctrl + Z	To undo the last command
Ctrl + F4	To close the current window
Ctrl + F2	To activate focus to the object selection dropdown
Ctrl + F8	Run to Cursor
Ctrl +F9	To set Next Statement

Ctrl + F10	To activate focus on the menu bar
Ctrl + Tab	To cycle through all open Visual Basic windows
Ctrl + Spacebar	Autocomplete current word
Ctrl + Backspace	To delete one word to the left of the cursor
Ctrl + Insert	To copy the current selection
Ctrl + Delete	To delete one word to the right of the cursor
Ctrl + Home	To move the cursor to the start of the current module
Ctrl +End	To move the cursor to the end of the current module
Ctrl + Page Up	To move the cursor to the start of the current procedure
Ctrl + Page Down	To move the cursor to the end of the current procedure
Ctrl + Up	To move the cursor to the previous procedure

Ctrl + Down	To move the cursor to the next procedure
Ctrl + Left	To move the cursor o the left by one word
Ctrl + Right	To move the cursor to the right by one word
Shift + F2	To go to variable declaration or object definition
Shift + F3	To find the previous item from the cursor for the last item selected
Shift + F4	To find the next item from the cursor for the last item searched
Shift + F8	Step Over (Equivalent to Debug)
Shift + F9	Quick Watch (Equivalent to Debug)
Shift + F10	Equivalent to right click to show menu
Shift + Tab	To remove one level of indentation from a highlighted block of code

Shift + Insert	To paste the last item copied to your clipboard
Shift + Home	To select from the cursor to the start of the current line
Shift + End	To select from the cursor to the end of the current line
Shift + Page Up	To select from the cursor to the top of the module
Shift + Page Down	To select from the cursor to the top of the module
Shift + Page Down	To select from the cursor to the bottom of the module
Shift + Up	To extend the current selection up to one line
Shift + Down	To extend the current selection down one line
Shift + Left	To extend the current selection to the left by one character
Shift + Right	To extend the current selection to the left by one character

Ctrl + shift + I	Parameter Info (Equivalent to Edit)
Ctrl + Shift + J	List Constants (Equivalent to Edit)
Ctrl + Shift + F2	To move the cursor to its previous position
Ctrl + shift + F8	Step Out (Equivalent to Debug)
Ctrl + Shift + F9	Clear all breakpoints (Equivalent to Debug)

CONCLUSION

Having gone through this book, I am sure you must have realized how important and useful Microsoft Excel is to the organizations in the world especially that of 2021 coupled with the features it entails.

As a businessman or woman, Excel is meant solely for you; You don't want to waste your time doing what you could have done in little or no time with Excel 2021 you can do well to recommend this to your family and friends even your colleagues at work.

As a student, there are a lot of added advantages you get to see by taking your time to learn how to use this app, you never can tell where you will find yourself in the future. Moreover, it is dangerous to live in this world without any basic knowledge regarding the use of Microsoft Excel.

With Excel 2021, you are on your way to taking your business, career, etc. to another height.

Also, having taken your time and energy to go through the hurdle of learning VBA, you are already aware that learning the VBA is not a child's play, especially in the area of creating custom functions and custom user forms.

It's no doubt by now, that you are now versatile with the use of VBA to automate tasks that could have been executed repeatedly, thus, causing waste of time, energy, and resources. With these skills learned, you can still use the following Excel resources to also boost your skills to a higher level

- **The VBA Help System:** You can find useful information about objects, properties, and methods on the VBA. This can be access free and available at any time but for Excel 2013 and later version, you will require a strong internet connection to access
- **Microsoft Product Support:** This is where Microsoft provides a wide range of technical support in the usage of VBA. Some services here are free and while others come with a fee charge. To access this service, go to http://support.microsoft.com.

- **Internet Websites:** Of a truth, this has been helpful. Here you get to access a lot of websites that contain Excel-related materials.

With all that has been said so far, I wish you all the best as you take your VBA skills to another dimension

See you at the top!

Was this book helpful to you?
Are you satisfied with the contents of this book?
If yes, I would like to hear from you, please kindly leave a review for this book after purchase. Thanks.

ABOUT THE AUTHOR

My name is James Jordan, I am an author who is passionate about my customers' satisfaction and always puts my customers' needs at the front line. I am a content writer and a publisher who drives passion in providing solutions to people in online businesses.

Follow my author page for updates on my other books.

One of the things that makes an author do more is getting customers' feedback and reviews.

Kindly leave a feedback after reading this book.

I will really appreciate it.

James Jordan

INDEX

M

macro, 281, 283, 284, 285, 288, 289,
290, 291, 292, 293, 295, 296, 297,
298, 299, 306, 312, 313, 315, 316,
337, 338, 342, 343, 344, 345, 346,
347, 348, 354, 396, 398, 422, 427,
431, 434, 435, 456

Macros, 283, 284, 288, 291, 297, 315

Main Tabs, 286

malicious, 293, 297

manipulating, 298

manually, 283, 431

maps, 289

MATCH FUNCTION, 174

Match_type, 175

MATH FUNCTIONS, 97

MAX FUNCTION, 132

MEDIAN FUNCTION, 134

message, 292, 293, 294, 295, 335, 339,
355, 367, 369, 376, 379, 383, 401,
404, 406, 407, 412, 413, 414, 415,
446, 456

Microsoft, 281, 285, 293, 300, 303,
329, 407, 467

microsoft excel terminologies
AutoFill, 7
AutoSum, 8
Cell, 4
Cell Formatting, 7
Cell Range, 6
Cell Reference, 6
Column and Row Headings, 5
Columns and Rows, 5
Data Validation, 8
Error Code, 7
Filter, 7
Formula, 7
Formula Bar, 7
Function, 7
Item, 9
Merged Cell, 6
Operator, 6
Pivot Area, 8
Pivot Chart, 8
Pivot Table, 8
Ribbon, 5
Source Data, 8
Template, 6
Values Area, 9
Workbook, 4
Worksheet, 4
Workspace, 5

MICROSOFT EXCEL TERMINOLOGIES, 4

micrososft excel terminologies
AutoFormat, 8

MID Function, 208

MIDB FUNCTION, 210

MIN FUNCTION, 130

Minus Sign, 94

Minute, 239

Mistakes, 283

MOD FUNCTION, 105

modify, 283, 326

MODIFYING THE COLUMN WIDTH, 37

MODIFYING THE ROW HEIGHT, 38

module, 292, 306, 307, 308, 312, 313,
314, 316, 318, 321, 322, 331, 333,
334, 335, 336, 339, 342, 344, 346,
348, 402, 453, 454, 456, 458, 461,
463, 465

modules, 292, 303, 307, 312, 318, 336,
398, 404, 416, 457

money, 281

Month, 148

MONTH FUNCTION, 221

moving, 283, 303, 443

multiple, 332, 365, 400, 418, 440, 443

N

N/A, 91

NAME, 91

NESTED IF FUNCTION, 157

NESTED PARENTHESES, 87

NETWORKDAYS, 89

NETWORKDAYS FUNCTION, 235

NOW FUNCTION, 237